THE PROPHET'S ARMY

THE PROPHET'S ARMY

Trotskyists in America, 1928-1941

Constance Ashton Myers

Contributions in American History,
Number 56

GREENWOOD PRESS

Westport, Connecticut ● London, England

Library of Congress Cataloging in Publication Data

Myers, Constance Ashton.
  The prophet's army.

  (Contributions in American history ; no. 56)
  Bibliography: p.
  Includes index.
  1. Communism—United States—1917. 2. Socialism
in the United States—History. 3. Socialist Workers
Party—History. I. Title.
HX83.M9   329'.81   76-15330
ISBN 0-8371-9030-4

Library of Congress Catalog Card Number: 76-15330
ISBN: 0-8371-9030-4

First published in 1977

Greenwood Press, Inc.
51 Riverside Avenue, Westport, Connecticut 06880

Printed in the United States of America

For
Robert C. Donaldson
and
John Scott Wilson

Contents

Preface

This study is a narrative account through the 1930s of the events and personalities in an American radical party, bolshevik in organization. The Trotskyists were an archetypical radical group in that they were an assorted body of people united by a sense of alienation from American culture and a rejection of many of its values. They were unique, however, in revering a living, brilliant leader-theoretician, Leon Trotsky. Like other American radicals, they claimed a vast body of doctrinal literature from the radical past and one historic occasion, the Russian Revolution, when the spirit of the overthrow of tyranny left the airy realm of speculation and vision and became manifest. And they tenaciously clung to their faith in the classless, stateless radical future.

Flexible and pragmatic in certain limited instances, on bolshevik party structure with its implicit elitism and explicit doctrinairism the Trotskyists were intractable. This intransigence would render them ineffective in the 1930s. Moreover, they unrealistically glorified the blue-collar proletariat as redeemer of the world. Yet their intellectualistic traditions and appeals meant little or nothing to most production or industrial workers. The Trotskyist leadership relegated to second-class citizenship in the party those people to whom their message had great-

est attractiveness—the white-collar lower -middle class.* These high-
school- and college-educated folk chafed at chronic depression cycles,
inflation, unemployment, job insecurity, and climbing taxes; but they
also internalized the ideals of parliamentary democracy. When such
people joined the party, they frequently found uncomfortable the
elitist, rigidly doctrinaire nature of party life, wherein entrenched leaders could not be deposed and hallowed "principles" could not be ex-
amined. Any effort to initiate reform brought slander and ostracism,
and often fragmentation of the party. Trotsky, who was himself from
the middle class, and his working-class American henchman, James P.
Cannon, ceaselessly excoriated these "petty bourgeois" influences and
fought to recruit more "real proletarians."

These policies destined the Trotskyists to failure in an advanced capitalist nation such as the United States, where ruling-class domination
depended on internalized ideology and self-policing rather than on overt
repression. The Leninist concept of party organization was simply un-
suitable for the American environment. Americans repelled by industrial hierarchies and job bureaucratism would hardly welcome these phe-
nomena in a radical party. Moreover, to so exalt the blue-collar "proletariat" and denigrate the views of those in the organization who had

---

*"Middle class" in this preface is used in the sense given currency by
much twentieth-century sociology and does not mean the "bourgeoisie"
of the Marxian categories: those persons who either own or control the
means of production, therefore who exercise great power over many
lives other than their own. These lower middle classes tend to be salary
or wage earners who have traditionally believed that education, dili-
gence on the job, proper standards of housing, dress, and conduct, and
responsible management of personal income would bring higher status
and security. People holding such attitudes may be found anywhere
from the small midwestern town to the big city ethnic neighborhoods.
Studies show that among them the old certainties have lost their force;
these persons feel inadequate and powerless. C. Wright Mills called
them "the new middle classes" in his *White Collar* (New York, 1951),
and prophesied that augmenting alienation would awaken a dormant
class consciousness which could incline them toward political activism.
Their generally higher level of educational attainment than that of
the production worker has made attractive to some of them the intellectualistic theories of Marxism-Trotskyism.

come from the rapidly growing white-collar classes showed tunnel vision of the worst sort. A radical group seeking to attract American working-class members would have to include as proletarians such labor force members as small store owners, farmers who work alongside a few employees, homemakers, health-care workers, technicians, office and sales workers, and transportation or communications workers. American Trotskyists briefly gave promise of enlarging their appeal when they merged with A. J. Muste's American Workers party and, soon after, entered the Socialist party. But both experiences had limited value. While membership increased slightly, non-Bolsheviks were alienated and dropped out of the movement.

Particularly interesting in the narrative are the successive efforts to gain free expression for dissenting opinions in the Communist, the Trotskyist, and the Socialist organizations. A pattern emerged wherein a dissident minority demanding such expression was denied it by party leaders carrying a majority with them. When the mavericks refused to depart voluntarily, party leaders expelled them. After organizing a new radical sect, the former dissenters proved equally repressive of free speech when in leadership roles in their new groups. Men holding power, even if only the ephemeral "power" of leadership in a party, seemed to fear a challenge within the ranks far more than oppression inflicted by government authorities. Leaders demanded docility in their "revolutionary" followers—a dangerous demand for a radical party, because with increasing submissiveness inevitably comes a weaker and less creative critique of capitalist values. An effective revolutionary organization in the American context probably would have had to provide encouragement for criticism in an atmosphere of full collective accountability and support.

The story of the American Trotskyist movement in its first twelve years gives proof that strictest bolshevik structure was inappropriate for a radical party in an advanced industrial state in the 1930s. For all the high intelligence, purpose, and administrative talent of its leadership, the group made only an indirect and sporadic, impact on American life. An "all-inclusive" radical party, the kind envisioned by Norman Thomas for the American Socialist party, was clearly better adapted to American attitudes and traditions. Even the Communist party perceived this truth in adopting the line of the "people's front." Still, neither the Socialist nor the Communist party realized success in the true sense of the word in this nation: neither one ushered in the class-less, stateless society, nor even the transitional "dictatorship of the proletariat" expected by some of them.

Serious radicals in the 1930s would have had to develop fresh forms of organization, new techniques for maintaining revolutionary dedication, to have justified any realistic expectation of a socialist triumph. This study shows that faith in the old forms, old techniques was faith misplaced. Promise could have lain only in innovation devised specifically for the American reality.

American Trotskyists wrote voluminously; as a consequence memoirs as well as commentaries on issues agitating the movement abound. James P. Cannon's *Ten Years of American Communism* and his *History of American Trotskyism,* published by the Trotskyist press, along with Max Shachtman's *Reminiscences* in the Columbia University Oral History Collection, are the most comprehensive of the memoirs, and formed the backbone of the present research. Many lesser figures in the Trotskyist movement, as well as Socialists, and even Communist recanters of the 1950s, commented on their brushes with Trotskyism. Their works provided details from the nonleadership perspective. The present study depended heavily on Leon Trotsky's theoretical works and his essays mapping party strategy. Most of Trotsky's writings are collected in volumes published in the 1960s and 1970s under the auspices of the Socialist Workers party. In addition to the above, the author proceeded systematically through the official and unofficial Trotskyist periodical literature (1928 through 1941) for reportage and interpretation of American, international, and party affairs: the *Militant,* the *New Militant, Socialist Appeal, New International, Fourth International* (the foregoing on Greenwood Press microfilm), *Internal Bulletin, Modern Monthly,* and many irregularly printed pamphlets.

Special collections consulted were Papers of the Socialist Workers party in the Wisconsin State Historical Society (on microfilm); selected radical papers in New York University's Tamiment Institute Library; certain documents in the personal files of Bertram D. Wolfe at the Hoover Institution on War, Revolution, and Peace at Stanford University; several sets of reminiscences in the Columbia University Oral History Collection including those in Betty Yorburg's Socialist Movement Project; the Norman Thomas Papers at the New York Public Library; and lectures in the Socialist Workers party's tape collection at the New York office.

The spirit and atmosphere of party life were elaborated in the interviews granted the author by many who participated in or observed the movement in the period discussed here. And certainly this work would be unwieldy and incomprehensible had it not had from its inception the expert advice and criticism of John Scott Wilson at the University of South Carolina. Indeed, the research that culminated in the book began in June 1969 in his seminar on conservatism and reform in modern America. John Duffy and James Kuhlman also read the manuscript and made helpful suggestions and encouraging comments. Bernard K. Johnpoll of the Graduate School of Public Affairs at the State University of New York at Albany gave the study detailed attention, made valuable recommendations for further interviews beyond the initial research, and posed questions needing satisfactory answers in the text.

John P. Diggins of the University of California at Irvine and Daniel Horowitz of Scripps College read portions of the manuscript and gave useful criticisms. I am grateful to all of them for their help. Of course I assume full responsibility for the book as it stands.

A grant from the President's Office at the University of South Carolina funded two trips for interviewing and research and the preparation of the manuscript, and funds from the National Endowment for the Humanities made possible three interviews in the summer of 1976. I greatly appreciate these indispensable gestures of support. Georganne Browder's skilled typing gave the final finishing touch. Cecil Myers provided the atmosphere of moral support during the entire undertaking, first to last, the kind of thing so necessary its value cannot be measured and for which there are not words adequate to express thanks.

Constance Ashton Myers

THE PROPHET'S ARMY

1

Introductory: Trotskyists and the American Radical Movement

Revolutionary Socialism in America Before 1919

Marxist socialism and communism as well as syndicalism and the trade union movement supplied the compound in which world Trotskyism germinated. The patriarch of American Trotskyism, James Patrick Cannon, came through three such groups: the syndicalist Industrial Workers of the World (IWW), the Socialist party, and the Workers (Communist) party. Leon Trotsky's first American protagonists, Ludwig Lore and Max Eastman, were Socialist party members. Still, the revolutionary compound that nurtured Trotskyism had to withstand the addition of a combustible additive and pressure from the intense heat it generated in the American environment. This combustible factor was, of course, the Russian Revolution, with the inevitable influx of new Russian variations on the familiar Marxist themes, variations that had survived the pragmatic test of a genuine political revolution.

The importance of the 1917 upheaval to American radicalism cannot be overemphasized. It infused new spirit and hope in the slumping socialist movement that had suffered several crises and fractures. Born in 1901 with the shearing away of the Socialist Labor party sectarians, the Socialist party reached its apex of electoral success in 1912. One year earlier the Wobblies of the IWW had been expelled by an increasingly accommodationist Socialist party for advocacy of sabotage and for anti-political agitation. (IWW philosophy held that workers' loyalties to each other must transcend national borders and allegiances. In America, IWW leaders sought to organize unskilled workers such as lumberjacks, miners, agricultural laborers, textile mill hands; workers and leaders alike regularly encountered violent resistance from employers, and newspapers covered such episodes in lurid, exaggerated detail, arousing public hostility to the Wobblies.) The onset of World War I produced a rift in international socialism which was duplicated in the American movement over the question of patriotic support for one's own capitalist government in a war for the fruits of imperial conquest.[1] Although American Socialists unlike their French and German comrades issued an official proclamation from St. Louis in April 1917 pledging nonsupport of the Allied war effort, a minority vowed loyalty to President Woodrow Wilson's commitment in the war to end all wars. Thus the Socialist movement lost some of its best known members such as Charles Edward Russell, W. J. Ghent, Gustavus Myers, Jack London, Algie Martin Simons, Upton Sinclair, Rose Pastor Stokes, and J. G. Phelps-Stokes. They contributed their journalistic talents to such props and arms of the Wilson administration as the Creel Committee on Public Information, the Civic Federation, and the Loyalty Legion; and occasionally spewed invective against their former Socialist comrades.[2]

In February 1917, the first of two revolutions erupted in Russia, ushering into power a democratic government professing constitutionalist principles. The February revolution found Leon Trotsky in New York, writing for the radical Russian publication *Novy Mir* in a dirty, uninviting cellar. On January 13, 1917, he arrived in New York as an exile from Spain seeking a modicum of political freedom. He was prepared to settle in New York and labor for the left wing of the fractured Socialist party in the hope of uniting it under a left program and of personally editing a new publication for it. The revolution also found Nikolai Bukharin in New York similarly enjoying a more open political atmosphere and intending to work for the American revolutionary movement. An adherent of the bolshevik wing of the Russian Social Democrats, Bukharin hoped to influence the American Socialist left wing to split from the party and form a new party. Trotsky's plan prevailed. Indeed, some New York Socialist leaders expected to promote Trotsky to the leadership of the imminent American revolution. But his preference that the party remain intact and that it publish a new left-wing organ was the last policy decision he made on American soil for the American movement.[3] Events in Russia summoned home the Russian exiles, now amnestied. In October 1917 Trotsky and Bukharin were to play commanding roles in the second revolution in Russia, altogether unanticipated by both of them while they were in New York early the same year. Americans as yet did not know of Lenin.

The year 1917 crystallized the Socialist party's left wing, chiefly, but not solely, over the war issue; it brought official American entry into the European conflict; it gave Russia two revolutions; it gave world socialists a model plus a constellation of new leader-theoreticians.

Personalities in Revolutionary Socialism

Before the solidification of its left wing in 1917 over the war question, the Socialist party in the United States was a hodgepodge of social classes and interest groups.[4] Shorn of many middle-class and native American members, "intellectuals, millionaires, and ministers," the remaining ones could be lumped into three broad categories with a variety of subvariations: worker and intellectual immigrants, native American trade union leaders, and city-bred party professionals.

Worker and intellectual immigrants. Immigrants from a range of educational levels and a handful of talented theoreticians swelled the movement especially after the Russian Revolution. They would be the core of the Communist parties created in 1919. They constituted the large membership of the foreign language federations, 40 percent of the total party roster before the revolution, 53 percent two years after it.[5] The most clever and literate members edited the federation organs. Trotsky and other Russian exiles fell naturally into this group until February events lured them home, and Trotsky, certainly thinking of himself as its prospective editor, had urged the creation of a paper for the new left wing. After Trotsky returned to Russia, his collaborator in party work, Louis Fraina, assumed the editorship of the first organ of the Socialist party, the *New International.* An American of Italian birth, of working-class origin, and a self-taught intellectual, Fraina was the first propagandist to emerge in the embryonic communist movement, by no means

a party yet. Cannon, who did not meet Fraina until 1920 or 1921, recognized him as "the founder of the movement."

> Fraina was the first *writer* of pioneer American communism. He
> did more to explain and popularize the basic program of the Russian
> Bolsheviks. American communism, which stems directly from the
> primitive American left-wing movement, owes its first serious in-
> terest in theoretical questions primarily to Fraina.[6]

Indeed, the historian of the early communist movement, Theodore
Draper, called Fraina "The first American example of the political Jack-
of-all-trades that a first-rate radical leader must be."[7] Editorially he
fused the syndicalist "revolutionary unionism" outlook with political
socialism and set the new ideology before the backdrop of the Russian
Revolution, a necessary step before a new party could come to birth.
For the purpose, Fraina drafted the phrase "mass action" recently
brought to America from strike scenes in Europe by S. J. Rutgers of
the Socialist party's Dutch Federation. Rutgers and Fraina, laboring
together on the *New International,* claimed that the Russian success
proved "mass action" to be a winning formula. Although prominent
partisans in the confused initial period of American communism, both
men dropped out after a few years. At a later time Cannon would eval-
uate Fraina as "undoubtedly the most original popularizer of communist ideas." He reemerged later as author of economic treatises under the pen name Lewis Corey.[8]

Another prominent immigrant theoretician was Ludwig Lore, who
edited the *New Yorker Volkszeitung,* the oldest continuous Socialist
daily in the world. Marxian socialism in America had its oldest link with
the Germans, and Lore fit solidly into that tradition as an orthodox
Marxist. Additionally, he was Trotsky's most intimate friend and would
remain loyal to Trotsky during Trotsky's difficult days in 1926 and
1927. Although not a disciplined Trotskyist, Lore would be the American movement's closest image of the foreign theoretician, so important
in American radicalism. In actuality, Trotsky himself would have to
play that role for his American following.

Native American trade union leaders. A second category of early
left-wing, revolutionary socialist was the native trade union leader, most
notably James P. Cannon and William Z. Foster. Cannon, born in 1890

of Irish parentage in Rosedale, Kansas, and Foster, who (possibly spuriously) claimed Irish immigrant parentage too, boasted solid American credentials. Finding themselves allied factionally against shifting combinations of European theoreticians and city-bred intellectuals, the two made peace for tactical reasons with white-collar radicals of the type of Kansas-born Earl Russell Browder and Minnesotan Martin Abern. For a short time the Foster-Cannon caucus enjoyed the journalistic services of one of the European theoreticians active in the Jewish Federation, Alexander Bittelman, who remained loyal to the official party when Cannon embraced Trotsky's cause in 1928.[9] By and large, the "proletarian" wing held together with a more practical (yet more strike- and confrontation-prone) orientation. Foster had come to the Socialist party through past affiliations that included leadership of the Syndicalist League of America as well as Samuel Gompers's American Federation of Labor (AFL). He consistently opposed the Socialist Labor party's and the IWW's program for dual revolutionary unions. He later found it difficult to play down the fact that he morally and financially supported the Allied effort in World War I. To compensate for this blot on his good Marxist name, Foster and his following made much of his personal leadership of the unsuccessful steel strike in 1919. In this strike Foster had gambled to win the leadership of the AFL, but all it had done was to certify Foster as committed to the cause of the worker. As the 1919 strike occurred when the Communist line condemned confrontations except for the purpose of overthrowing capitalism, his actions were not applauded by revolutionists. Foster "discovered" the Bolshevik revolution in 1921, and entered the two-year-old United Communist party where, until the rupture over Trotskyism in 1928, he was often associated with Cannon in efforts to keep the party united for specific mass action projects.[10]

Foster's story is tragic, for he almost succeeded in the major tasks he set for himself. Leadership in the Communist movement became his chief aim toward which it was alleged he moved unscrupulously. Time after time he was left only second in command. When at last in late 1929 it appeared he had the Comintern blessing, Earl Browder was given the mantle instead.[11] Browder went on to become general secretary of the Communist party, a post he held through the New Deal and World War II.

Browder and the later chief of the Trotskyist sect, Cannon, were associated in the Socialist party's Kansas City local and in editorship of *Worker's World* from 1917 to 1919. To boast leaders from the American heartland and especially of working-class origin was a significant asset to a party inspired by Marxism, a German doctrine, and a revolution in Russia, and to any party professing to lead the world's masses to a place in the sun. Marxist ideology was tainted in American eyes with foreign origin. Moreover, exponents of Marxism were often described inaccurately but vividly as wildly gesticulating bomb-throwing aliens or as foreign "slick" armchair subversives. Browder and Cannon belied such imagery.

Cannon, like Foster, typified the proletarian wing in early communism, and when the Trotskyist party polarized itself in 1939 and 1940, Cannon continued to hold the proletarian banner aloft. The " 'High Priest' of Trotskyism in the United States and the 'Patron Saint' of the Fourth International," he was a shrewd and capable politician, described once as a miniature Boss Murphy of Tammany Hall.[12] Had he elected a business or mainstream political career, he would surely have "gone very far and very high," as he did in the radical movement, a later opponent admitted, adding that he was "the most superb speaker that the party had."[13] He knew no foreign languages, but went regularly to Moscow, and after he was expelled from Russia he corresponded regularly with Trotsky. In 1915 he was general secretary of the IWW, protégé of its first general secretary, Vincent St. John. His being an authentic rebel in addition to his proficiency in labor matters gave Cannon an extraordinarily high status in his radical group. Chiding Cannon for being short on theory, Max Shachtman, his 1940 antagonist, noted that the defect did not detract from his leadership but did affect his personality. Aware of his shortcomings, Cannon cultivated a sneering attitude toward intellectuals and a corroding contempt for theory.[14] Nevertheless, Cannon wrote voluminously and lectured all over the nation interpreting current events and devising programs in the light of "Leninism-Trotskyism." The four Dunne brothers, Vincent Ray, Grant, Miles, and for a time, William; Farrell Dobbs; and such "proletarian-wing" radicals as Arne Swabeck and Karl Skoglund followed Cannon's lead.

City-bred intellectuals. Jay Lovestone, Bertram D. Wolfe, and others from the major cities (but mainly from New York) and largely of Jewish second-generation immigrant stock, constituted the third category, the city-bred intellectual. In their orbit were a number of young men such as Benjamin Gitlow still given to romanticizing revolutionary potentialities, who tended to oppose Foster and Cannon on such issues as legalizing the early Communist party and later uniting with progressives for electoral activity in farmer-labor party schemes. Dubbed the "City College boys" because many had attended classes at the City College of New York, in these first years some were revolutionary conspirators (an underground, illegal party seemed more authentically revolutionary), all were intraparty intriguers, and hair-splitting theoreticians.[15] Not one of the three mentioned—Lovestone, Wolfe, or Gitlow—joined the Trotskyist party; each ultimately left American communism having recanted or been expelled or both. However one "City College boy" did ally with Cannon and rose to become the Trotskyist intellectual mainstay. That person was Max Shachtman.

Shachtman was born in 1904 in Warsaw, Poland, of Jewish parents who brought him to America when he was not yet a year old. At their home in the Bronx the elder Shachtmans welcomed the socialist *Jewish Daily Forward* and discussions of socialism. The young Shachtman attended City College for about a year, browsed in the radical literature at the Lane Bookshop of the Rand School of Social Science, and listened to Communist soapbox oratory and informal discussions at what later was called "Trotsky Square," the small Central Park circle at Fifth Avenue and 110th Street.[16] During the 1920s he matured within the communist movement, but his remarkable journalistic and propaganda-making capabilities flowered in the next decade after the Trotskyist rupture. He and Cannon tolerated and leaned on each other, with a few hostile exchanges punctuating the relationship in the 1930s; in April 1940 Shachtman left the party after an eight-month verbal duel with Cannon in the pages of the *Internal Bulletin*. It is a tribute to Shachtman's integrity and commitment that despite the Cannon-Shachtman split and the fact that Trotsky took Cannon's side in the dispute, Shachtman was, after Trotsky's death, named administrator of Trotsky's literary estate. Twenty-four years later he was a member of the national executive committee of the Socialist party of America.[17] His impact on the Trotskyist strand of revolutionary socialism was profound. He exerted a powerful attraction on radical youth and served as their advocate in numerous party disputes. When he left the party, much of the youth membership left with him.

Another city-bred intellectual deserves note in this context. Like

Ludwig Lore, Max Eastman was in radical journalism before 1917 as editor of *The Masses;* like Lore, he joined the early party, but despite his nominal membership he never seemed one with the others; and like Lore, he adopted Trotsky's cause when the rift in the Russian party grew. Unlike Lore, Eastman came from a well-to-do old Yankee family, had a preparatory school background, and held an earned Columbia University Ph.D. "The first American Trotskyist was undoubtedly Max Eastman," Cannon said. On a trip to Russia in 1922, Eastman had an audience with Trotsky; in fact, Eastman introduced Cannon to Trotsky on that occasion. The journey and meeting were the first steps that later would bring Eastman's publication of an exposé of the Stalinist state, an exposé whose royalties still later financed the printing of the first Trotskyist organ. Eastman never joined Trotsky's party, but like Lore, he enrolled as a publicist for conservative Americanism in the 1940s. For the desertion, Trotsky denounced him as a dilettante in his final published article. Eastman was the strongest type of a coterie of literary Trotskyists that hovered on the fringes of the movement, damned by the Communists for Trotskyism and damned by the Trotskyists for unwillingness to submit to revolutionary discipline.[18]

The left-wing socialist leadership on the eve of 1919, the year a true American communist movement was founded, comprised, then, the three styles of revolutionary personality: the foreign-born theoretician, the more radical of the American labor unionists, and the city-bred intellectual. Although the three squabbled, and sometimes a few of their number seceded in a huff, from 1905 through the 1930s what united them was of more importance than what transient issue may have briefly divided them. All three came from the syndicalist and socialist movement to profess Marxism-Leninism. Therefore, the Russian Revolution shone as beacon for all three personalities because they shared a vision of a classless society where cooperation rather than competition would one day reign, and each was convinced this goal was attainable only through cataclysm. Therefore, all realized the urgency of press and podium propaganda and strike actions to proselytize the masses who were, after all, expected to precipitate the cataclysm under the guidance of a vanguard disciplined party. By 1919, first the utopian Socialists and next the reformist and patriotic socialists had been sheared away. The militant left-wing Socialists remained, to give birth to American Communism out of which would spring American Trotskyism.[19]

Party Characteristics

When Trotskyists formed a real party they duplicated the Stalinists' approach to doctrinal dissent. In being expelled, they excoriated the parent party for stifling free discussion with threat of explusion. Finding themselves in like straits, a small radical island in a hostile capitalist sea, they believed it necessary to require absolute accord. If a short period of theoretical debate over new policy turns or the wording of the program failed to yield harmony, the uncompromising ones faced ouster. Again and again this occurred in the 1930s, producing myriads of tiny purist "parties" that sparkled briefly and then expired. What stand should be adopted toward other radical parties? To what extent should Trotskyists participate in the electoral process? Which should receive programmatic preference: immediate demands for bread-and-butter measures from government and employers or a maximum program of struggle to precipitate the revolutionary moment? How should Trotskyists greet Hoover's and Roosevelt's foreign policies? What must a revolutionary Socialist do when his capitalist country is at war? To what degree should Trotskyists propagandize within established trade unions? Should new, more militant unions be formed? How should an American party differ from a European one? How do you adapt a European example to an American setting? What position should a Marxist take toward Stalinist Russia: slavish emulation, critical support, or total opposition? These questions fomented the debates that kept meeting halls humming far into the night.

For the twelve years from the birth of the sect until his death by assassination, Leon Trotsky furnished the answers to these questions. From exile the aging revolutionist attempted the impossible: to keep thoroughly abreast of political developments in each country whether or not he had a following there, and to watch closely and to analyze the augmenting world crisis. On the basis of his distant observations and from the standpoint of the Marxist dialectic, he prescribed the "proper" party line toward governments and events.

His two fundamental assumptions were (1) that Stalin had led the Soviet Union away from Marxism-Leninism onto the path of bureaucracy, his policies a prostitution of true socialism, and (2) that the reliability of dialectical materialism as interpretant of social change was unquestionable.* Scarcely an issue of the party press appeared without an article or letter from Trotsky; from these seeds the party line grew.

The same battles that were fought inside the Socialist parties and perhaps to a lesser degree within orthodox communism raged in other Trotskyist parties, wherever they existed around the world. As in every section, in the United States the role of party theorist or expositor of Marxism for the American context was significant. Marx had expounded an instrumentalist theory of knowledge, saying knowledge is indissolubly bound up with action, and his disciples consistently maintained that theory and action are one. Lenin decreed, "There can be no revolutionary action without a revolutionary theory," and he insisted the party should be directed by a central organ.[20] The press was the last vehicle a declining party would allow to crumble; it was an important adhesive, an emblem of unity in adversity and repression. A squadron of intellectuals who could bring the words of a classic or contemporary master to bear on current problems and a paper with loyal readership were equally needed by each other and by the party.

A member who submerged himself in theoretical matters often did not have time to organize workers or plan and participate in demonstrations and strikes. Usually the intelligentsia who did this work for revolutionary socialism came from the college-trained. A kind of elitism was therefore inbred within the radical movement, the elitism of the "City College boys," for instance. In reaction grew the reverse elitism of those with a labor activism orientation. The latter hold particular importance in Marxism with its supine faith in the redeeming role of the proletariat. The cultist of the proletarian mystique, busily organ-

---

*Dialectic materialism, a mainstay of Marxist economic analysis, holds that any existent condition calls forth its opposite. The two come into conflict and the clash produces a synthesis of the two poles. In reaching the synthesis, only the more socially useful elements from both are preserved. Thus the term "dialectic." Marx explained that this drama takes place repeatedly as the social manifestation of fundamental economic necessity—i.e., the clash of social forces reflects bases of subsistence, or, virtually survival tactics for both. Sustaining ideologies emanate from material need. Therefore, Marx added "materialism."

izing strikes and marches of the unemployed, played down the role of the easychair pontificator, but bolshevik discipline demanded a facade of unanimity to confront a hostile public. The American Trotskyist party's *Internal Bulletins* furnished an effective safety-valve for intra-party disputation.

Sometimes the questions found no resolution, but before each splinter broke from the main branch, debate filled *Bulletin* pages and meeting halls. Each splinter reflected in miniature the 1929 rupture that produced the Trotskyist movement. Cannon did not care that he had demanded freedom of discussion for airing differences when he and his faction were expelled for "Trotskyism." He as adamantly stuck to the line once adopted in convention and as determinedly stifled dissent as ever did Stalin or a representative to the American section from the Communist ("Third") International, such representatives always being specifically dispatched to member "sections" to ensure conformity. Dissenters in the Trotskyist organization who could not be brought to heel were as promptly and unceremoniously expelled as was Trotsky from the parent party in 1927. So new parties formed, replete with mimeographed news sheets and moral imperatives. But without the luster, romance, and glamor of a gen-uine Bolshevik like Leon Trotsky, they proved ephemeral. The Trot-skyists created a viable party. A pale reflection of orthodox com-munism but free of Moscow's domination, Trotskyists behaved as orthodox Communists did, opportunist in tactics, dogmatic in Marx-ian analysis, bolshevik in structure.*

By 1941 after the conviction under the Smith Act in Minneapolis of eighteen leaders (see Chapter 9 for explanation), the faithful had been whittled to a core of proletarian-oriented members. Fusion politics in the 1930s had brought in numerous young intellectuals from urban areas,

---

*Bolshevik organization consists of a party structure from neighborhood "local" through district branch and state executive committee to the national committee. When the national committee is not in session, a political committee settles questions that arise. Decisions are made on the basis of "democratic centralism." This means that after consider-able freedom of discussion at the lower levels, delegates are sent to an-nual convention which decides the program for the year; party discipline exacts undeviating adherence to the adopted program.

most of whom left the party during the consequent wave of expulsions and departures. The proletarian element, members of the blue-collar or "working" classes, kept its grip on organizational leadership while battling verbally with the remaining intellectuals. Both these wings, intellectual and proletarian, nevertheless acknowledged that dedication to total change had to supersede factional grievance. Both wings represented discontented fringes in society which had united in a radical commitment, and that fact presupposed willingness to yield "enormous energy and sacrifice" for moral ends. To get the job done made discipline necessary. Thrashing out issues to the point of fission was the sad truth about radical parties and in part accounted for their relative impotency in American politics.[21] "We do not envy the future historian of the American revolutionary movement when he faces the problem of tracing the course of the ephemeral sects. . . ." a leader who himself founded a splinter sect declared, and Max Eastman quipped, "The factional division of radical groups in America is like an onion trying to commit suicide."[22]

Although they failed to attract the wide following the philosophes drew, in some respects American radicals resembled their eighteenth-century French predecessors, whom Peter Gay described as carrying "on an unending debate with one another," their "exchanges . . . anything but polite . . . . To the delight of their enemies, the philosophes generated a highly charged atmosphere in which friendships were emotional, quarrels noisy, reconciliations tearful, and private affairs public."[23]

Gay went on to conclude, however, that these antagonists were really "a *petite troupe,* with common loyalties and a common world view." As with American radicals, "harassment or the fear of harassment drove the philosophes to remember what they had in common and forget what divided them. The report of a book banned, a radical writer imprisoned, a heterodox passage censored, was enough. Then, quarrelsome officers faced with battle, they closed ranks." The entire radical movement was capable of closing ranks in the face of severe "red scares," as in 1919 and 1952. This was true of small sects and large parties. These people devoted themselves to a grand design for human improvement. The devotion commanded a considerable and admirable, and under attack a ferocious loyalty.[24] Reflecting with nostalgia on the New York of the 1930s, Irving Howe felt "with pleasure and old stirrings of faith and conviction, that love for the unborn future which may yet redeem the past."[25]

In spite of the internal convolutions that sometimes threatened to dismantle the Trotskyist movement's structure, the prophetic vision of which Howe spoke, added to the work at hand, held it together and gave it historical continuity that other like sects did not sustain.

2

The First Trotskyists and the Communist Rupture

Forging the American Communist Party

The driving force behind left-wing socialism in 1919 was a profound conviction, in the words of James P. Cannon, that "Soviet Russia is a strike—the greatest strike in all history."[1] Embattled American radicals attached themselves firmly to the October revolution whose astonishing successes revived spirits almost crushed by enforcement of sedition and espionage legislation, post office censorship, raids, and deportations.

Since 1917 and the war question crisis, left-wing Socialists had met separately from the main party. Before the February revolution, Leon Trotsky and Nikolai Bukharin, sojourning in New York, had served actively at such conferences. In 1918 Cannon resigned from the declining Industrial Workers of the World and, because of its evident strength, joined the Socialist party left wing. When the call went out in April 1919 for a "National Conference of the Left Wing" to meet in New York in June, he had full credentials to participate in what was a preliminary convention of a new communist party. The April call-to-convention only suggested the conferees would create a "general council" to "conquer the Party for revolutionary socialism." But the June meeting concluded with a call to another, this one in Chicago, of "all revolutionary elements to unite with either a revolutionized Socialist party or with a Communist party."[2]

Prior events in 1919 furnished impetus for these actions. In Russia in January, Lenin had called together the third, or Communist, international. In February, occurring almost simultaneously were the Seattle general strike; a textile strike in Lawrence, Massachusetts; and a miners' strike in Butte, Montana, replete with "Soldiers', Sailors', and Workers' Council," evidence of a revival of dissent. In March, Lenin's third international, the Comintern, held its first congress, voted itself into existence,[3] and called for affiliates all over the world. It was in response to this summons that left-wing Socialists convened in June. By the time of the Chicago meeting that opened September 1, a new Communist party was a certainty. Unanswered still was the question, which group in the American radical movement would lead a new party? Nor had the questions that perennially agitated radical parties been settled. Would the party organize according to a menshevik, open membership model? Or should it be narrow and conspiratorial, the kind of revolutionary party Lenin demanded, and thus organize on the bolshevik model? And, how would the political requirements of the hour be accommodated to Marxist doctrine?

The new party had to hack out its answers from experience. Two Bolshevik parties formed, the foreign language federations filling the "Communist party," and native Americans predominating in the "Communist Labor party." Both followed the Socialist party's structural pattern and both pledged allegiance to the Comintern. But they disagreed over orientation, the Communist Labor party affirming commitment to an "American movement" (hazy and undefined) rather than a foreign one, its rival asserting that problems of American workers duplicated those of workers all over the world, a syndicalist (therefore an internationalist) tenet. Both necessarily professed Marxism. In the membership roster of both Russians had a clear majority, followed closely by Jews, Finns, Germans, and Italians. Noticeably absent were blacks and women.[4]

In 1920 in keeping with the spirit of the "united front" just enjoined on affiliates by the Comintern, the two parties merged into the United Communist party, underground in nature because of the conspiratorial tradition in bolshevism and fear of raids and reprisals. Unity was short lived. Tactical quarrels provoked the first split into factions. The "liqui-

dators," in which Cannon, Earl Browder, William Z. Foster, and Jay
Lovestone had coalesced (the final instance of their cohesion), wished
to emerge from underground as a fully legal party, thus "liquidating"
the secret apparatus. Bertram D. Wolfe's "rurals" argued to be alert for
a propitious moment to surface in this period of government repression.
Benjamin Gitlow and others constituted the "goose caucus," who
"cackled like geese," Lovestone complained, to remain underground
and conspiratorial as their Russian predecessors had done before 1917.
A disagreement over trade union policy also erupted. Foster, fresh from
his experience in the 1919 steel strike, favored action in established
unions, "boring from within," to avoid the isolation endemic in radical
sectarianism. The IWW men, Cannon among them, cherished the dual
union tradition.[5] Just as budding factionalism in the American party
became evident, officials in Moscow took the helm and gave detailed
directions. Beginning that relationship of guardian and ward between
Comintern and section party that typified communism until 1943,
Grigori Zinoviev, chairman of the Comintern, sent H. Valetski, his first
in a succession of representatives, over to the United States in the summer of 1922 to settle the question in favor of Cannon's liquidator faction, and to endorse Foster's boring from within as the method to reach
American workers. With Valetski came Joseph Pogany, a Hungarian
intellectual.

John Pepper, alias Joseph Pogany, became in 1923 the national
leader and was caught in the bitterest faction fighting yet to take place
in the communist movement. Because he was an authentic European
radical, he appealed to both immigrant and American-born workers. He
is of interest in the story of American Trotskyism because in 1924, after
the first official condemnation of Trotsky, Pepper usurped Ludwig Lore's
influence in the party. Lore had become a prime target as first spokesman for Trotsky. Conversely, Pepper, "the father of American anti-
Trotskyism," aligned with the American Stalinists until he was recalled
to Moscow.[6] Cannon, Pepper's "antagonist from first to last," chiefly
on account of disagreement on trade union policy and not over defense
of Trotsky, called Pepper "an orator of dazzling facility and effective-
ness," whose design was "to single out the more stubborn, more inde-
pendent-minded leaders of the left side for political annihilation" in his
own bid to make himself personal dictator.[7]

Pepper implemented in the American section the call for a mass legal party issued by the Comintern. Lenin's publication *Ultra-Left Communism, an Infantile Disorder* had deplored the isolation, ineffectiveness, and foolish romanticism of conspiratorial sects. In 1919 Russian revolutionary leaders had believed absolutely that world revolution would come in a matter of months. By 1921 (as Michigan communists, the first expelled from the American party, had predicted) those leaders admitted it might, after all, take years. After the underground organization had been "liquidated" at Pepper's behest, the legal "Workers party of America" held its first convention in July 1923. Cannon, just back from Moscow and his initial meeting with Trotsky, delivered the keynote address and was elected chairman of its national committee.[8]

After an abortive move to capture the Chicago-based Farmer-Labor Federation and foist on it a revolutionary program (as directed by the Comintern), the Workers party next considered entering the Conference for Progressive Political Action (CPPA), an organization of liberals, labor unionists, and Socialists who backed Robert M. La Follette of Wisconsin for the presidential nomination. Cannon and Foster, allies in opposing Pepper's domination of the Workers party, disapproved the farmer-labor party venture. Cannon noted in his memoirs that he nevertheless favored Lovestone's plan to approach the CPPA; in his older (1943) history of Trotskyism he termed both of these early fusion projects "wild adventures" because they represented dabbling in two-class, or class-collaborationist, politics.[9] Communists at their March 1924 meeting formally recommended national support for the CPPA. But the Communist party of the Soviet Union by May 1924 had changed its tactical program in the wake of Lenin's death in January. It recalled Pepper and ordered the American party to keep aloof from the La Follette organization, but to announce a slate of Workers party candidates for the general election.[10] So ended communism's first brief flirtation with the wider world of reformist politics.

A profound struggle for succession to party control was to take place in the Soviet Union in the spring of 1924 following Lenin's death. Kamenev, Zinoviev, and Stalin singled out Trotsky for excoriation and ordered each party section to denounce him. Serge Ivanovich Gusev (alias P. Green), new representative to the American section, effected the policy shift and guided opinion toward the Stalinist position. Trotsky, a lone individual and relative newcomer to the Bolshevik wing of the Russian Social Democratic party, was now accused of revolting against the Leninist Old Guard within the central committee of the Communist party of the Soviet Union. Stalin, emerging as strongest man in the triumvirate, first voiced "socialism in one country" in 1924 although he did not as yet pronounce it national policy. In subsequent months Zinoviev fell from grace in the Communist party of the Soviet Union and from chairmanship of the Comintern, replaced in the latter by Bukharin. On Comintern orders, P. Green saw that Charles Ruthenberg moved into the leadership of the American section, against Zinoviev's wishes and disappointing Foster's hopes. Clearly to prosper in the party a member had to denounce Trotsky.

Cannon did not, with the others, censure Trotsky, but neither did he raise objections to the policy changes or argue Trotsky's cause. Rather, Cannon promptly formed a center faction, the nucleus of the future Trotskyist grouping, aided by the organizational ability of Martin Abern, the budding journalistic talent of Max Shachtman, the support of trade union specialists Arne Swabeck and William Dunne (who would later leave Cannon's retinue).[11] Cannon reflected, "I think the beginning of the degeneration of the internal life of the party, from conflicts of clearly defined political tendencies . . . can be traced to the year 1925," implying that the conflicts centered on the question of denouncing Trotsky.[12] Gitlow later said Cannon hoped to assume sole leadership with his personal following inside the Cannon-Foster caucus, from which vantage point he could strike for leadership of the entire party. Foster did not bite this worm; he too wished to be party leader, not simply the trade union specialist ("spets," in party jargon) within a fresh Cannon caucus. Cannon's bid failed, as did Foster's. The singular fact in the selection of American leadership was that it was made in Moscow, not by the American comrades, and was made to ensure Stalin's ascendancy.[13]

Lenin's Testament

Trotsky and Stalin had contrasting personalities. Trotsky was an intellectual, a brilliant orator, theoretician, and organizer and deployer of men for vast enterprises, a character with considerable romantic appeal. Stalin was the drab, behind-the-scenes manipulator, master builder, and controller of the political apparatus, formulating policy pragmatically

according to his view of the requirements of the Soviet state, realistic
to the point of moral equivocation.[14] Trotsky held in his hands what
Max Eastman considered a trump card. As both attended in early 1924
the Thirteenth Congress of the Russian party, Trotsky informed Eastman privately of the "drift and essential details of the suppressed document called 'Lenin's Testament,' " the last lines of which Trotsky claimed
were written on January 4, 1923. The document hinted at Trotsky's
and Lenin's embryonic plans to "open fire not only against the state
bureaucracy, but against the Organizational Bureau of the Central Committee . . . ," and not only "to remove Stalin from his post of general
secretary, but to discredit him before the party as well." Lenin did not
recover sufficiently before his death to implement the design.[15]

Kamenev read the document aloud to the Thirteenth Congress assembled together and in separate delegations under pledges of secrecy;
he instructed delegates not to take notes or refer to the testament on
the floor. Greatly impressed, Eastman submitted the document to the
New York Times to publicize the current Soviet aberrations and to validate his own critique. The *Times* printed it on October 18, 1924, during the heat of the succession struggle in Moscow. Then, to Eastman's
embarrassment, Trotsky disavowed it as "so much mischievous inven-
tion," charging Eastman with slandering the Central Committee and
foreswearing any further relationship with him.[16] Trotsky and the party
press next disavowed Eastman's book, *Since Lenin Died* (1925), as essay
exposing and deploring party regimentation.

Trotsky's departure from the truth rose up to haunt him during the
Dewey Commission hearings in 1937. The subcommission conducting
the hearing had reason to question his veracity, for Trotsky from exile
in Russia's Alma Ata had in 1928 retracted the disavowals, excusing
them as an effort to stifle factional bitterness in the Communist party
of the Soviet Union. He had yielded, he claimed, to a politburo ulti-
matum that he take a public position on the testament. The testament
and *Since Lenin Died* appeared before the world events which would
bring Trotsky's exile. "We had to maneuver to win time, and the Troika
wanted to use this—to provoke an oppositional abortion." "It was not a
lie, but it was not the full truth," he confessed at the hearings in 1937.[17]

Eastman deserved better of Trotsky than the curt disclaimer and
lame recantation later. Eastman was "the champion of Trotskyism in a
literary way, and the first one to make the position of Trotsky known

in this country," commented Shachtman, and, in Cannon's words, Eastman had been "the first American Trotskyist."[18] With Trotsky, Eastman was saddened by the growth of bureaucracy in the revolutionary state and wished to reveal how Lenin's intentions had been corrupted.

What was in the controversial testament? In the form of a memorandum, it resembled a personal reminder, the jotting down of private rumination. It was succinct to the point of terseness. Lenin apprehended danger and instability in the relationship between Stalin and Trotsky: Stalin was unable to wield power with sufficient caution. Trotsky, although "distinguished by exceptional abilities and the most able man now in the Central Committee," exhibited "too great self-confidence, and is too attracted by the administrative side of affairs." After critical remarks about Bukharin ("not fully Marxist," too "scholastic") and Pyatakov, the "two most able forces," Lenin prescribed raising the Central Committee's membership to fifty or one hundred to forestall split.

The memo's postscript (dated January 4, 1923) contained the stern warning, "Stalin is too rude, and this fault, entirely supportable in relations among us Communists, becomes insupportable in the office of General Secretary": remove him and replace him with "another man in all respects different from Stalin."[19] Clearly the complexion of the Russian party and the Comintern would have been different had Lenin acted or had this been put into effect upon his death. Because of failing health, Lenin could not act and the document remained suppressed until Eastman released it. Even then Trotsky, his party days numbered, had tried to restore harmony to a party embroiled in a power struggle.

The incidence has significance in that an unflattering critique of Stalin later associated with the term "Trotskyism" had been made public and subjected to debate through a newspaper of international scope, a critique that questioned the legitimacy of the current Soviet regime since it had been articulated by the father of the Soviet state.

Events of 1926 and 1927

Strikes punctuated 1926 as they had 1919, sparked by an abortive general strike in Great Britain. Al Weisbord, a young Harvard-trained lawyer in the Workers party, alone organized the "unorganized, unskilled, and low-paid" textile workers in Passaic, New Jersey, "neglected by the A.F.L.," and called a strike which the Workers party entered. When the AFL Textile Union, brought in at the last hour, negotiated a poor settlement, the party blamed the defeat on Weisbord's dual union organizing method.[20] Three years later, however, during the Communist party's third period and possibly inspired by the Weisbord episode, the comrades endorsed a new textile workers' industrial union formed independent of the AFL—clearly a dual union.[21]

The year 1927 was a notable one for American Communists. In March, Workers party leader Charles Ruthenberg died. A replica of the Russian succession struggle took place in the American party. The Cannon-Foster caucus maintained majority support until August when the Comintern promoted Jay Lovestone to general secretary in order to counter the factionalism within the Cannon-Foster group.[22] Quarrels between the two had resulted from difference over trade union policy and rivalry for leadership. Buttressed with Comintern pressure, Lovestone obtained majority support at the August 1927 plenum* and kept his status until August 1929.

Lovestone was known as chief propagator of "American exceptionalism," a thesis that viewed the United States apart from the mainstream of the world revolutionary movement due to special conditions resulting from the peculiar staying power of American capitalism and treated American capitalism as on the ascent and destined for more and better things, surging toward a "Victorian age." Considered a right-wing, or conservative, approach, "exceptionalism" implicitly rejected confrontations as useless under the circumstances and prescribed the same policy of biding for time that Stalin was implementing in the Soviet Union. Since no country shares identical conditions with another, Trotskyists believed that exceptionalism furnished a convenient alibi for inaction to armchair socialists in any capitalist society, and was a close cousin to Stalin's "socialism in one country." Paradoxically, Trotsky had advanced a like doctrine. He noted in American life exceptional circumstances which, for instance, "would make a revolution in Germany far more important for France than for America," due to unevenness of

---

*The plenum was a crucial kind of meeting of party officials regularly held to settle major questions, a kind typical of American Marxist parties.

historical development in the two countries.[23] Presumably France, whose industrial revolution came earlier than America's and whose capitalist arrangements lacked the special viability of America's, was more incipiently revolutionary. Embraced under other labels by Lovestone's rivals and opponents, the thesis drew encomium only when termed "exceptionalism" and attached to his name. In a party dependent on theory, theoretical dissension is sometimes thrown forward as a smoke screen for the feuding that accompanies personality clashes during scrambles for position.[24] In any case, the Comintern intruded to settle such squabbles in the interest of the Stalin regime and Soviet policies. These interests, officials believed, were best served in 1927 by having Lovestone elevated to leadership to break the Cannon-Foster deadlock.

The Russian party by 1926-1927 had advanced socialism in one country to dogma, elevated Bukharin to chairmanship of the Comintern, and begun in earnest to root out "Trotskyism." As in the American section, Trotskyism in the Communist party of the Soviet Union, was in part political rivalry masquerading as ideological irreconcilability. True, Trotsky had opposed the official Comintern line on the British general strike and in 1927 he had opposed Comintern support of Chiang Kai-shek and the Kuomintang in the Chinese Revolution. These were tactical disagreements. Certainly Trotsky was not "counter-revolutionary" as charged. Nor had Stalin abandoned the doctrine of permanent revolution. The plain truth was that a dynamic and influential figure like Trotsky posed too formidable a threat to the monolithic regime Stalin thought necessary to bring industrial technology quickly to a technically and socially medieval land. Proof lies in the fact that as soon as Trotsky was out of the way, through a series of expulsions Stalin made a ". . . left turn, deposed Bukharin, and appropriated much of Trotsky's program. He rose to power by uniting the opposition to his rival, Trotsky, then destroying the united opposition, section by section. He chose his apparatchiks by the criterion of anti-Trotskyism, replacing independent and gifted men by mediocrities who owed their posts entirely to him."[25] He was then free to apply the opposition's ideas in his own way. Already removed from politburo and central committee, at the Fifteenth Congress of the Russian party in December 1927 Trotsky was expelled and placed at the disposal of the GPU (the Soviet secret police) who transported him to Alma Ata on the Turkestan border.[26]

Professing that he did not know the issues, Cannon stayed aloof and did not denounce either Lore or Trotsky. Reflecting later on his behavior in 1927, Cannon found he had been "deeply oppressed by the developments in the Russian party and the expulsion of the Opposition."[27] Probably he failed to speak out because he wished to have more time to observe closely how these dramatic occurrences would affect the American section and his own chances for obtaining leadership. By the time the Sixth Comintern Congress convened in 1928 he had progressed further in evaluating his chances. The news that Cannon had stepped forward as supporter of the Russian opposition came as a bombshell, Gitlow reported. "Why the sudden conversion?" he asked, skeptically.[28]

From August 1927 when Lovestone had won his majority to succeed Ruthenberg until the Sixth Comintern Congress in Moscow in July 1928, Lovestone was in uncontested control. In February 1928 a plenum reviewed the six months of Lovestone's rule and prepared for the forthcoming congress. No one posed the question of Trotskyism, nor did it come up at the May 1928 plenum. "There was no one in the American party in 1927 who might even be considered a 'Trotskyite,'" said Cannon.[29]

This was true because Ludwig Lore was no longer in the party. He had outspokenly favored Trotsky's cause in 1926 and was the very first to be expelled from international communism for "Trotskyism," fully two years before the wave of expulsions. Lore refused to accept the monolithic concept of the party and the rigid military discipline. For this he might in subsequent years have clashed with Trotsky himself. After his ouster in 1926 Lore declined to go to Moscow to plead his case. As Irving Howe and Lewis Coser remarked, Communism wanted "weak men, obedient men"; Lore did not fit, and was thought "an alien irritant in the otherwise healthy body of American Communism." Lore later merged into the American mainstream as a columnist for the *New York Evening Post*. The Trotskyist party in which he had by then enrolled and to which he still belonged demanded prior censorship of his column; he refused to permit it and melted away from the movement, a man who held personal independence foremost.[30]

In 1928 so clear was Cannon's name of Trotskyist taint that the plenum elected him delegate to the Moscow congress. Aware that Fosterites hoped a Comintern decision would repudiate Lovestone's secretaryship and knowing that this might indeed happen, Cannon preferred not to go. No man in his caucus faction, a buffer group between the trade union specialists such as Foster and William Dunne and the organizers and propagandists, had a chance to win leadership. Representing a minority faction-within-a-faction, Cannon could see that even if the leadership changed, the Cannonites would remain a minority; the Russian leaders did not take them seriously. But Shachtman, Abern, and others insisted that Cannon join nineteen delegates to the Sixth Comintern Congress.[31] Thus it was that he went to Moscow.

The Sixth Comintern Congress

Three events occurred at the congress that would have importance for Trotsky's supporters. First, the questions of Lovestone's and Bukharin's respective posts were raised. The Cannon-Foster caucus delegates drew up a statement against the "Right Danger in the American Party" as the July 1928 "Opposition Platform." The document, written by Alexander Bittelman and signed by Cannon, Foster, Dunne, and others, assailed "exceptionalism" and related "serious opportunist errors": the viewpoint that the depression was merely a "recession," Lovestone's campaign to "Americanize" the party by drawing on the American Revolution for heroes and events to celebrate, his continued insistence that "objective conditions" in the United States rendered unfeasible the development of a mass communist party. The "Opposition Platform" urged agitation and liberal use of Marxist clichés.[32] In 1972 Shachtman reassessed the "Right Danger" as "a trumped-up 'program' of which a round nine-tenths was political and economic rubbish."[33]

Lovestone and Bukharin were riding the same wave. If the gossip that Stalin intended to depose Bukharin was correct, that event could precipitate Lovestone's fall in the American section. Bukharin denied before the Senioren Konvent (a committee of elders) any rift between himself and Stalin, and public measures bore out the denial awhile longer. He was reelected Comintern chairman. This was outward show, however. Formal declarations meant little. In the corridors, or the "corridor congress," Stalin undermined and shattered Bukharin's support. Bukharin's and Lovestone's days as leadership figures were numbered.

In the American section Foster's second bid for leadership represented by the joint warning against the "Right Danger" failed. Nevertheless the Russian party had been seeking fresh American leaders. Foster's record of bond purchases during World War I (not really pertinent now but raised at issue by Lovestone) and his known factional bellicosity thwarted his bid. Gitlow reported that Stalin rejected Foster and chose William F. Dunne as a promising leader, an intellectual who projected a proletarian image. But Dunne's reputation for excessive drinking made him ineligible.[34] Lovestone retained his post for a few months longer.

The second significant event at the congress was the emergence of Earl Browder as candidate for American leadership. A respectable-looking white-collar worker of old American stock, he reflected well on the party and gave promise of following policies exactly as instructed by Kremlin leaders. Another Comintern representative with plenipotentiary powers would oversee the American section, edit its organ, and make its decisions. Had Cannon been a serious candidate (which he was not), he would never have submitted to such an arrangement. To obey orders handed down to him from a strong international figure like Stalin, a head of state and director of an international network of organizations such as the Comintern threatened to become, was a far cry from being American spokesman for a powerless, exiled revolutionist (however charismatic and brilliant) like Trotsky. Due to immobility, an exile must accept Cannon's evaluation of American developments. The situation would allow far greater scope for the strong-willed Cannon to exercise his own discretion in party affairs. Browder understood the political reality of American leadership and knew his personal limitations. He had already proved his ability to function as loyal bureaucrat on his current tour of duty as secretary of the Pan-Pacific Secretariat in the Far East. He knew the intimate workings of the international movement. Most important, he recognized Stalin as strong man in the CPSU. Browder's time had come.

The third major event at the congress was the circulation of a critical document, "The Draft Program of the Comintern: A Criticism of Fundamentals," written by the expelled, slandered, and exiled Trotsky. Only one-third of the paper, the theoretical portion, made the rounds. On the first page appeared the command, "Must be returned to the secretariat immediately after reading." Congress directors did not want

any delegate to return home and publicize the document as Eastman
had done with Lenin's "Testament."

Why the directors circulated the document remains a mystery. Shachtman speculated that Stalin may have done it to undercut Bukharin's
authority, for in the section given out, Trotsky criticized the draft program as Bukharin's work. Cannon was drawn to Trotsky's deprecatory
analysis. Maurice Spector, a leader in the Canadian section who had
been close to the Cannon-Foster faction, had sympathized with Trotsky's
"criticism." But Cannon's fresh inclination toward Trotsky may have
surprised Cannon himself. Trotsky's stance was known as a leftist one,
and the Cannonites, accused of many things, had never been labeled leftists or ultra-leftists.[35]

Shachtman explained later that the gamble for factional, then party,
leadership had led the Cannon faction up a blind alley. Cannon's factional slogan, "Unite the Party in the Faction Fight," failed to suggest
how to "unite." When racked by factional disagreement any party will
seek unity. Cannon merely said the comrades should fall into rank behind
him. Perhaps he sensed the weakness of his position for, according to
Shachtman, he was glum and morose about his prospects.[36]

Cannon described differently his mood at the congress. He claimed
his faction meeting in caucus in Moscow begged him to fight for the
party leadership, assuring him of their backing until the time Lovestone
could be overthrown. He delayed a reply to them while he and Spector
conferred. Apparently he decided the outlook for success was bleak; in
any case another option lay to hand at precisely that time. Cannon
could embrace Trotsky's cause with its genuine, logically presented,
and convincing viewpoint (which his own factional cause had lacked).
He decided in favor of Trotsky and probably did so under this impulse.

Spector and Cannon "concluded that the cause of Trotskyism would
be served better in the long run if we frankly proclaimed his program
and started the education of a new cadre on that basis, even though it
was certain to mean our own expulsion and virtual isolation at the start
of the new fight." But neither spoke out at the congress in favor of
Trotsky's "criticism." Cannon recalled,

> We let the caucus meetings and the congress sessions go to the
> devil while we read and studied this document. Then I knew what
> I had to do, and so did he . . . . It was as clear as daylight that

>Marxist truth was on the side of Trotsky. We made a compact
>there and then—Spector and I—that we would come back home
>and begin a struggle under the banner of Trotskyism.

Cannon and Spector spoke only to one British delegate about Trotskyism and gave no inkling to the rest of the delegation of the position they
had decided to defend. They tried to smuggle their copies of the criticism out, but as a precaution they stole an extra one from another
commission member in case theirs had to be surrendered.[37]

Party members in the United States knew nothing about the episode.
"We'd have denied it indignantly" if someone had reported it then, "as
a factional slander against Cannon and our group," Shachtman recollected. Yet when Cannon returned, he chose Shachtman as the first
comrade beside his wife, Rose Karsner, to read the criticism, first feeling out their responses cautiously, mentioning the hopelessness of party
advancement. Shachtman immediately swung to Trotsky's side, as did
the other four comrades who saw it (the only ones to do so before expulsion): "All burned with indignation that Trotsky's viewpoint had
been viciously misrepresented by the Russian leadership."[38]

The small core of initiates, understanding the consequences of their
Trotskyism whether in the Russian party or any other, chose to delay
and secretly proselytize among the Cannonites. It was necessary to proceed carefully, to ask leading questions such as, "What do you really
know about the Trotsky opposition? Have you read much by Trotsky?
Are you sure he is wrong? Could the Comintern leaders possibly be
wrong in opposing him? You and I know they are wrong in supporting
Lovestone and wrong in opposing our faction, for example." The growing number of converts diligently studied the documents of the Russian
opposition. Max Eastman had translated the opposition platform under
the title, *The Real Situation in Russia,* and it became "the arsenal of
the Trotskyists."[39]

Despite precaution, by October 1928 suspicions were aroused. It
seemed astonishing that Cannon, Shachtman, Abern, and other key
people could favor Trotsky. Foster preferred to dismiss the possibility.
An exodus would weaken his faction. Surely the Cannon-Foster faction
could not have harbored in its own midst a nest of heretical Trotskyists?
But if it had, and Lovestone found out first, the disgrace would magnify.
For that reason the Trotskyists were accosted at a joint caucus meeting

in New York and asked by comrades either to confirm or to disavow
their position on the Trotsky question. For about four weeks, Cannon,
Shachtman, and the others stalled, objecting to the caucus's raising the
Trotsky issue, a settled question, at all. But the comrades contended
that now disavowing Trotsky was vouching for him. When they finally
asked the direct question, by a predesigned plan Cannon abstained,
Shachtman voted "no," and Abern "yes." The Fosterites called a special
central committee meeting chaired by John Pepper and Lovestone "to
investigate the charges against Cannon-Shachtman-Abern of harboring
Trotskyist ideas and carrying on Trotskyist propaganda in the party."

Lovestone's followers promised an open trial and free speech for the
accused hoping to embarrass the Fosterites by making a public show of
the Trotskyism that had grown under Foster's nose. The new Trotskyists cheered the chance to propagandize further. "The more we'd talk,
the more they'd learn," Shachtman observed. The Foster and Lovestone
people voiced their hatred of Trotskyism.

> Some of the evidence against us was absolutely fantastic and
> hilarious. I remember the manager of the party bookstore on
> Union Square testified, "Shachtman came into the bookstore and
> asked if there's a copy of Eastman's book there." That was the
> sum and substance of his evidence. I [Shachtman] had asked for
> a copy of Trotsky's book to read. It was almost taken for granted
> once you read anything on Trotsky you would be a Trotskyist . . . .
> The only sure way of maintaining an anti-Trotsky position is not
> to read what Trotsky had written. It was good enough to know
> what Trotsky's opponents said about him.[40]

The accused were questioned on their views of Trotskyism leading
toward the pivotal issue, What did they think of Trotsky's position? Day
after day they hedged, the audience to the inquisition growing steadily.
Finally Cannon, Shachtman, and Abern were forced to a clear declaration. Cannon "read to a hushed and somewhat terrified audience of
party functionaries a statement wherein we declared ourselves 100 percent in support of Trotsky and the Russian opposition on all principled
questions . . . ."[41] The central committee promptly arraigned and indicted all three. Foster, spurred by Browder, drew up a sharp motion
against them. Lovestone contrived a milder motion, hoping to protract

the inquiry and utilize the issue to smash the Foster faction by harping
on the fact that out of the ranks of that caucus sprang, overnight, no-
torious Trotskyists. On October 27, 1928, Cannon, Shachtman, and
Abern walked out, expelled from the group they had helped found.[42]

Now began the actual struggle for American Trotskyism, the struggle
to build a party to take power in the United States, a struggle that began with no resources except human determination and the exhilaration
of fresh purpose.

The Workers (Communist) Party, Left Opposition

Initially the Trotskyists intended to reform the Communist party,
not construct a rival one. Since Trotsky was right, one day he would
be redeemed and recalled to the Communist party of the Soviet Union
and the Comintern; subsequently the party would reinstate his followers in their rightful, leadership roles. Moreover, the comrades still in the
party (in the Trotskyists' eyes) remained comrades with different opinions. For four years the expelled members sustained this erroneous analysis of their situation. During the next two months expulsions took
place in the party branches. The first issue of the American Trotskyist
organ announced the expulsion of Arne Swabeck and Albert Glotzer in
Chicago. A telegram from Minneapolis dated November 18 announced
expulsions of sixteen, including Vincent Ray Dunne, brother of William
F. Dunne who stayed with the main party. In Kansas City two left-wing
Socialist party members who had come through the Communist Labor
party were expelled; three were ousted in Philadelphia. Expelled also
were some Slavic factory workers in Cleveland, an Italian group, and
Spector, the Canadian leader. More than sixty expulsions were executed
in six weeks. The Stalinist press reported that 150 of Trotsky's aides in
military and political work were arrested in the Soviet Union. A later
report indicated that 300 were arrested. Victor Serge, communist ideal-
ist, revolutionist, and journalist was exiled to Central Asia.[43]

In the heat of immediate reaction Cannon addressed a central committee plenum, and taking his cue from Trotsky's criticism, he charged
the party with "monstrous distortions of Lenin's teachings," with denial of party democracy, with rampant suppression. The party expelled
the Trotskyists in the same manner in which the Socialist party expelled

its left wing in 1919, he complained. Some had believed there was no need to create a new "communist" party in 1919, if only the Socialist party had permitted discussion of important questions. Today, true democracy would allow Trotskyists to voice their ideas and debate them *within* the Workers (Communist) party. But alas, instead of permitting the open airing of opinion, "fascist gangster tactics" were used by Stalin's "regime of bureaucratic strangulation" which lopped off good proletarians leaving a party of unqualified middle-class careerists to take leadership jobs: "professional dentists, professors, journalists, etc." If the speech was calculated to provoke a groundswell of demands for reinstatement, it failed. Nor did an appeal against their expulsion bear fruit.[44]

An organ to promulgate their ideas assumed priority. Looking toward this, before expulsion Shachtman made arrangements with a printer, a personal acquaintance and former IWW member, Joe Cannata, to produce a newssheet in his small shop. Shachtman's friend at that moment was "out of the movement but in sympathy with it. Cannata suggested the name *Militant*. We snapped it up right away—an excellent name," and the radical printer offered to extend them credit, recalled Shachtman. Funding came to the *Militant* from some Hungarian communists led by Louis Basky; from an expelled group of Italian Trotskyists in New York, followers of Amadeo Bordiga; from a small group in Boston; and from Max Eastman. Eastman actually furnished seed money for the *Militant*. Shachtman and Cannon found Eastman "immensely excited by the prospect of a Trotskyist group being organized and led by real party people such as he never was, who might have influence over Communist party militants such as he, Eastman, could never exercise." He handed over for the *Militant* the two hundred dollars paid him as translator of *The Real Situation in Russia*. By these means the new organ of the left opposition came into existence.[45]

The first issue appeared on November 18, 1928, featuring the headline, "FOR THE RUSSIAN OPPOSITION! AGAINST OPPORTUNISM AND BUREAUCRACY IN THE WORKERS COMMUNIST PARTY OF AMERICA!" Under the headline marched diatribes soon to become watchwords of the Trotskyists. The editors were astonished at the Fosterites who signed the "Right Danger in the American Party" presented at the Sixth Congress; now these Fosterites coalesced with Lovestone against caucus comrades. The editors contrived a respectable age for their faith. It was born in 1922 when Trotsky struggled to keep rich Russian peasants and technocrats from rooting themselves in power, then adopted by Zinoviev and Kamenev in 1926, boasted the *Militant.* Trotskyists pledged to combat socialism in one country, to defend the Soviet Union as a workers' state while opposing the Stalinist canker within it, and to tell the truth that "centrists and reformists" would not tell. They demanded publication of Trotsky's documents and insisted that Trotsky be brought from exile and reinstated. The editors would expose errors of Stalinist policies (as yet they were not ready for an all-out attack on the party and regime they hoped to reform and reenter). They would reveal the injustices in capitalist society: the execution of Sacco and Vanzetti and the twelve-year imprisonment of Tom Mooney and Warren Billings, for instance. Last, and significantly, the first *Militant* bragged, "We're still Communists. The CP [Communist party] is our party too, we helped build it, and only want the right to express our viewpoint."[46]

In December 1928 Maurice Spector, former editor of a Canadian Communist publication, joined Cannon, Shachtman, and Abern, as editors of the *Militant.* Two years later Arne Swabeck, former Chicago organizer and national committeeman on the party-sponsored Trade Union Education League, joined the staff.[47] Although others came and left, for the next twelve years Cannon and Shachtman stayed on the board, gradually coming to represent the proletarian and intellectual wings. The world events that mandated theoretical reevaluation also brought Shachtman's departure from the Trotskyist fold in 1940. This shattered the duo.

The Boston Branch and *Bulletin No. 1*

In early November 1928, six isolated communists in Boston decided to call themselves the Independent Communist League and organize against Stalinism. Two had recently returned from brief visits to their native Russia dismayed by the hardening bureaucracy, and in the case of the one woman, with the deteriorating and "brutal condition of females." A physician and pioneer in the birth control movement, spokeswoman for the tiny fellowship, Antoinette Konikow had joined Plekhanov's Emancipation of Labor group in Switzerland. In 1893 she emigrated to the United States, got caught up with Jewish workers in

Boston, founded a Workman's Circle, and enrolled in the Socialist Labor party. Expelled from this party, she moved into Eugene Debs's socialist movement in 1897, the movement that soon fused with others to form the Socialist party. Twenty-two years later she joined the vigorous young Communist party. The American branch, or party, paid particular attention when she refused to vote Trotsky's expulsion after a two-and-a-half-hour speech by Lovestone in Boston. She rose and gave a ten-minute rebuttal, indicating that they in Boston had not had a chance to read Trotsky's own statements and could consequently reach no correct conclusion. "The remarks of Comrade Trotsky, the . . . right hand of Lenin, may well be considered by us as an S.O.S. to the comrades of the world, warning of the great disaster Soviet Russia is facing."[48]

When ordered by Lovestone to come to New York, she refused to go. Since the Boston group could not get a majority to expel her, her notice came by mail from headquarters in New York.

Early in December 1928 the first (and only) issue of *Bulletin No. 1, The Independent Communist League* went to press. Shortly before, Konikow as the league's secretary received mimeographed material by Shachtman, Cannon, and Abern for inclusion in the *Bulletin*. Her group joined Cannon's right away. "We were rightly proud of our little *Bulletin* and were heading in the right direction," Konikow reflected ten years later. "We still swim against the current, but so did Lenin."[49]

George Weissman, a Trotskyist organizer at Harvard University in the mid-1930s, remembered Konikow as elder stateswoman in the Boston branch. Already an "old lady, she attended branch meetings quite regularly, brought to the door by her son Willy, also a member; gave a class at her house for young comrades; turned out for all affairs; and took a great interest in everything." Although she did not serve on the executive committee in Weissman's years there, "it was only because she didn't want to. She was an important and active member whose advice was heeded on all policy matters."[50]

The Boston branch grew by 1936 to about fifty members, attracting at first a few middle-aged Communists and some women from the garment industry. Then in came a "whole gang, about a dozen, of Irish fellows, both South Boston and Mission Hill Irish, who became radical on their own and began shopping around the various groups." They found the Trotskyists most persuasive. "When these Irishmen had been

assimilated, they developed the actual working leadership," and Konikow turned over the role of organizing to them. From there the Boston
branch went out to battle Communists as well as Coughlinites (followers of the anti-Semitic, anti-Wall Street radio priest Father Charles
Coughlin) for the right to free speech, all the while beset by the pro-
Coughlin police, on the streets of Boston and Lynn.[51] Thus fared in its
infancy the first branch to declare unanimously for Trotsky.

Communist Party Reprisals

Retaliating swiftly, the parent party sanctioned threats and acts of
hooliganism against Konikow's unit, against purveyors of the *Militant,*
against speakers at Trotskyist meetings. Gitlow recalled that the Communist party insisted on absolute and sole right to stage street corner
rallies, and would heckle, push, spit on, and break up with pocket knives,
cudgels, and iron pipes any gathering of other radicals. Brass knuckles
and blackjacks were the weapons most often reported in *Militant* accounts. When a meeting would disperse, the Stalinists "cheered, sang
the Internationale with raised fists" and held their own meeting on the
spot. The Communist party had sworn not to let Trotskyists get a toe-
hold in the United States. The Trotskyist press logged disruptions at
meetings in New Haven, Cleveland, Los Angeles, Chicago, Minneapolis,
and Salt Lake City, all within three months after the first expulsions.
As a defense, Trotskyists hired strong-arm men to protect their speakers.
The IWW sent "seamen, lumberjacks, stevedores, and bindlestiffs, etc.,
all itching to get their hands on Communists who they said ruined their
organization."[52]

Such melees persisted on into the 1940s. In the wake of the 1928
expulsion, however, they happened with great and predictable frequency.
Some meetings were canceled due to fear that Stalinists would provoke
a riot. Every issue of the *Militant* after November 18 recorded fresh
episodes. A real anomaly, the hated capitalist police sometimes had to
be called to break up fighting among radicals. Most cowardly were the
Stalinists' assaults on lone *Militant* salespeople. One issue of the *Militant* detailed an attack by forty on a single saleswoman in New York
City; another told of two women selling papers being attacked by thugs
and called "counterrevolutionary prostitutes." Two others were as-

saulted and given black eyes. Harry Roskolenko claimed that once while he was peddling the *Militant* three leather-jacketed Communists jumped him, knocked out three teeth, and pulped his testicles. In Philadelphia, two *Militant* salesmen were beaten by Communists wielding brass knuckles and clubs. Perhaps exaggeration entered these gruesome stories, the kind to which a propaganda sect inevitably resorts. With finality, the Communist party denied responsibility, asserting that "obscure militant workers" did these violent deeds. Shortly, though, Trotskyists met force with superior force. True, *Militant* salespeople alone were always in some hazard, but rallies could proceed peacefully when sluggers and other undesirables were escorted out by burly guards.[53]

To prove Trotskyists were counterrevolutionary, Stalinists broke into Cannon's and Rose Karsner's home in late December 1928 to steal the group's files and records. Allegedly Lovestone and his cohorts entered and "took everything there was, including the money and our huge correspondence which could have been carried in one fist." A few days later the Communist party press printed its exposé of the counterrevolutionaries. Any letters that would have belied the tale were discreetly omitted. The opposition was accused of cohabiting with "dark reactionary forces, government forces," and with a mysterious millionaire. "It was just a big squib," recalled Shachtman, noting that if a tiny minority party would burglarize and steal here as part of the fight against Trotskyism, one could expect worse offenses in Russia with state and police power at its command, indirectly validating the American opposition's portrayal of a despotic bureaucracy in the Kremlin. Nevertheless the Communist party "simply brazened it out," in Shachtman's words, making no effort to conceal its nefarious act.[54]

Answering the charge of complicity with the political right, Trotskyists confessed: Yes, we have connections with Max Eastman and are selling his book. We communicate with left opposition groups abroad. We do have Amos Pinchot on our subscription list. But we have no relationships with a "mysterious millionnaire" or with Calvin Coolidge. Nor do any capitalists finance us in a propaganda war against the Communist party. But if Pinchot's subscription is significant, what of the *Daily Worker's* subscribers, who include the Commander-in-Chief of the U.S. fleet, a Catholic Archbishop, Warner Brothers, and an official of the Chicago *Tribune?* No, the attack is "cheap two cent sensationalism, falsification, and political bankruptcy."[55]

The new sect survived the assaults. The *Militant* rolled off the press regularly and new members came in, the street-brawling attracting a few liberals interested in free speech. Radicals, even some Stalinists, were won over, the *Militant* purred. Because of their nationwide scope, Trotskyists soon had a skeletal national structure, and on February 15, 1929— urged by Trotsky—they published a "platform," a statement of principles and position on current issues drafted by Cannon, Shachtman, and Abern.[56]

In the spring of 1929, the Soviet government indeed deposed Bukharin from the Comintern chairmanship and editorial board of *Pravda,* and replaced him with Vyatoslav Molotov. The Soviet government dispatched Trotsky into exile in Turkey, and published an open letter indicating that it was correcting its policies—changes obviously based on Trotsky's criticisms. With his ally Bukharin's demotion, by the opening date of the national conference of the Trotskyist opposition in Chicago, May 17, 1929, Jay Lovestone's leadership in the American Communist party was undermined and his days in the party numbered. Seven months after the Trotskyist expulsions, the American politburo suspended Bertram D. Wolfe, ousted Gitlow from the secretariat, and expelled Lovestone from the party for "opportunism."[57]

Despite the changes, it became increasingly apparent that hostilities engendered between Trotskyist and Communist leaders made it unlikely that the apostate sect could ever return to the parent party.

3

The Communist League of
America (Opposition): First Years

Lovestone's faction supported a motion to allow the suspended or expelled Trotskyists an appeal to the next plenum of the central committee, but James P. Cannon and Max Shachtman snubbed the concession. The Fosterites had voted "instantaneous and irrevocable expulsion." The dissidents well knew the Lovestone plan was to keep them around as an internal factional issue, but they left peacefully because they knew, too, that prospects for full reinstatement were bleak.

The International Labor Defense (ILD)

Just as bleak appeared the prospects for survival as an independent organization. The outcasts had no resources: "zero—in personal possession, organizational fund, we didn't have a nickel," no salary, no severance pay.[1] Cannon felt a keen disappointment, too, in being expelled from the International Labor Defense (ILD) which he had helped the party establish in 1925. Supposedly nonpartisan, and under Cannon's administration scrupulously limited to labor defense, the ILD had been affected least by factionalism of any of the Communist operations. Its sole departure from principle lay in a reluctance to work with the Socialist party. Cannon had run it smoothly and had kept it autonomous and financially sound. He later remembered, "The ILD was born in Moscow in discussion with Bill Haywood," both dismayed over persecution of workers in America. Haywood "to the end of his life . . . continued to be an active participant in the work of the ILD by correspondence." In its first years it aided "class war prisoners in the United States—scores of IWW members railroaded . . . under the criminal syndicalism laws. . . ." Furthermore, the ILD helped in the highly publicized J. B. McNamara, Sacco and Vanzetti, and Mooney and Billings defense cases. Its purpose, Cannon explained, was "nonpartisan defense without political discrimination,"[2] and according to historian Theodore Draper, the ILD represented the most mature expression of a front organization thus far achieved by the American Communists. In its bailiwick Cannon assembled the nucleus of his subsequent political faction: Martin Abern, later Trotskyist district organizer in Chicago and New York, and Max Shachtman, intellectual, journalist, and perennial editor of Trotskyist publications. Abern served the ILD as assistant national secretary, and Shachtman, as editor of its organ, *Labor Defender*.[3] "We thought of the ILD as a factional fortress," commented Shachtman.[4] The Lovestoneites had the party machinery, the Fosterites the trade union machinery, while the Cannonites gravitated around the ILD.

The ILD furnished attorneys, agitated for release of prisoners, raised bail monies, and attempted to obtain retrials and pardons. When a case was up for trial, the staff held protest meetings, circulated petitions, and carefully cultivated good relations with other radical groups: it was a successful united front operation. After the Trotskyist exodus, expulsion from the "factional fortress" followed as a matter of course.

With Cannon, Shachtman, and Abern out of the ILD, Lovestone ran it for awhile, then Foster; at last it was dissolved. Recognizing a need for a like defense agency because the Communist organization absolutely refused to assist other radical groups, Cannon's party established the Nonpartisan Labor Defense (NPLD) by the mid-1930s. Although the NPLD did not serve such spectacular cases as the ILD had, it functioned to the same end.

American Politics in the Early Depression

The opposition faction faced a dismal economic environment. Prescient economists warned that the 1927 employment and productivity levels could not be sustained. Demand for consumer goods and services fell because wages lagged behind prices. The union movement had slumped in the 1920s. Agricultural prices dropped, and fresh construction in mid-1928 trailed the 1927 figures. Few as yet noted the change. Americans exulted in such bubbles as the Paris Peace Pact, a new bill for cruisers, and flamboyant politicians like Huey Long. Optimism still colored the 1928 elections. The Socialist party, affiliate of the second international, ran its newest personality, a former Presbyterian minister named Norman Thomas, and attracted 72 percent of the total vote. Thomas was to change the party's following and image in the next decade, when electoral politics would loom more and more important for Socialists.[5]

Trotskyist leaders coaxed the rank and file to stand by the Workers (Communist) party candidates in national, state, and municipal elections. The Workers party candidate, William Z. Foster, attracted an infinitesimal .000846 percent of the vote. "No one is moved but his own followers," carped Shachtman after the election. He saw reason for hope in the 1928 count for the Republicans and Democrats, viewing Al Smith's huge popular vote as indicative of the political backwardness but the growing radicalization of the masses, for Smith, a New Yorker with part-Irish background, purported to speak for the common man.

The stockmarket crash and deepening economic depression with resultant unemployment, foreclosures, and wage and price reductions delivered an altered election outlook to working people by 1932. The crisis at home eclipsed foreign distress, although abroad Germany's chronic defaulting in reparations payments brought French occupation of the Ruhr Valley, a sliding schedule for payments devised by American capitalists, swelling inflation of the Mark, and President Herbert Hoover's moratorium in 1931 on all war payments. The ineffectiveness of the president's domestic programs in the face of bitter strikes and the wave of bank failures infused a sense of great urgency in the 1932 elections.

Norman Thomas this time drew 2.22 percent of the total votes, and did better than he ever would again in areas with well-established Socialist party organizations. Foster, again the Communist candidate (and again supported by Trotskyists), drew .26 percent of the votes. With James Ford his running mate, he attracted a flock of disciples from the middle classes, as a "League of Professional Groups for Foster and Ford" collected around him. Its roster comprised such literary luminaries as John Dos Passos, Sherwood Anderson, James T. Farrell, Edmund Wilson, Sidney Howard, Sidney Hook, Erskine Caldwell, and Granville Hicks, some of whom would swarm into the Trotskyist orbit. Franklin D. Roosevelt's election, carrying forty-two states with nearly 23,000,000 votes, represented the voice of discontent heard once again, speaking in 1932 more loudly with the mounting economic predicament. By 1936, even the promising Socialist party, torn within by fratricidal strife, did poorly. Much of its leadership drifted into the Roosevelt "brain trust."[7]

The Communist party in 1936 underwent a policy change due to the popular front dictate at the Seventh Comintern Congress. From 1928 when its leadership ousted the Trotskyists, Communist policy had demanded boycotts of liberal and radical ventures, and harsh censure of New Deal measures as "social fascist"—a sham facade of social reform masking intensified repression. Because a pre-revolutionary government remained (according to Marxist analysis) the arm of the ruling class, New Deal government controls were construed in the interest of that class and not for the people as a whole.[8] From 1928 to 1935 the Communist party was in its "third period."

In Germany Communists had united with Nazis against Social Democrats and democrats ("social fascists"), an anomalous union that Trotsky blamed for the triumph of Hitler in early 1933. The victory of German fascism caused the Comintern to review official policy. The Seventh Congress therefore ordered the popular front, an approach designed to serve Soviet foreign policy requirements. The fresh line enjoined an alliance against war and fascism *with* democratic and Social Democratic forces, the forces that had been labeled "social fascist" and scorned from 1928 to 1935.[9]

The first five years of the Trotskyists' existence were acted out against the backdrop of the Communist party in its third period, deepening depression in the United States, and the rise of fascism in Europe.

Trotsky As Opposition Leader

Leon Trotsky, veteran of the 1905 Petrograd uprising, during the Bolshevik revolution was president of the Petrograd soviet and after the revolution commissar for foreign affairs. In June 1919 he assumed com-

mand of the 400,000-man Red army and led it to victory in October
1920. From the earliest organization of the Soviet government, Trotsky
played a leading role, and as a consequence his name commanded respect both in and out of Communist circles.

He claimed the growth of his opposition movement began in the
early 1920s when he led a struggle against the creeping abridgment of
party democracy. By January 1924 a definite polarity had crystallized—
machine bureaucrats on one side, the growing Trotsky opposition on
the other. Trotsky published *The New Course: A Manual of Democratic
Centralism* prescribing a democratic regimen, but in accordance with his
view that only one party, unopposed, could carry out the tasks of building a Socialist state, the regimen was democratic for Bolsheviks alone.[10]
His interest in free expression within the party resulted from a desire
that his opinions on rapid industrialization be heard. With Lenin's
death and the emergence of Stalin, the polarity hardened with deep antagonism; international issues rose to prominence too, and Trotsky was
exiled to Russia's Alma Ata. When Stalin banished him even from
Soviet territory, Trotsky spent four years on the island of Prinkipo in
the Sea of Marmora, then went to France for two years where he moved
about, incognito, pursued and hounded. For eighteen months, from
June 1934 to December 1936, he lived with friends in Honefoss, Norway. The first of the Moscow purge trials took place while Trotsky was
in Norway. Under pressure from the Soviet regime, the Norwegian government required him to seek refuge elsewhere. When Germany, France,
England, and the United States denied him asylum, a committee of
American liberals and Socialists persuaded the president of Mexico to
admit him. From Mexico he attempted to guide his followers in the
path of Marxism as he saw it; he remained in Mexico until his assassination in August 1940.

Irving Howe accorded him this tribute: "As exile, harassed, powerless, Trotsky achieved greatest moral stature." No more cheering listen-
ers, "no longer armies to spur into heroism; no longer parties to guide to
power," relatives and friends assassinated, children hounded, still Trotsky continued to "cry out his defiance, unbent and unyielding, caustic,
and proud: a solitary Promethean figure, he continued to write his
trenchant analysis of the totalitarian regime in Russia . . . ."[11]

The American Trotskyist movement had two advantages. One was
the local leadership of Cannon, a direct link with the native revolution-

ary movements: the IWW, the Socialist party, the Communist Labor party, and the Workers (Communist) party which he had served as its first national chairman. His strongest point was an ability to propagandize among workers, and in local sections, to debate the issues in factional disputes. Less attractive than Trotsky because less adept in theoretical matters, Cannon's deficiency was compensated by Trotsky's personal leadership from exile.

The second advantage the American movement enjoyed was the aura of Trotsky. His followers believed that Trotsky's ideas and leadership, "obviously the really decisive factors in maintaining the integrity and cohesiveness of the American movement," made possible the training of "a small but precious generation of militants . . . in an understanding and respect for the achievements of socialist thought, a knowledge of its history and traditions, a realization of the innate shortcomings of that unique American brand of vulgar practicalism which is . . . the curse of the radical and labor movements."[12]

Trotsky As Ideologue: The Tenets of Trotskyism

Although his followers emphasized two of Trotsky's tenets, the permanent revolution and "the degeneration of the workers' state," six others stand out as characteristically (if not in all cases uniquely) Trotskyist. First was the certainty that his own Marxian analysis was absolutely true. According to his claim, his was the sole authentic legacy from Marx and Lenin. Belief in an ineluctable progress of events toward the dictatorship of the proletariat informs Marx's work, and Lenin shared this firm expectation, reflected in his own programmatic and analytical writings. Before the revolution, Trotsky had been associated with the Menshevik wing of the Russian Social Democrats and Lenin with the Bolshevik, but Trotsky had swung to bolshevism. From then the two revolutionists had basic theoretical agreement. Lenin endorsed Trotsky's slogan, "All Power to the Soviets!" Both swore by the dialectic: "Here let us say briefly: history goes forward not along a straight line but along a devious one; after a gigantic jump forward there follows as after an artillery shot a rebound."[13] Even though Trotsky was convinced his later movement remained tiny because "we are living through a period of economic, political, and social reaction," he never wavered

because "the vindication and the victory of our ideas in time is assured."[14] A chiliastic vision of a redeemed world informs the writings
of Marx, Lenin, and Trotsky. After the dictatorship of the proletariat
when the state shall have withered away, a new type of person will develop, a "new man." Lenin and Trotsky agreed that the perspectives of
communism were infinite and sure, and their labor for it indispensable.

The doctrine of the permanent revolution maintained that the gains
of the revolution in Russia would evaporate if revolutions did not occur
in the more developed countries. A state cannot remain socialist in a
capitalist world:

> But to overthrow the power of the bourgeoisie and establish that
> of the proletariat in a single country is still not to assure the com-
> plete victory of Socialism. The chief task, the organization of
> Socialist production, is still to be accomplished. Can we succeed
> and secure the definite victory of Socialism in one country with-
> out the combined efforts of the proletarians of several advanced
> countries? Most certainly not. The efforts of a single country are
> enough to overthrow the bourgeoisie; this is what the history of
> revolution proves. But for the definitive triumph of Socialism, the
> organization of Socialist production, the efforts of one country
> are not enough, particularly of an essentially rural country like
> Russia; the efforts of the proletarians of several advanced coun-
> tries are needed. So the victorious revolution in one country has
> for its essential task to develop and support the revolution in
> others.[15]

A second Trotskyist tenet was the law of combined, or uneven, development. Industrial technology, the fruit of capitalist production and ex-
pansion, developed in the Western nations with its governmental twin,
parliamentarism, progressing through three successive stages: (1) handi-
craft, (2) manufacture, and (3) factory production. To attain the modern economies necessary to survive in an industrial world, that is, the
"factory production" level, backward peoples cannot afford luxuries
like popular government and the slow march through the prior two
stages. Because of the reluctance and slowness of such peoples to abandon ancient folkways, the social reorganization required to reach industrial goals has to be arranged by technocrats with military and police aid

for social control. While in some areas this occurs under harsh colonial
rule, thus creating the condition for nationalist revolution, in other
geographies only a prior revolution can bring about the necessary restructuring of society for the age of technology. Either way, under the
whip of external necessity backward cultures are compelled to make
leaps more convulsive than in other preceding epochs. In his own theory of uneven development, Stalin insisted that stages could not be
skipped. He justified the brief constitutionalist, Lvov-Kerensky government from February to October 1917 in Russia and the "republican"
Kuomintang victory in 1927 in China on the grounds of "non-skipping
of stages." Trotsky held firmly to his "law," that stages could be and
often were combined or compressed.[16] The two of them simply analyzed
events from differing theoretical vantage points.

Consistent with the doctrine of the permanent revolution was the
third tenet of Trotskyism, the injunction to spread communist ideas inside established workers' councils or trade unions to "bore from within"
the unions where daily contact, hence influence, is possible. Dual,
"red," unions were ineffective because isolated, surviving only from
crisis to crisis and, in general, speaking a language the average worker
does not grasp. William Z. Foster had embraced "boring from within"
and the Communist party endorsed it except during the third period.
Cannon, the IWW veteran, disagreeing initially, came around to this
view probably during his International Labor Defense work, where the
impact of the small communist group had been visible within the larger
working class and radical movement. "Boring from within" was based
on the ideas of class struggle, the militant minority, and the strike, and
on the demand for amalgamation with other unions, the goal being industrial unionism. The small corps of communists in a given factory
had as its duty to guide other workers to an awareness of the source
of their oppression, the employer class, the owners of the means of production, who also oppressed fellow workers in other industries. The
strike called forth the collective working-class consciousness and hopefully delivered bread-and-butter benefits. Where a trade union existed
in his particular trade or profession, the Trotskyist was expected to belong, and where none existed, the Trotskyist was expected to take the
initiative in organizing the unorganized. The aim was unity of the entire working-class movement in industrial unionism attainable through
the overthrow of a second antagonist, the labor bureaucrat. Every issue

of the Trotskyist party press reported developments in the world of labor from the perspective of these strategies.[17]

Trotskyists saw the established unions, led by powerful individuals who fraternized with top management officials, as a kind of political police. Union leadership, the *Militant* charged, was "a main instrument of the capitalists in strangling this spirit [of] resistance in the ranks of the working class." Labor leaders divided the workers, deliberately limited potential strength of unions by refusing to organize the unorganized, entered into struggles alongside workers but betrayed workers to the capitalist, and generally served as "agents of the enemy in our ranks."[18]

Using the same logic, Trotskyists enjoined periodic participation in united front actions for specific limited purposes. Examples of Trotskyist cooperation with another radical, or even a liberal, organization were the united demonstration against the Scottsboro trials, rallies for the release of specific groups of political prisoners, or marches against war and fascism and unemployment.

It was easy for such mutual united front efforts to degenerate into "class collaboration," the bugaboo of abandoning principle that caused Trotskyists to shun the Communist party's popular front. In joining united fronts, Trotskyists were to seek to control the project, steering it in the desired direction, keeping their own discipline and integrity all the while. "A united front is only a temporary agreement on immediate demands in action and must be preserved as long as it functions for the class interest"; its rationale, an attempt to exert pressure on the capitalist class. A united front operated for certain specific demonstrations toward specific goals, or against specific threats to the working class. Ideally it drew otherwise passive workers into political motion, broadened the base of action, and provided a chance for Trotskyists to present their line undisturbed and "uncorrupted by the political views of other members." To bore from within the trade union movement was perpetual united front activity, putting pressure on both labor czars and the employer class.[19] In America where socialist ideas simply did not strike deep root, the task was to persuade a working class to accept the "dim blessings of communist cooperation, when incentives to private acquisition and bourgeois cooperation are so overwhelming."[20] The solution was for communists to refuse to risk sterility by isolating themselves in doctrinally "pure" revolutionary unions as the Socialist Labor party continued to do, but instead to employ the tactic of boring from within.

A fourth Trotskyist tenet excited extensive and intense intraparty debate. The Trotskyist interpretation of Marxist doctrine forbade combining in "class-collaborationist" farmer-labor party movements. Despite Marx and Lenin, on Comintern orders American communists wavered, became involved in the Federated Farmer-Labor party debacle in 1924, and prepared to enlist in the Conference for Progressive Political Action (CPPA) until they were brought to heel by new Moscow directives. On the face of it, a farmer-labor party would seem to offer an excellent opportunity to bore from within. But according to Marx (Trotsky pointed out) peasants or agriculturalists are essentially bourgeois and have interests irreconcilable with those of the proletariat; any alliance between the two can only exist "within the iron frame of the dictatorship of the proletariat." "A workers' and peasants' party merely camouflages the bourgeoisie—repeats bourgeois society: exploited, deceived masses below, the contented and the fakers at the top." Trotsky reminded his followers of Lenin's warning that "peasants are a reactionary and anti-proletarian force."[21] There could be no merging for revolutionary purposes with them.

When it seemed propitious, radical parties had turned their backs on Marx. The American Communist party in adopting the popular front in 1935 and urging farmer-labor unity appeared to violate a Marxist stricture. When Trotsky berated the Stalinists in 1926 and 1927 for not guiding the Chinese communists to a proletarian triumph, he strayed from strictest Marxism, which predicted revolutionary surges for industrialized nations with growing, yet alienated, industrial working classes. China in 1927 was a peasant nation. When in 1933 Trotsky announced a fresh policy of "entrism" and to expand the influence of his movement prompted his followers individually or as a group to join mass parties previously labeled "centrist," he veered from Marxism again. Entrism was a fifth tenet of Trotskyism. In 1933 he asked Trotskyists in France to join the big Socialist Federation of Workers and his American disciples to fuse with the Musteite conglomerate of intellectuals, laborites, and pacifists.

A sixth tenet was the Trotskyist position on pacifism and militarism. Although Trotsky explicitly repudiated terrorism, he preferred not to truckle with pacifists. Pacifism, he reasoned, came directly from bourgeois democracy in its effort to rationalize human behavior in the interests of profit. William Jennings Bryan's petty bourgeois pacifism was as naive as the Jeffersonian "harmony of interests" theory, both predicated on the assumption that an environment unfettered by the demands and hazards of military conflict better promoted capitalist trade relations.[22]

But what about the requirements of revolution? Did Trotsky sanction force and violence to meet them? He argued that Marx found violence, part of the means-and-ends question, repugnant. But when it erupted in a revolutionary situation, revolutionists had not advocated it—they had simply predicted it—and repugnant or not, it appeared an essential ingredient in social rebellion. "The struggle for power organized and led by the revolutionary party is the most ruthless and irreconcilable struggle in all history," and to win, the dictatorship of the proletariat will necessitate "armed insurrection as the means of smashing the bourgeois state apparatus" out in full panoply to resist the rebels.[23] Violence will be dictated to counteract the "legal" violence imposed by increasingly repressive regimes in the final agony of capitalism, so Trotskyist programs proclaimed. Middle classes, economically squeezed at both ends and vacillating between the proletariat and big capitalists, are finally driven in the name of justice, or law and order, to align with capital for fascist control in the new "supernationalist state, an imperialist empire to rule over continents, to rule over the whole world." Workers then must think of matters of power, declared an article by Trotskyist theoretician James Burnham in 1938, recapitulating a theme from Trotsky's latest manifesto, *The Death Agony of Capitalism and the Tasks of the Fourth International.*

Fascism creeps in using the "language of love" and dressed "in the garb of anti-poverty schemes." It arrives in the form of planning and centralization of control, demanded by the petty bourgeoisie but actualized by the "monopolist class" in its own interest. The moment of truth is at hand when the big bourgeoisie loses faith in the ability of "democratic" politicians to preserve the regime of capital, at which time it may halt the electoral process. Fascism comes inevitably in an advanced democratic-capitalist system. "Nothing will 'stop fascism' short of the overthrow of capitalism," warned Cannon, but the overthrow will occur because the working class will be goaded into insurrection by unemployment, inflationary spiraling, fruitless foreign wars. A general strike, or a series of them, may precipitate the final, armed class conflict. United front demonstrations for limited aims would serve as dress rehearsals for this climax.[24] Trotskyists found it beautiful to contemplate and satisfying to discuss: this powerful, ineluctible march of events.

Trotskyists in no sense condoned pacifism, yet remained staunchly antiwar when a war involved bourgeois-imperialist governments contesting with each other for world spheres of influence. Rather than support a national war effort ("social patriotism") even against reactionary or fascist powers communists were expected to embrace "revolutionary defeatism"; they were to sabotage the home government to precipitate revolution in obedience to the slogan, "Turn the Imperialist War into a Civil War!" "Defeatism" meant to carry the class struggle to its highest level, civil war, never flinching for patriotic niceties. "Defensism," on the other hand, was critical support of a regime.[25] "Critical support . . . simply meant, we would criticize hell out of a movement, condemn it, attack it, but say, 'in spite of all these things, there's this and that good about it, and therefore we're for it'," explained Shachtman.[26] For instance, while relentlessly condemning Stalin for having betrayed the revolution and allowed the Soviet Union to degenerate into a corrupt bureaucracy, Trotskyists still affirmed defensism: critical support of Russia. It was "the absolute duty of every revolutionist to defend the U.S.S.R. against imperialism, *despite* the Soviet bureaucracy," Trotsky testified in Mexico on April 17, 1937.[27] He never relinquished faith that Stalin would be overthrown and the course of socialist progress resumed in Russia.

Trotsky was sure the degeneration of the workers' state in the Soviet Union resulted from abandoning the strategy of permanent revolution. Antibureaucratism was another tenet, and was explained thus. For expediency, Stalin halted activity in Communist revolutionary centers in foreign countries and restrained incipient revolution, causing it to fail as in Germany in 1923 and again in 1933, in the latter case making Hitler's rise possible.[28] He built military alliances with capitalist powers and nurtured a coterie of technocrats at home dedicated to supervising the implementation of his agricultural and industrial plans with force and political police. His program was centrist in slogan and inspiration, reactionary in policy, Trotsky contended, elitist and fascist, Shachtman insisted.[29] "The GPU [Soviet secret police] has become the defensive arm of the Soviet bureaucracy against the people. The hate the bureaucracy bears me stems from my struggle against their monstrous privileges and their criminal absolutism. And that struggle is the very heart of what is called 'Trotskyism.' "[30]

In contrast with the ossified officialdom in Russia was the highly fluid United States, in the death throes of capitalism, hence sinking into economic, political, and social reaction. Trotsky's opposition remained isolated and tiny because of the social regression enveloping it. Fascist-style leaders had already emerged, such as Mayor Frank Hague of Jersey City, New Jersey, because of an encroaching sense that society could "no longer be run on democratic means." Moreover, the whole world had become "a sort of colony for the United States." Given these facts, "the hour of revolution is near," proclaimed Trotsky in 1933, and Americans were fortunate to have a revolutionary legacy.[31] Indeed theirs "is a history of uninterrupted revolution," the right of revolution being the "most precious and inalienable of democratic rights . . . the foundation and safeguard of all others." Trotskyists reminded Americans that in condemning force and violence they condemned "the whole course of American history."[32]

The Soviet Union, a degenerated workers' state, then, needed a restoration of revolutionary purity, while the United States hovered on the brink of social revolution. To unify them, and the world, under the banner of a brand new international and to bury the decaying Comintern was Trotsky's burning vision.[33] In keeping with this prospect, he drafted a call to a fourth international:

> The First International has given you a program and a flag
> The Second International has stood the great masses on their feet
> The Third International has given an example of tough revolution-
> ary action
> The Fourth International will give you world victory.[34]

The Communist League of America (Opposition)

A difficult five-year battle for members and attention faced the left opposition. Gradually the ranks filled. Some recruits came, one by one, from the Communist party, but most of the newcomers were unaffiliated young radicals. Cannon remembered that the tiny movement attracted "certain elements which might properly be called the lunatic fringe," a hazard of new movements in general. "Freaks always looking for the most extreme expression of radicalism, misfits, windbags, chronic oppositionists who had been thrown out of half a dozen organizations . . ." asked for admission. Once the sartorially conservative Cannon excluded a garish dresser with long hair from membership in the New York branch on the grounds that such a person would alienate the ordinary American worker who, after all, was the prime target for recruitment.[35]

Some who sought to join the Trotskyist opposition had left the Communist party because they refused to yield to its discipline, only to find as rigorous a discipline exacted of oppositionists. Still others wished to enlist because they believed the new sect to be a forum for protracted political debate. This trial-and-error period was necessary. The chaff eventually drifted away, leaving the wheat: a "fragile nucleus of the future revolutionary party."[36] But in addition to having to select out a membership, there was the hardship of dire poverty; there was so much to do, a message to spread through newspaper, pamphlets, and meetings, and never sufficient resources to do it. The stiff conditions persisted "not for weeks or months, but for years."[37] The isolation of sectarianism made the path even thornier. Members turned in among themselves arguing fiercely, very often over trifles.

Certainly there was no hope of replacing the parent party, but there was certitude about the correctness of Trotskyist vision and long-range prospects, the same kind of certitude found in the parent party and endemic in Marxist organizations. To hurry up the radicalization of the working class, oppositionists made it their revolutionary duty to translate and print Trotsky's writings, publish the suppressed documents, analyze events chiefly in the labor movement in the light of Marxism-Leninism, and educate themselves further through meetings which were really large classes. Justification came from Trotsky himself, who wrote that their work was important because "all the problems of our planet will be decided on American soil . . . . It is necessary to prepare," a heady potion for a tiny splinter group to swallow.[38] Finally it was faith in their program, psychological boosts from Trotsky, plus inner camaraderie that sustained the oppositionists.

Marxist parties customarily instructed members to run for office and campaign vigorously, using elections as valuable occasions to disseminate communist ideas. Although Trotskyists supported Communist candidates in the national elections in the first years after expulsion, in 1929 a Trotskyist, C. R. Hedlund, stood for election in the Minneapolis mayoralty contest and drew more votes than the Communist party candidate. This occurred even before the Chicago meeting in May 1929 that had formally called into existence the Communist League of America (Opposition), making Hedlund, a railroad worker, the very first Trotskyist to run for public office. His platform, like those in so many future contests, called for a campaign to organize the unorganized and a slate of workingmen's rights—to organize, strike, and picket without police interference.[39]

A few weeks after the Minneapolis election, thirty-one voting delegates and seventeen alternates from twelve cities convened in Chicago to adopt a platform and a constitution, elect a national committee, and determine future priorities and details of membership. At the convention Cannon, Shachtman, Abern, Spector, and Swabeck were designated to serve on the national committee along with Karl Skoglund of Minneapolis and Albert Glotzer of Chicago. As a forgone conclusion, the constitution as drafted embodied democratic centralist, or bolshevik, structure. To be sure, the spirit of mutual purpose prevailed during the proceedings, possible support for a future labor party provoking the sole disagreement. The majority adopted the platform statement but nevertheless agreed that the important question of a labor party would be raised again one day.[40]

The Chicago congress delegates disclaimed any intent to build a rival party. Never one to confess an impolitic move, Cannon said he believed this tactic gained many recruits from the ranks of communist workers, and perhaps it did.[41] Some who deplored bureaucratic tendencies within the Communist party nonetheless declined to leave it altogether. To such persons, the Communist League of America may have seemed a regenerate wing which would rejoin and reform the main party. In fact, the new group's leaders fully anticipated this result.

For the next two years the *Militant* showed Trotskyists running for local office and campaigning for themselves and comrades, but the major labors of the new splinter group were education and propaganda. Branch cities hosted classes in Marxism, the *Militant* announced. The New York branch held an open forum series. Contributions paid for the ongoing publication of Marxist works. The national committee scheduled lecture tours, and by 1931 planned a theoretical magazine, the *New International,* to supplement the *Militant.* As left oppositionists organized in Europe, a plethora of foreign-language or foreign-origin Trotskyist organs appeared: *Truth* (French), *Our Message* (German), *Our Struggle* (Yiddish), *Bulletin of the Opposition* (Russian, French, and German), and *Bulletin of the International Communist League (Bolshevik-Leninists)* published in Brussels. Joseph Carter (party name for Joe Friedman),* Manny Garrett (party name for Emanuel Geltman), and Martin Abern edited an American organ for younger Trotskyists entitled *Young Spartacus,* replacing the youth section in the *Militant.* By the end of 1930, the *Militant* staff moved to larger headquarters at 84 East 10th Street, and early the next year began to solicit "the $2,000 fund" for an ambitious publishing program that included an English edition of *Bulletin of the Opposition,* regularly written by Trotsky at Prinkipo, and a Marxist classics series.[42]

The *Militant* of July 25, 1931, summoned Trotskyists to a second national conference in September, and published an agenda which, although calling for discussion of the trade union question and an outline for the priorities of the Communist League of America, made no mention of the labor party issue. It surfaced at the conference anyway, and the comrades agreed on a policy of cautious support to be accorded only after careful scrutiny of a prospective party. This action revised the former stand which opposed in principle any support for what in the American environment would necessarily be a two-class party, and revealed that the group hesitantly began to feel its way out of an intolerable situation. To agree in 1931 to think about working with a labor party was a step toward the large policy of fusion embraced two years later. The meeting ended with a call to comrades to penetrate more deeply into the Communist party, a wistful backward glance, but added

---

*Comrades frequently assumed names other than their own specifically for party work with the intent of derailing U.S. or state government investigators. The names with no exception were short, simple, ordinary—and English in origin. In the case of the numerous second-generation European Jews in the movement who adopted them, the aliases it was hoped would help dispel a common assumption that most radicals were Jews or aliens.

the forward-looking note, "The Left Opposition is more firmly establishing itself—and members are strengthening themselves for more active
and direct intervention in the class struggle."[43] A year later at the third
conference a nine-point program repeated the theme, urging Trotskyists
to draw closer to the Communist party to create "organized Left Opposition fractions within" it and prodding them to join "fronts" and trade
union left-wing associations.

Communist League of America comrades realized that the battle to
win over the orthodox party for "truth" was a hopeless one. Moreover,
membership made no sweeping gains, hovering as it did between 150
and 170 at the time.[44]

First Intraparty Conflicts

Two minor quarrels punctuated the early years of the Communist
League of America. Even though members made no effort to lure a
mass following, they keenly felt the diminutive size of their grouping.
Protest has an irresistible appeal for youth; understanding this, Trotsky
instructed his opposition to steer away from "Socialistic Babbits as are
in the CP and SP, and address proletarian youth," each oppositionist becoming "personally responsible for the tutelage in scientific socialism
of several young fourteen- or fifteen-year-old boys, and for their introduction to the revolutionary politics of the proletarian vanguard."[45]
Leftist youth movements did recruit successfully in the 1930s: the National Student League (NSL) and the Student League for Industrial
Democracy (SLID) were examples; but they had no proletarian emphasis. The Young People's Socialist League (YPSL) and the Young Communist League (YCL) busily and fruitfully enrolled members. For
specific demonstrations these leagues fused into united fronts, and in
1935 the NSL and the SLID merged to create the new American Student
Union (ASU). Why could not oppositionists, with their charismatic exiled leader, tempt a youthful following too? To this end Joe Carter,
Manny Garrett, and a few others in New York began publishing *Young
Spartacus.* By March 1934 about 200 young members doubled the
party's roster. Attitudes toward the novitiates precipitated the initial
squabble in the Communist League of America, and lines formed in a
pattern that persisted through major disputes until in 1940 when a per-

manent breach occurred. Wishing to keep his growing image as patriarch unchallenged, Cannon, with Swabeck's backing, scolded "young up-starts" under Carter's "intellectualistic" tutelage for allegedly carping and disdaining policy decisions made by the national committee. Shachtman jumped to defend the young comrades from New York, praising youth as "our most precious material." Cannon with scant justification retorted that Shachtman tried to set young against old, and wished to replace "elder comrades with the younger comrades."[46]

Trotskyism exerted a powerful appeal to New York Jewish youth. Shachtman who had entered the Marxist movement through the Young Communist League in New York sprang to stave off what he apprehended as calcification in leadership: Cannon could not tolerate criticism! The brief flare-up subsided, but subsequent quarrels between Shachtman and Cannon turned on the identical issue. Possibly Cannon's fury over young Carter's critique gave Carter the germ for the theory of bureaucratic collectivism. Possessed of a sensitive and fertile mind, Carter has been described as the most brilliant theoretician of the party, one who seldom, however, set forth his ideas on paper but who exchanged them freely with comrades.[47] The theoretical bent in Trotskyism particularly lured the Jewish youth of Carter's kind. Cannon's so-called proletarian wing harbored a persistent, smoldering envy of the strength these members enjoyed in the party. The pattern took definite shape: internal squabbles over points of doctrine forced the two wings apart, then just as regularly pressure or persecution from outside pulled them together again.

The second conflict was triggered by a communist splinter sect's effort to merge with the Communist League of America. The heavy-handed reaction of the Passaic, New Jersey, authorities to the textile walkout called in 1926 by Al Weisbord was well publicized and inspired not only massive sympathy demonstrations but an avalanche of material aid, and visitations by Manhattan's theatrical, literary, and ecclesiastical elite. The strike failed, but Cannon exulted, "As a strike leader he was first class, make no mistake about it," and Lillian Symes said the walkout "marked an outstanding achievement of American communism in the 1920s."[48] Nevertheless, the Workers (Communist) party had expelled Weisbord and his cohorts for showing too much initiative; whereupon Weisbord founded the Communist League of Struggle. Impressed,

Trotsky at first hoped to see Weisbord's splinter, a bold and courageous few who seemed to share his values, fuse with his own.[49]

Repetitious and jargon-studded statements of "principle" and "program" replete with long, wordy definitions struggling for absolute exactitude seemed always to follow talks about fusion. The *Internal Bulletin* (for members only) and the *Militant* (the "public" press) spotlighted one declaration after another on fusion with the Weisbordites. It was a healthy arrangement to keep two party organs humming. Doctrinal differences between the Communist League of America and the Communist League of Struggle were aired before the entire readership, the open press playing a vital role in this policy matter as it would in later ones. An open press made it possible for those engaged in flirtations with Trotskyism to view the party at work, and if they did not like what they saw, to slip away quietly.

Negotiations between Weisbord and the national committee bogged down over statements of policy toward centrists; the committee accused Weisbord of defending his mistakes instead of making clear his opinions, and altogether failing "to meet with our requirements." Piqued, but reluctant to be shoved aside summarily, Weisbord complained that the consequent collapse of fusion talks rested wholly with the Communist League of America. A letter closed the case. "The national committee has decided that it cannot accept comrade Weisbord for membership in the League," and as Weisbord's was "an impossible mixture of loans made from the viewpoints of the three other groups . . . ." his application was rejected.[50] A subsequent evaluation of the matter charged: "His political line in general represented an attempt to substitute for the principle line of the Left Opposition on nearly all the main questions, a melange of opportunism and confusion borrowed in part from the Right wing and in part from the Centrists."[51]

William Isaacs in his study of modern Marxism found significant distinctions between the two groups, one of them turning on Weisbord's advocacy of "direct action" tactics: flamboyant demonstrations at food stores, utility offices and plants, and against evictions. Picketing, marching consumers, workers, and tenants carrying bold placards Weisbord believed must logically lead to insurrection. Trotskyists called such schemes "adventurism." Another difference lay in Weisbord's approach to the race problem in the United States. Generally he approved the black na-

tionalism adopted as policy by the Communist party's Sixth Comintern
Congress, "Self Determination for Negroes in the Black Belt," but added his own flourish, a plan to "lynch the lynchers" in the South. Trotskyists rejected black separatism, endorsing the idea of full integration
of blacks into all American institutions.

Then, Weisbord believed it a fine plan for communists to enter a labor
party.[52] From 1929 through 1931 Trotskyists refused to consider collaborating with any labor party except for the most limited united front
actions. Of course, in 1931 the political committee within the national
committee reassessed the policy in view of their failure to draw a sizable
membership. By late 1933, the Communist League of America welcomed unity "with leftward moving groups," changed its official policy,
and abandoned "propaganda group" status to become a revolutionary
party with appeal for the depression-ridden masses. But in the fall of
1932, League leaders were not ready to move in that direction and they
turned down Weisbord's bold proposals.

In the early years Trotskyists established principles and patterns of
activity that would remain with them. In the first place, the Communist
League of America was born as an evicted splinter and as time progressed,
it would be plagued by further fragmentation. Second, Trotskyists rig-
orously honored their educational priorities such as Marxist classes and
the ambitious publishing schedules they prepared in the first months.
Third, the Cannon-Shachtman rift had already appeared and Carter had
raised the issue of bureaucratic rule, one that would rear its head with
devastating effect in a few short years. Fourth, the sect for solid practical reasons moved toward scrapping one programmatic point in order
to adopt its opposite hoping to enlarge itself. Yet another pattern took
shape. Once Trotskyists embraced a doctrine or program, every member had to take it as his own and a prospective member to profess it
without a hair's deviation.

4

The Communist League of America and Labor

For several reasons, the role of the American Trotskyist organization as a propaganda group directed at purifying the Communist party ended in 1934. As a tiny sect, it was ineffective in American labor and political life and its members knew this. The rise of Hitler and the Nationalist Socialist party disenchanted the Trotskyists with the Communist party; it had proved unable to seize a chaotic moment and take power. As Cannon phrased it, "Fascism triumphed without even the semblance of a civil war, without even a scuffle in the street."[1] Trotsky himself began in 1933 to urge wider participation in the working-class movement through possible merger with a broader-based radical party, in France at first, and active organizing and striking in existing trade unions. Disenchanted with the parent party, bored with being a propaganda sect, and pessimistic about their potential to attract new members, his American followers considered now a change of policy toward what they had previously labeled "centrism." In 1934 the Communist League of America emerged from its cocoon onto the labor scene as active participants and dickered with a freshly formed party of radical labor intellectuals for merger.

American Labor in the Early Depression

Alarmed, Trotskyists estimated that labor union memberships had
fallen by almost a million between 1920 and 1930.[2] Massive reprisals
against strike leaders and striking workers had been remarkably successful. Old line American Federation of Labor (AFL) leadership had betrayed the workers. Still, the Communist League of America annually
stated its determination not to establish new "red," or dual, unions
("ultra-leftism"), or new class federations modeled after the American
Federation of Labor. It would continue to make trade union activity
the primary endeavor, to enter "joint movements with the progressives,"
and to seek the overthrow of reactionary labor bureaucrats," the old
Foster program from the Stalinist party of the 1920s. The goal remained the amalgamation of all unions in one great industrial union. As
Trotsky explained, the union movement was forced to confront a mon-
opolistic capitalist structure resting on centralized command (not free
competition) and state power, and workers had to contend with the
fact that invariably labor czars, unofficially policing the labor force and
vying for capitalist rewards, exercised control over their unions.[3] Therefore the main party task consisted "of gaining influence over the trade
unions—more of winning through the trade unions influence over the
majority of the working class."[4] Under its present leadership, the AFL
had miserably failed its constituency: it had failed to grasp opportunities to organize in the South, failed to realize membership gains for ten
years, failed to push for old age and unemployment pensions, and failed
to protect workers' rights.[5] Even the Congress of Industrial Organizations (CIO), the "one big union" for which so much was hoped, failed
to adopt a radical program. The CIO capitulated when John L. Lewis
endorsed the reelection of the capitalist president, Franklin D. Roosevelt, who during World War II passed resolutions condemning Trotskyist "seditious activity" and condemning Trotskyists as "enemies of the
labor movement."[6]

Nor did the Communist party have an unassailable record, according
to the *Militant*. In its third period, the Soviet representative treated established unions as hopeless in the revolutionary sense and advocated a
"new revolutionary trade union," or dual unionism. In those years the
party refused united front actions and required its people to pull out of
the AFL. Later, in the mid-1930s having undergone a change of

"line," the Communist party completely reversed itself and made common cause with the "labor bureaucrats," including Lewis of the CIO, and with President Roosevelt as well. Of course, through these tactics in the 1930s the Communist party made the greatest inroads of any Marxist grouping in the labor movement, partially because the CIO took in the Trade Union Unity League (the old Trade Union Educational League) organizers.[7] Recanters of later years recollected that Communists even entered government service.[8] Trotskyists, unable to exert comparable influence, had cause for envy.

They now contemplated standing independently, ceasing to think of themselves as merely opposition appendage to parent party. After extended observation and criticism of developments in the labor movement, in 1934 alone they found themselves prepared to furnish leadership for two big and dramatic strikes—one, of hotel food workers in Manhattan, the other, of truck drivers in Minneapolis. While caught up in these events, now recognizing a clean separation from the main party, they boasted "we were the more militant, the more aggressive wing," taking the more uncompromising position, and in their reflections, certain participants said they believed that in unions and strikes Trotskyists made their greatest impact on American life.[9] Such involvement would have been inconceivable for a Communist party faction waiting contritely in the wings for readmission to the party from which it had been expelled.

The high rate of unemployment made it difficult to organize American workers and suppressed any militance workers might have otherwise shown. Men whose jobs are insecure are extremely reluctant to challenge their employers. Only desperate circumstances drive them to strike. But so driven, workers in 1929, even before the chaos of the depression, walked out of factories and coal fields from Manhattan to Elizabethton, Tennessee. Strike news was parlayed critically in the *Militant,* most often by trade union editor Arne Swabeck. In 1929 the *Militant* reported that 8,000 members of the new Needle Trades Workers Industrial Union struck New York dress contractors, but in spite of their being a Trade Union Unity League affiliate were unhappily guided by "reformist" leaders who failed to prepare them adequately and failed to make appropriate demands, such as week-work rather than piece-work. And, the report continued, workers finally capitulated to this "Right" leadership "who collaborated with 'organized' bosses and state and city authorities," even calling in the Tammany Hall mayor, Jimmy Walker, and Governor Herbert Lehman. A five-week-long fur strike involving 2,000 workers slipped into the same rut, its leaders pursuing wrong-headed tactics and irresponsibly halting the strike with no gains made.[10]

Nor did the *Militant* soften the blows aimed at the leaders of the astonishing textile revolts in the South. *Militant* critics found the AFL policy of refusing to permit different unions in southern mill towns to cooperate in strike actions impossibly reactionary. But after the arrests of Communist strike leaders and textile workers at Gastonia, North Carolina, *Militant* headlines reproached the International Labor Defense, now under Communist party control, because it failed to assemble a united front made up of sympathetic groups such as the IWW, the Socialist party, the Socialist Labor party, certain unions, the new Conference for Progressive Labor Action, and the Trotskyists. The *Militant* asked: "American Working Class: rally to the defense of Gastonia—employ a United Front" to defend the fifteen "indicted in Gastonia for the major crime of arousing the serfs of the textile barons to struggle."[11]

The coal fields near Harlan, Kentucky, seethed too. Swabeck, noting the incipient clash in early 1929, observed that the National Miners Union (NMU), spawned in Pennsylvania under Communist party auspices, had moved into Kentucky, and concluded it was a dual union created to compete with the United Mine Workers of John L. Lewis. Swabeck complained that the Communists, entering the conflict, did not conduct their effort wholeheartedly either against Lewis or against the operators, failed to exert command in organizing the unorganized fields, and were sluggish in setting up union activities where they had once existed in the former strike areas of Pennsylvania and Ohio. When the NMU, evicted from Kentucky, returned to its fields of Pennsylvania, it did so in time to have its leadership "co-opted" into the CIO giving Communist party labor specialists the chance to bore from within. By 1933, the Progressive Miners Union and other independent groupings had organized and thought of federating. Noting these developments, Trotskyists dispatched James P. Cannon to their federation conference and got him on their program as speaker.[12] By this time Trotskyists were emerging from their shell and seeking wider contacts for a possible new party. They stood ready to offer direction in the ongoing struggle for labor organization.

The year 1934, an exhilarating season for young radicals, witnessed
a remarkable upsurge of labor activity. Hope was replacing depression
despair; a modest economic recovery was evident in the summer of 1933.
Workers, reminded that they could now legally organize for collective
bargaining into unions of their choice under the provisions of Title I,
Section 7A of the National Industrial Recovery Act, sensed that they
must seize the hour and "demonstrate their collective power to recalci-
trant employers through the strike." The principal radical parties were
happy to help, the only question being under whose auspices unorganized workers would form unions and strike. Indeed, the year 1934 saw
1,856 work stoppages involving 1,470,000 workers, and some of the
strike actions were virtually social upheavals.[13]

The Communist League of America in the
Labor Movement

In the winter of 1934 Trotskyists helped initiate and then com-
mandeered two strikes, the first evidence that the formerly small propaganda sect, "the Pharisees of the Revolution," was ready for a debut in
the labor movement. But the conduct of these actions showed clearly
the difference between the New York hotel workers' organization, top-
heavy with strong-willed and egocentric intellectuals, all wishing to
lead, none willing to be led, and the Minneapolis branch of the Communist League of America, baptized in the labor movement and so in-
ured to the requirements of successful struggle: discipline and unity.

Two unions, an independent one and a small Stalinist one, in early
1934 held hotel workers' memberships. Some Trotskyists happened to
belong to the independent union, the Amalgamated Food Workers,
whose members were growing restive with their low pay, long hours,
and heavy workload. The Trotskyists managed to channel the unrest
of these union brothers and take the helm in their strike. The League
sent in B. J. Field, just returned from working with Trotsky in Europe
for four months, a man who had some proficiency in economics and had
astounded his comrades with his knowledge of the stock market. Field
also spoke French with ease and could therefore discuss the issues in
some depth with the French chefs. The chefs promptly elected him
secretary of their union. After initially protesting that Field was not a

food worker and therefore should not officiate in a chef's union, Cannon and Shachtman at last relented. Aristedemos Kaldis, leader of the Greek chefs, called the strike—gathering in bellhops and doormen as well as waiters, waitresses, dishwashers, and bus boys—and waved his butcher knife, shouting "Out, out of the kitchens, proletariat of Greece-in-America, off with your black jackets!" Subsequently Harry Roskolenko reported, "Soon we had dozens of gently-maddened Greeks entering our Trotskyist ranks."[14]

The Communist League of America turned all its energies to the strike. At some sacrifice it printed three (rather than one) issues a week of the *Militant* and took full advantage of this change to propagandize for bolshevism by assigning seasoned Trotskyists as messengers, clean-up crew, and other indispensable functionaries. Mass meetings, culminating in a rally of 10,000 at Madison Square Garden in New York City, featured Trotskyist speakers. Stalinists, not to be outdone, sent in an Italian-speaking comrade, adding another international touch. And Lovestone people came. The disruption of orderly hotel service was so total that mediators from the National Labor Board came up from Washington, D.C. Confusion reigned among the striking employees simply from the conglomeration of radical parties involved, each group purporting to give direction to all of them; adding to the melee was the genuine distress of hotel management and the drama of rallies and pickets.

Years later Cannon remembered that Field, heady with the power gained from leading 10,000 strikers, ceased to find time to confer with the national committee of the Communist League of America, so caught up was he in negotiating with Mayor Fiorello La Guardia and government agencies and giving press interviews. In a surprise move, the national committee put Field on trial in mid-strike for breach of discipline on the grounds that he failed to consult regularly with party leadership, and expelled him and his wife Esther. Neither even spared the time to attend the "trial."[15] In his own defense statement later, Field, with Kaldis and others, insisted that while he tried to negotiate a just settlement and was trying realistically to benefit from the services of the government mediators, Cannon and Shachtman agitated unceasingly to oust him from the leadership because he refused to allow them to dictate strike strategy from behind the scene, even forming "unprincipled blocs" with Lovestoneites, such as Benjamin Gitlow, with Louis Budenz of the Musteite American Workers party, with Stalinists, and with others to accomplish his ouster. Field reminded the League that he had built the membership of the Amalgamated Food Workers from "less than 100 to nearly 8,000 members."[16] Standard epithets as "cliquism," "bureaucratism," and "red-baiting," flew back and forth among the Communists, Trotskyists, and Field's supporters, but in the meantime the strikers won, and the Trotskyists had shown members that they "meant business" by daring in mid-action (with questionable wisdom) to expel a leader whom the national committee thought had broken discipline and consorted with the class enemy.[17]

Field and eight others went on from the League to ally with Gitlow to form the "League for a Revolutionary Workers Party," carping in their organ against Trotskyist policies. After abortive efforts to negotiate merger with two other splinter groups, the Field party disintegrated in May 1935.[18] As a consequence of the strike, two League members were sentenced to prison on charges of assaulting a chef, but the Nonpartisan Labor Defense aroused the New York labor movement to demand their release. Their convictions were reversed and the prosecution dropped the charges.[19]

In spite of the inner dissension that riddled the strike effort, radicals and the labor movement knew well enough that Trotskyists, formerly thought to be merely sectarian hair-splitters, had played a part in the generally satisfactory episode. The Communist League of America had in its first five years of sequestration hammered out its principles, produced a qualified body of chiefs, and so come of age.

In the wake of the hotel strike the three Trotskyist Dunne brothers—Vincent Ray, Miles, and Grant—guided a coal yard drivers' strike in Minneapolis. With them were Karl Skoglund, local labor and radical activist; Farrell Dobbs, who joined the League one month after the strike; and William Brown, organizer for the International Brotherhood of Teamsters' Local 574 in the Twin Cities. The Trotskyist leadership in Minneapolis presented a real contrast to the New York leadership, chiefly Jewish and non-working class. The Dunnes, from a Catholic, midwestern background, had been labor activists and political radicals and had suffered firings, blacklists, and expulsions as "reds" from the American Federation of Labor. A fourth brother, William, stayed in the Communist party when the other three followed Trotsky and remained a Stalinist to his death. Dobbs, another midwesterner, was a self-taught engineer before the depression and a coal yard worker during it. Skoglund, a Swedish organizer and strike leader blacklisted in his native land, had emigrated to America, joined the Communist party, and been one of the first expelled for Trotskyism after October 1928. The Dunne brothers, Dobbs, and Skoglund decided in late 1933 under the provisions of Section 7A to organize the coal drivers.[20]

Thirty years before, Minneapolis employers had formed a Citizens' Alliance, dedicated to preserving individual bargaining and the open shop. In spite of the passage of the National Industrial Recovery Act in the summer of 1933, the Citizens' Alliance resolutely set their course to frustrate efforts to organize labor in Minneapolis and St. Paul. At that time Minnesota had a farmer-labor governor, Floyd Olson, supposedly sympathetic to union aims. He once had been quoted as affirming, "I am not a Liberal, but what I want to be—a radical."[21] The Citizens' Alliance intended to thwart the designs of the Olson administration and for good reason believed they would succeed. No strike in Minneapolis since World War I had gained anything for the strikers. Minneapolis workers' wages were pitifully low. But workers there as in other cities generally felt a welling of confidence in late 1933, and coal yard drivers decided to cement an affiliation with the Teamsters' local, hoping with the backing of this strong union to demand decent wages. Management refused to recognize the affiliation, the National Labor Board came in, and both management and Teamster officials procrastinated making a decision through the coldest and thus most crucial weeks of the year for the delivery of coal.[22]

Suddenly, on their own initiative the drivers struck in whirlwind fashion, tying up sixty-five truckyards and 150 coal yards from Wednesday to Friday, February 7, 8, and 9. This forced the hand of the National Labor Board, who hacked out with employers an agreement granting the workers their demands, yet preserving to the employers the face-saving mechanism of having the union acceptance vote taken at separate, "individual," coal yards. In the settlement the coal companies formally recognized General Drivers Union No. 574—AFL, and the victory enlarged the union's membership by nearly 3,000.[23] The radical, or pro-union Farmer-Labor party administration of Governor Olson had no part in delivering these gains to the Minneapolis coal yard workers. According to the Trotskyists, the farmer-labor organization was a fraud in any case because it violated the cardinal principle of "no two-class parties." Trotskyists claimed that the gains were won by workers acting collectively under the able and determined guidance of the Dunnes, and the organizing abilities of Dobbs and Skoglund.[24] In the following summer the same men would help the entire body of Teamster drivers in the city to win like gains.

Cannon, deploring the conduct of the hotel strike, applauded this one for the good Leninist unity and discipline. Unlike B. J. Field and the hotel strike leadership, the coal yard strike leaders together declined to confer with either "class enemy," employer or government agency, until the yard operators yielded to important demands. Whether or not they regularly sought counsel from the Trotskyist high command, Cannon did not say. But by enlisting in the labor movement and participating in both strikes, the Communist League of America had come smashing out of its sectarian closet.

The Unemployed Movement

To ease the distress of the jobless a plethora of organizational schemes concocted by both radicals and mainstream altruists were unfolded. A few scattered Communist League of America comrades marched in unemployment demonstrations from time to time, but the League itself with its tiny roster of about 150 did not try to unionize the jobless; rather it commented on and criticized how other radicals tried to do so. Tom Stamm, Hugo Oehler (a veteran labor organizer who came to the League fresh from Gastonia), and Arne Swabeck regularly from 1929 through 1934 wrote articles for the *Militant* on developments in the unemployed movement.

By 1930 the Communist party had put together its Unemployed Council, its slogan "Unemployment Insurance at Full Wages," and carried on a single-minded campaign to frustrate Trotskyist involvement in meetings and marches. The next year, the Industrial Workers of the World (IWW) created an Unemployed Workers' Industrial Union, asking "Bread Lines or Picket Lines?" and calling for the six-hour day and the five-day week. Lovestoneites had their Association for the Unemployed. The Socialist party, too, tried to organize the jobless into a Workers' Alliance of the Unemployed. Though the leaders of the different groups would never have admitted it, their goals and tactics were very much alike: the chief cause for contention was the question of leadership in the overall movement. Most of the groups agreed on basic immediate demands, whether or not the demands were incorporated into the slogan rhetoric: the six-hour day with no pay reduction, full union wages on all public works, unemployment insurance, no evictions for nonpayment of rent (soon a subgrouping of tenants' leagues formed around this demand), and, for the Communist party, the League, and the Musteites, "large and long-term credits extended to the Union of Soviet Socialist Republics."[25] The Roosevelt administration hoping to activate a new market for American products formally recognized the Soviet government in 1933, yet did not advance funds for purchases in the United States. Leaders of some of the unemployed organizations believed that credit extended to Russia would bring so great a Soviet demand for American manufactured goods that the jobless would be rehired to fill the orders. Strategically, the groups agreed on two points: they should aim toward a broader movement comprising both the employed and the jobless, and unemployed groups should try to unify, preferably into a federation.[26]

Militant accounts and comments by on-the-scene observers showed unemployed alliances staging marches and demonstrations in local communities all over the country, striking fear in the breasts of city fathers who sometimes reacted hysterically by summoning police to stave off riot. Squad cars obediently moved in to disperse demonstrators. Hunger marches and rallies with inevitable confrontations occurred as early as 1930 in St. Louis, Cleveland, Detroit, and New York. Occasionally elaborate preparations preceded these events. For two months radicals planned a massive demonstration for March 6, 1930, in New York City. However, New York authorities arrested and jailed several Communist party officials who had planned it, William Z. Foster among them, on charges of inciting to riot. Tom Stamm later affirmed, probably puffing the figures, that all told 1,250,000 people demonstrated in 1930. In the spring the Communist party sponsored in Chicago a national unemployed convention to "Organize for Action!"[27]

City officials and "respectable" citizens observed these events with alarm, viewing them as incipient rebellion. To arouse public antagonism against marchers, officials and newspaper editors referred to them as public nuisances and a real menace; then to feed growing fears prated further about "red" riots. Evidently the jobless did not see things that way. Witnessing the hunger marches from Cleveland, Len de Caux recorded,

... the communists didn't scare the unemployed. In hundreds of jobless meetings, I heard no objections to the points the communists made, and much applause for them. Sometimes I'd hear a communist speaker say something so bitter and extreme I'd feel embarrassed. Then I'd look around at the unemployed audience— shabby clothes, expressions worried and sour. Faces would start to glow, heads to nod, hands to clap. They like that stuff best of all.[28]

In an era of unemployment, communists were fully employed in organizing the unemployed, de Caux commented, for they were an integral part of every such protest he witnessed: anti-eviction fights, rallies at relief offices, hunger marches, even the 1932 "Bonus March." Unemployed veterans of World War I staged the latter, convening in Washington to persuade congressmen to pay them immediately the full value of their adjusted compensation certificates and so relieve economic distress. The apprehensive President permitted military forces to scatter the veterans. De Caux continued,

Marching columns of unemployed became a familiar sight. [Cleveland's] Public Square saw demonstrations running into tens of thousands. The communists brought misery out of hiding in the workers' neighborhoods. They paraded it with angry demands through the main streets to the Public Square, and on to City Hall. They raised particular hell.[29]

Throughout the early 1930s the unemployed formed the backbone of social protest. In 1930 and 1932 collaborating radical groups planned frequent attention-getting projects. Sixty-nine delegates from twenty-two local groups convened in Pittsburgh in November 1932, among them the A. J. Muste Unemployed Citizens' Committee. Through the winter and spring of 1933 local conferences met, Stalinists and Trotskyists vying to dominate them. Communists and Socialists held rival conferences in February 1933. In March the *Militant* reported a demonstration in New York's Union Square with all radicals in unison pledging to keep up the front against unemployment. After the rally the crowd marched on the State Capitol building in Albany to present demands to Governor Herbert Lehman. James P. Cannon was there, marching to the state capitol representing the League. In June 4,000 from "every jobless union" in New York assembled before the Board of Estimate to demand relief. In July at Columbus, Ohio, Musteites organized the National Unemployed League with a network of state-level affiliates. Through 1934 the unemployed movement continued on as before.[30]

Other programs beside hunger marches and relief rallies surfaced, proof that discontent smoldered far beyond the little radical movement. Liberals and businessmen devised bizarre schemes. At the Shrine Auditorium in Los Angeles a group met regularly hoping "to provide plenty in a land of plenty" with their plan for all Americans to work twenty years, then retire at forty-five—a forerunner of the Townsend Plan. Father Coughlin too had his predecessor. A St. Louis priest, Father Cox, toured distressed cities hailing himself as chief of the "Jobless Party," its panacea free coinage of silver and outlawing of usury. The "Jobless" platform excoriated communists of all stripes, the *Militant* reported. Cox had no trouble winning over businessmen, who gave him a rousing welcome in Pittsburgh; 70,000 persons turned out to hear his message in Pitt Stadium. The Jobless party later merged with the Liberty party, confirming the *Militant's* warnings that the Coxites represented incipient fascism.[31]

A self-help movement for vegetable gathering and bartering drew 165,000 in Los Angeles. Born early in the depression in Seattle, it spread quickly due to press support. Its basic premise was that capitalism was tired and needed a little push.[32] By 1934 the self-helpers maintained a mutual exchange in New York City to coordinate a national barter system. The Seattle founders had claimed their purpose was to get the jobless to produce their own necessities—"to build a 'society within a state.' " The barter boom reached its apex in 1932-1933 and enlisted the encouragement of some well-known personalities—economists, clergymen, publicists, manufacturers, and businessmen such as Dr. Arthur E. Morgan, president of Antioch College and soon to head the Tennessee Valley Authority; Stuart Chase, economics analyst; and Leland Olds of the New York Power Authority. In Marxist style Hugo Oehler branded self-help and barter exchange "a class collaboration move to prevent the free play of the class struggle development of the working class" calculated to bridge the crisis until the return of normal capitalist exchange.[33]

Out of the self-help movement came the radical leader Abraham John Muste and his following in the American Workers Party, with whom the Trotskyists would fuse in one year's time. By early 1933 Musteite Unemployed Leagues had sprung up in urban areas hard hit by unemployment. Indeed, Art Preis, later a Trotskyist labor historian, from an American Federation of Teachers local in Toledo, Ohio, founded in 1933 the Lucas County Unemployed League, the branch of the Muste organization that would bring Muste nationwide publicity as strike leader and radical. The center of the Toledo Auto-Lite strike grew out of this active branch.[34]

At the time Musteites first organized, they would not permit "communists" to cooperate in their drives, lumping Stalinists, Trotskyists, and Lovestoneites together. When in May 1933 a National Federation of Unemployed Workers' League (NFUWL) met in Chicago, the Musteites had apparently reconsidered; they sent delegates to Chicago to mingle with other radical groupings and the NFUWL named one of them, Ludwig Lore, to its national committee. (Oehler represented the Communist League of America in Chicago.) In July 1933 the NFUWL met again, this time in Columbus, Ohio, and the Muste group had clearly assumed command. Arnold Johnson, a Musteite, chaired the meeting; Louis Budenz, Musteite labor activist, moved among the delegates authoritatively; while Muste with leading Stalinists Clarence Hathaway and Dennis Batt collaborated to draft a Muste-designed "declaration of independence." The Musteites had decided to enter the broader radical movement through their unemployed leagues and were making great strides. Muste had delayed uniting with Marxists because of their "foreign" ideology and the "foreign" connections of the Stalinists and the Trotskyists, because he firmly believed the time had come to build a radical organization peculiarly adapted to the American scene.[35] Now that the Communist party quoted Thomas Jefferson and Tom Paine, Muste felt assured that the hour was right to work with them.

A. J. Muste and the American Workers Party

By the winter of 1933-1934 when Musteites and Trotskyists discovered each other , Cannon, Shachtman, and Muste had given about the same number of years to labor and radical movements. For instance, in 1919 Cannon had enrolled in the Communist Labor party; Shachtman, a City College student, listened to soapbox oratory at "Trotsky Square" and read radical literature at the Rand Bookstore; and Muste, thirty-four years old, was executive secretary of the committee that was preparing the Lawrence, Massachusetts, walkout of 30,000 textile workers. But Muste's radical path in the 1920s traced a different course from that of Cannon and Shachtman, who had spent those years in the Workers (Communist) party.

Muste sprang from dissimilar origins. Born in the Netherlands, he studied for the ministry at New Brunswick Theological Seminary. After his training he left the Protestant mainstream, attracted to the Quakers because of their pacifism and to the labor movement because of his own awakened and sensitive social conscience. Before the Lawrence strike, he shuttled for ten years between Quaker meeting house and union hall. Then in the 1920s he founded Brookwood College, a workingman's "resident college" in a two-story farmhouse and barn in Katonah, New York. Under his direction Brookwood College became briefly an important theoretical center in the labor movement. It offered a two-year course: a first year in the three "R's," and a second in training for activity in the labor struggle. Possessing the fascination of novelty, the college attracted a galaxy of intellectuals as visiting lecturers: David J. Saposs, Everett Dean Martin, Harry A. Overstreet, Harry Elmer Barnes, Reinhold Niebuhr, Sumner Slichter, Norman Thomas, Roger N. Baldwin, Bill Haywood, James Maurer, William Z. Foster, and John Strachey, among others.[36]

Muste tried to steer Brookwood on a dead-center course between on the one hand conventional, democratic, party politics and unionism of the kind that would shortly flourish in the New Deal, and on the other hand the communist ideologies with their Russian orientation. Speakers for a wide spectrum of viewpoints were welcome at Brookwood, but Muste eventually became a victim of his open forum ideal. In 1928 officials of the AFL, particularly Matthew Woll, led a campaign against the college accusing Brookwood of showing "anti-religious" and "red" tendencies. As a result almost all union support was withdrawn and Muste's ouster was assured. Woll's influence was doubly strong, for he held office in two groups, the AFL and the pro-capitalist National Civic Federation which he served as acting president.[37]

Marxists took an opposite tack in their critique of Muste's perform-
ance at Brookwood. They accused him of firing left-wing scholars from
teaching posts, expelling students who outspokenly agreed with the communist "line," preventing students from having a voice in the direction
of Brookwood's policies, and using the college's time and resources to
build the Musteite Conference for Progressive Labor Action, forerunner
of the American Workers party.[38] Actually in such matters he simply
decided issues pragmatically. He felt himself unable to became a disciple
of a political or religious sect; he had already found the church too
bound up with the status quo. A revolutionary party was too willing to
condone violence. The sole stand to which he adhered tenaciously was
pacifism. Christian pacifism led him into the Fellowship of Reconciliation, to a deep admiration for Gandhi, and to perennial involvement in
antiwar congresses, no matter under whose auspices they were held.[39]

Trotskyists certainly did not revere Gandhi. Cannon or Shachtman
showed up too at the antiwar congresses in the early 1930s solely to
read the League "statement" into the record: pacifism was "poison for
the masses," disarmament, a lever for war ("who has the weapons?"),
the League of Nations and national defense, "humbug." Such congresses, labeled by Trotskyists "ceremonial mass meetings," were in
those years staged by ad hoc committees of liberals and radicals. In
1932 the American Committee of the World Congress against War comprised people active in the creative arts—Henry Barbusse, Maxim Gorky,
H. G. Wells, Upton Sinclair, for example—and civil libertarians such as
Roger Baldwin. After 1934 the League against War and Fascism arranged antiwar gatherings. Muste's position stayed the same: "Convince American labor not to go to war and you have capitalism defeated." But to Trotskyists the congresses were ". . . a repulsively unc-
tious parade of studied respectability" replete with "generalities and
futile pacifist fulminations against war replace[ing] concrete programs . . . ."[40]

Muste and the Trotskyists were fundamentally incompatible. Shachtman and other contributors to the *Militant* perceived the doctrinal and
tactical disagreement back in 1929 when they chastised Lovestone and
Gitlow for pondering a merger with Muste. They branded Muste "progressive," accusing him of "genuflecting before the AFL and the forces
of anti-communism," and of waging "too respectable [a] campaign on
unemployment." "Their wordy radicalism is not costly and obligates

them to nothing; it is cheap," proclaimed the caustic Shachtman, and Cannon concluded that all progressive leaders, Muste certainly, have played decoy for the reactionaries.[41]

Muste was an honest philosophical socialist in a time when it was dangerous to be one. He had held office in the Intercollegiate Socialist Society and the subsequent League for Industrial Democracy whose organ, the *Socialist Review,* was metamorphosed in the 1920s into his own *Labor Age* (later *Labor Action*). After the campaign of harassment by AFL officials that led to his removal from Brookwood's board of directors, he sought an outlet for his proletarian sympathies and his administrative and leadership capabilities and so joined Socialists and labor unionists in 1929 to create the Conference for Progressive Labor Action (CPLA). In response to the deepening economic crisis, during succeeding years the CPLA grew increasingly radical forcing moderates out and leaving within it a body of militant labor intellectuals.[42]

Louis Budenz and Arnold Johnson were two of those who came into the CPLA for a brief time before moving into the Communist party. Ernest Rice McKinney, James Burnham, J. B. Matthews, Sidney Hook, J. B. Salutsky-Hardman, and other meteors of the left similarly stopped off briefly with Muste.

But these restless, energetic men desired a vehicle for greater political pursuits than a mere "action conference" afforded, and in 1933 they transformed the CPLA into the American Workers party, believing they had originated something on the political scene—a revolutionary party created out of American traditions for the American environment. In fact it was barely a party, with its dues-paying membership hovering around 1,000 and with roughly an equal number of sympathizers.[43] The American Workers party embraced European revolutionary doctrines such as war on capitalism, imperialism, and fascism, and that international staple, the "class struggle," all standard Marxist bogeys. It reproached Socialists as "hopelessly reformist" and branded Communists as "Moscow's puppets." It enjoined defense of the Soviet Union as the first and only workers' state, exactly as did the Trotskyists.[44]

Budenz, Johnson, Hardman, and several others had considerable experience in the labor movement and among the unemployed. Engrossed in business of this sort, they had not really taken time for theory. The critical "middle-American" public, with its strong nativist tendencies, had always pointed scornfully to the attachment of radicals to European philosophies and Russian events. The American Workers party believed it could surmount the nativist prejudices against radicalism and thought itself unique in promising a fresh "American approach," relying on native revolutionary traditions from the eighteenth century to propel the country toward "workers' democracy." Meantime, the party disseminated its ideas through *Labor Action,* continued its engagement with the jobless and labor movements, and in keeping with Muste's pacifist commitment polemicized against capitalist war.[45] From this background of CPLA and the American Workers party came the Musteite Unemployed Leagues, initially spreading the gospel of self-help, but soon combining with communists and socialists in militant marches and rallies.

The Great Toledo and Minneapolis Strikes

The hotel and the coal yard drivers' strikes, both steered by Trotskyists, barely ended when the workers at three Toledo plants—Auto-Lite, Bingham Stamping and Tool Company, and Logan Gear Company—walked away from their jobs and threw up picket lines. As at Minneapolis the issue was labor's right to self-organization and collective bargaining. April and May 1934 brought the Muste group before the public eye as effective leaders in a labor contest and as dangerous radicals. Trotskyists cheered every move.

Toledo, like Minneapolis, was a "cheap labor 'scab' town," containing sleepy local AFL and Federal Auto Workers unions. Musteite militants captured the AFL local briefly and brought off the strike, aided by the small Federal Auto Workers local and the Unemployed League.

The parts industry until May 1934 had refused absolutely to deal with labor organizations; and Auto-Lite, Bingham, and Logan, like the automobile manufacturers, wanted to deny the union the prestige of recognition. To avert a walkout in February, company officers had agreed to meet union officers on April 1, but backed out when the date arrived. Trying to make capital of the employers' refusal to bargain, Communists in the Unemployed Councils urged a general strike, and the Central Labor Union of Toledo, which had until then ignored exchanges between employers and union, took notice when workers left their jobs. What followed has been described as a four-day pitched battle, beginning April 13. Although Auto-Lite obtained an injunction against picketing, Louis Budenz picketed in defiance of the order, carrying a banner inscribed "1776–1865–1934" at the head of the line. Police arrested Budenz and tear gassed the picketers. Next, Auto-Lite imported 1,800 strikebreakers, and in late May, 700 national guardsmen arrived, battled with strikers, killed two, and injured twenty-five. In ensuing clashes, 200 strikers and onlookers were hurt and 200 arrests made. All but five of the 100 local unions had voted for the strike, but only when war was on its doorstep did the Central Labor Union appoint a committee to negotiate with stalling management representatives.

Hoping to drain off aggressions, authorities scheduled a big parade and hired speakers, including Muste, but when the appointed day arrived, the AFL struck Muste and other militants off the speakers' list, informing them the affair would be too lengthy and tiresome for participants. The parade, held on a Friday, drew a huge crowd, but instead of draining off steam and deflating the strike it ushered in a new phase. At the rally afterward as a succession of "safe" speakers addressed the throng, persons in the audience clamored for a general strike beginning the following Monday. Shouts and demands for the general strike swelled. Rather than face such a catastrophe, Auto-Lite yielded, granting a 5 percent wage boost and de facto union recognition valid for six months subject to revocation after that. It was a qualified victory, but labor historian Philip Taft claimed it was "the first important gain made by the United Auto Workers," because over 4,000 were employed by the three companies. By June 6 after some recalcitrance on the employers' part, all the strikers had been rehired.[46]

Taft said the settlement came "just in time to halt a move for calling a general strike," and that it was the work of federal mediator Charles Taft, brother of Senator Robert Taft.[47] He failed to cite the role of the Muste organization or to credit the strikers' strategies for the outcome. In his memoirs, Budenz recognized that unity between employed and jobless persons augmented the catalytic effect the revolutionaries had on the lethargic AFL and so helped the contest.[48] Muste believed the attitude of "calm defiance," plus the threat of general strike, delivered victory.[49]

As postscript, Muste recorded that the mediator, Charles Taft, made a slip of the tongue which revealed prejudice against the strike. Taft allegedly asserted in Muste's presence, "There was no justification for the strike anyway." Negotiations were in progress at that moment.

Muste informed Taft he intended to disclose the incident to the public so it could know the mediator was unfriendly to union recognition despite the new federal law. Taft thereupon asked Muste to confer with him in his hotel room. When Muste arrived, he found reporters already there. Taft confessed his slip, asking that they not print or repeat it. Subsequently Muste gave out a report, but no paper printed it, not the Associated Press, the United Press, nor the local Toledo paper. Only after negotiations ended a week later was one account printed.[50]

Toledo put one radical party on the labor map. Minneapolis, its strike erupting almost simultaneously, was to put another on it.[51]

After the coal yard drivers won their wage increases and union recognition in February, General Drivers Union Local No. 574 under its Trotskyist leaders began to expand to general cartage companies. Governor Olson had gone on record as "sympathetic to union aims" six weeks after the coal strike, one month before the broader strike in May, but as he failed to appear when invited to Minneapolis Teamster meetings, members questioned his sincerity. To bring members in, the local set up committees corresponding to the seven categories of hauling, and in March and April enrolled 2,000 to 3,000 men, making the General Drivers Union the largest union in Minneapolis. Recent triumphs emboldened the Trotskyist leadership. They were angry because other Minneapolis employers refused to discuss wage raises and union recognition with Local 574. Accordingly they called a strike for May 15 and in the intervening time made elaborate preparations.

Masterminding the arrangements, by May 12 Vincent Ray Dunne and Farrell Dobbs had installed an efficient multipurpose strike headquarters. A dispatch center for a motorcycle courier service equipped with four telephone lines protected by a code specially devised to foil wiretappers, the headquarters also contained a commissary with dining hall to feed 10,000 hungry pickets daily and a first-aid center staffed with three nurses and two physicians. It was indeed prescient to add the medical dispensary: injured strikers could elude arrest by avoiding city hospitals and ambulance services. Fifteen mechanics at headquarters kept vehicles running and four roof-top sentries equipped with tommy guns patrolled the site.

For this strike Trotskyists relied on the effective "flying picket squad" used in textile strikes in the South and in farm worker strikes in California. The flying squad captains' orders superseded all others. Stationary picket posts stood at the city limits on highways, at gasoline bulk plants and filling stations, at the wholesale market (six square blocks), at the loop retail district, and at truck freight terminals, each led by a "captain," with a "field commander" at every station. Finally, claiming to correct distortions in the capitalist press, union leaders published the *Organizer,* a one-page daily.[52]

On the eve of the strike the Citizens' Alliance met at a downtown hotel, confident from previous experiences in crushing labor. The Alliance had earlier announced if employers were to deal with the Teamsters, it must choose the union leaders. Local 574 had of course refused such interference. At the meeting, Alliance officers argued for a big wage increase for workers to disorganize the campaign for union recognition, but Alliance members by vote defeated the proposal, then pledged $200,000 to defeat the strike and planned to mobilize a "citizens' army" in a residential district. Subsequently the mayor had 155 upper-class men sworn in by the sheriff as "special officers," titles which (Arthur M. Schlesinger noted) were "accepted with Skull and Bones high spirits." And, "both sides armed themselves with lead pipes and baseball bats."[53]

Strike smashing efforts were bolstered by 2,000 strikebreakers and the Hennepin County chapter of the Minnesota Law and Order League, which kept a desk at Citizens' Alliance offices. Dan Tobin backed the resistance too: he disapproved of Trotskyism in his union local. On their side, the General Drivers Union had encouragement from the Central Labor Union and the state Farm Holiday Association. In its first days, 35,000 construction workers struck in sympathy. For four days in late May a "real war" took place in Minneapolis, its most publicized encounter the "battle of deputies run" at the city market. Associated Press releases described graphically (but inaccurately) the events: "Striking truckmen rioted today in the city market . . . police reddened the pavements with their blood"; "Pandemonium raged," spurred by "outside agitators intent upon prolonging the strike with its attendant violence"; a businessman was killed, "victim of the surging mob."[54] Pipes, clubs, sticks, pistols, and iron bolts served as weaponry wielded by women as well as by men, for, the *Militant* jubilantly proclaimed, "to involve the women is to double the strength of the workers"; indeed, "they raised hell generally," said Dobbs. In short, the *Militant* portrayed an "inspiring" and "grand spectacle."[55]

Fraternity men from the University of Minnesota volunteered as strikebreakers but fled the battlescene. As an observer for the *Minneapolis Star,* one such student wrote about how police dealt with the strikers. "Suddenly I knew, I understood deep in my bones what Fascism was." That young man was Eric Sevareid.[56] While conflict raged in the streets, the Regional Labor Board met at the Nicollet Hotel with union and company officials to hammer out a settlement. At last, on May 24 after Governor Olson entered as mediator, employers announced acceptance of the board's proposal; after some delay the strikers reluctantly accepted what the board required of them as a compromise. They won recognition for the union and some increase in pay "to be negotiated," but for the drivers only. "Not the best in the world but the strike was settled and it was a start," commented Dobbs.[57] It was in fact only a truce while terms could be negotiated.

On July 5, farm and AFL leaders in a display of unity paraded together through town and held a mass meeting. With the strike in its second month, the Department of Labor sent mediators to Minneapolis. Eugene Dunnigan "with pince nez and cigar" and Father Francis J. Haas, who had reportedly effected 125 settlements, arrived from Washington, D.C. Although by mid-July they had put together a settlement agreeable to the strikers, employers would not consent to pay the federally approved wage increase, nor would they honor seniority rights in relocating workers. They refused to recognize the union's right to represent all its members and they demanded that the union agree to a blacklist of workers most active in the strike. Nor did the Regional Labor Board act to expedite implementation of the terms. Their taste for battle with the ruling class whetted by the recent affray, the brothers in Local 574 voted by acclamation to go out again, shouting "Smash the Citizens' Alliance!" A second strike which began on July 16 was more devastating than the earlier one, and brought help from most labor groups in the Twin Cities. This time police swept down on working class clubs, offices, and radical party headquarters, making 300 arrests. Cannon and Shachtman had their hotel rooms ransacked by authorities and were among those seized and incarcerated in a military stockade.[58] As the tempo rose again, two trucking employers relented and signed the approved wage settlement. But several bankers in the Citizens' Alliance applied pressure on the remaining employers and kept them from signing. Building trades spokesmen complained to the Associated Press that by now it was "a struggle against the tyranny of the Branch Banks and the Citizens' Alliance . . . a handful of financiers wished to set up a dictatorship and prevent the strike from being settled by preventing businessmen from settling, through control of credit."[59]

The farmer-labor governor, Floyd Olson, who had voiced support for the May strike and who held office by the labor vote, called in national guardsmen and embargoed city trucking activity. On August 8, Olson visited President Roosevelt in nearby Rochester, Minnesota, and discussed the credit situation. Roosevelt contacted Jesse Jones of the Reconstruction Finance Corporation, who telephoned Father Haas suggesting that part of the multimillion-dollar government loan would have to be recalled because the collateral had shrunk in value due to the strike. Federal officials then ordered release of the militants in the stockade. In mid-August the Citizens' Alliance and forty-seven firms agreed to the Haas-Dunnigan settlement or a modification thereof. On August 21, the employers capitulated, yielding on every strike term. Subsequent elections in individual trucking houses, the compromise device that had served in February, rendered a general triumph for Local 574. By October 10, loose ends were tied in place. Down to the half-penny, General Drivers Union 574 got its demanded increases in addition to seniority rights and union recognition.[60] Communist party officials, who had carped at every step taken by the despised Trotskyist strike leadership, especially a tentative wage settlement agreed to in August but not made final until October 10, were silenced.[61]

The episode had cost taxpayers and businessmen heavily. During the thirty-six-day stoppage, city bank clearings were down $3,000,000 a day; $5,000,000 was lost in wages; and the taxpayers had funded the guardsmen's presence at $300,000. The city paid $50,000,000 for the spectacle, but the power of the Citizens' Alliance had been broken, albeit temporarily. The nonunion shop was overthrown, and the right of workers to organize unions of their choice vindicated.[62]

Such victories could only attract new members to the drivers' union and inspire an expanded organizing effort. In ensuing years, Farrell Dobbs brought the General Drivers Union to an eleven-state area which became by 1938 a federated system calling itself the Central States Drivers Council. Dobbs's major tactics were the secondary boycott, "leapfrogging,"* and area-wide uniform agreements. Dan Tobin, general president of the Teamsters, who regarded his union as the most powerful in the nation, grudgingly (and enviously) accorded Dobbs his personal admiration. Fearing that Dobbs's drivers would leave the AFL Teamsters and affiliate with the new, more aggressive CIO, Tobin in 1938 merged his rival Minneapolis branch of the Teamsters, Local 500, with 574 to create Local 544-International Brotherhood of Teamsters (AFL), and in 1939 named Dobbs as international organizer. It was against Tobin's protest that on December 6, 1939, just after Tobin offered him the secretary-treasureship of the brotherhood, Dobbs decided to work full time in the Trotskyist party.[63]

Dave Beck, utilizing Dobbs's techniques, went on to establish the Western Conference of the Teamsters, and Jimmy Hoffa, learning at Dobbs's feet as young business agent for Tobin's Detroit Local 299, later used similar methods in "consolidating his great power through the Eastern, Central, and Southern States . . . ."[64] Hoffa credited Dobbs for his contribution, although he quarreled with Dobbs's Trotskyist commitment:

> I wouldn't agree with Farrell Dobbs's political philosophy or his economic ideology, but that man had a vision that was enormously beneficial to the labor movement. Beyond any doubt, he was the master architect of the Teamsters' over-the-road operations.[65]

According to Hoffa, working conditions among one group of drivers affected working conditions for the rest. Hoffa knew that a militant union sworn to no compromise with employer associations and determined to obtain for labor a just share of the proceeds of labor cannot long keep its gains and strike for more if it is surrounded by the unorganized, by company unions, or by so-called "class collaborationist"

---

*"Leapfrogging" in this case meant refusing to load and unload cargoes in communities where workers in trucking were not organized into the Teamsters, or refusing to load and unload with unorganized workers. Usually the device produced energetic action to organize in the boycotted areas.

unions headed by labor czars. And he knew that by expanding its operation, the union could proselytize for the labor movement generally.[66]

Trotskyist victories in bringing Teamster membership to eleven states enhanced the authority of the sect. The Minneapolis strike propelled the Communist League of America out of its isolation. Suddenly the comrades had torn loose from their image as impractical theoreticians, preoccupied with Russian problems to the point of disinterest in American affairs, strangers to the labor movement, an "impotent bunch of intellectuals." Because of Minneapolis, the League looked attractive to the Musteites who were scouting opportunities to enlarge their little band. Similarly, Trotskyists had watched the American Workers party closely since its formation, noting with high approval the conduct of the Auto-Lite strike which had "mushroomed into nearly a national phenomenon in the big early days of the CIO."[67] But like the League, the American Workers party experienced very slow growth. Conditions were ripe for an initial contact looking toward merger negotiations.

5

Radical Fusion Politics: Musteites and Trotskyists

In July 1933 Trotsky left Turkey for France. His stay in France coincided with significant political events in Europe, and making full use of this proximity he studied the French repercussions with the utmost care and loyalty to detail. As a consequence his communications to the American branch—indeed, his writings in general—assumed a French coloration. He began to view France as prerevolutionary, therefore the key to the international situation.

"For a New Party and a New International"

Four months before his arrival in France the international left opposition denounced the Communist international for condoning the scandalous inaction of the German Communist party, a laxity (Trotsky charged) that made possible Hitler's rise to power. "Have no illusion— the CP [Communist party] has lost its vitality," a communiqué to the Communist League of America warned. When Zinoviev and Kamenev returned to Russia from exile and "praised Stalin unqualifiedly," Trotsky likened Stalin to Chichikov, who collected dead souls; and he demanded a new party: "the old one could not be reformed for it now bowed to an autocrat." The Trotsky opposition, eschewing "a dogmatic character," aware that "great events . . . may radically change the situation of the working class and could also oblige us to change our position," was "not too weak to proclaim a new party."[1] Three months later the League received clear instructions and a rationale: Prepare the new road. It has proved impossible to reform the Communist international; in the process of trying we educated the cadres of the Bolshevik-Leninists but did not reform the Comintern! The fall of the German party decided the fall of the party in its entirety. No longer does the League demand reintegration into existing parties. "It is high time an end were put to narrow propagandism." "We are no longer an Opposition, but an Independent Organization . . . . The C.I. is dead!"[2]

Accordingly, the plenum of the international left opposition at its Paris meeting planned a fourth international to supplant the corrupt third. Moreover, three independent groups, one from Germany and two from Holland, united with the international left organization in the "Pact of Four" announcing the new international. Max Shachtman remembered that because of League disenchantment with its role as opposition wing of the Communist party, a dissatisfaction gathering momentum since 1932, the international Trotskyist movement accepted the plan with considerable enthusiasm.[3]

Next the American rank-and-file comrades would have to be brought 'round. The *Militant,* that indispensable educational device, would do service here. Headlines called "For a New Party and a New International," proclaiming that "From this time onward the Communist League ceases to regard itself as a faction of the official Stalinist party." The *Militant* painstakingly explained the League's stand on major issues, hoping the new independent status would draw a wider readership who would wish to be instructed in Trotskyism. The "National Committee, Communist League of America" invited

> . . . all revolutionary workers, regardless of their present affiliation or non-affiliation in common efforts leading to the construction of a genuine Communist Party in America.
>
> Taking the necessity to create a new party as the point of departure, the Communist League proposes a frank and comradely discussion with other individuals, groups and organizations aiming toward the same goal and submits, for their consideration, the following points . . . .[4]

Its editors announced a transformation of the *Militant* from a propaganda organ to a "popular agitation paper appealing directly to the mass of American workers."[5] The League scheduled special lectures to explain the new course. Articles appeared speculating on the character of the proposed party, one premise being that the League was not that new organization. Nevertheless its twenty-eight branches would circulate and advertise a proposal that revolutionary groups collaborate to build the party and a fourth international. By the end of 1933 the League was running headlong down the way to which Trotsky had cautiously pointed in March.[6]

Trotskyist voices blended in a mounting chorus. The depression crisis evoked analysis and prescription of all varieties, from one pole to the other. Well-known liberals and radicals who disdained both the Communist and Socialist parties but who shared a conviction that capitalism heaved in its final, mortal crisis, also proposed creating a party to gather in the swelling ranks of revolutionaries. They believed the relentless crushing of the lower middle class would force many, alienated from the state, into these legions. But no existing party could thwart incipient fascism, because not one specifically appealed to these disaffected. There was no "aggressive, competently-led revolutionary party." These critics rejected the Communist party because it subserved Moscow. They scorned the Socialist party and the Musteite Conference for Progressive Labor Action as too opportunist. For instance, to deter fascism Mauritz Hallgren reasoned that revolutionaries would have to take over communications, transportation facilities, and power centers, at once, in a planned insurrection. No existing party was prepared to lead so bold a venture.[7] And according to John Dewey it really boiled down to a question of fascism or revolution.[8] Max Eastman thought a coalition "consecrated to the task of capturing the political power," an alliance of "the Left Wing of the technicians with the working class and the exploited farmers, led by men trained in economic, historical, and social science" might be able to do the deed.[9] J. B. Salutsky-Hardman, head of the Amalgamated Clothing Workers, said labor unionists liked the idea of a new party. Half the working force walked the streets, after all. Farmers could not meet mortgage payments. White-collar workers and professionals were ready for action; so were high school and college graduates with no job prospects. To channel this energy born of distress, Hardman advised a farmer-labor organization based on the Minnesota model.[10] The proposed party must not focus on European crises as Stalinists and Trotskyists tended to do, Muste cautioned, but should draw on the "American revolutionary tradition."[11] And repeatedly V. F. Calverton in *Modern Monthly* pointed out the signs of encroaching fascism and deplored alien Marxist ideas. With Muste he told home-grown radicals to "Americanize their Marxism."[12] One group, boasting that all its members were "native American radicals," met in Chicago in September 1933 expecting to found a new party through a temporary "Farmer-Labor Political Federation" chaired by John Dewey. Two years later the group still met, now under the name "League for Independent Political Action," the chairmanship having passed over to Paul Douglas.[13]

Such a coalition as these intellectuals planned flew in the face of the Trotskyist axiom "no two-class parties." Yet the record shows Trotsky contemplated the same thing as early as June 1932 when he broke ground venturing that a projected labor party would have to be considered on its merits given the circumstances. He speculated that as long as his followers kept their identity as a separate communist group, a labor party could "be an arena for successful struggle."[14] When the next summer (1933) he commanded the fresh strategy, the way was cleared and the Communist League of America found a sizable body of American intellectuals toying with the idea.

Approaching the American Workers Party

Some of these intellectuals had been Communists. Some of them, Muste, Ernest Rice McKinney, James Burnham, Sidney Hook, Budenz, Johnson, were already affiliated with the Conference for Progressive Labor Action (CPLA), a "labor" group that had drawn radical intellectuals who for one reason or another shunned union politics and the Socialist and Communist parties. What kind of labor group was it? The United Hebrew Trades had condemned the CPLA as a dual union movement. It was viewed as "a bunch of inexperienced professional radicals," as "half-Communist, half-I.W.W., half-liberal" (hence pointless) by Socialists who withdrew in 1931 when Muste, Budenz, and others took charge and announced the CPLA would be the nucleus of a new revolutionary, but non-communist, party.[15] To Trotskyists the CPLA revealed a growing hostility in the unions toward the "class collaboration methods of Green, Woll, and Company, and a . . . demand for more militant policies and action" (hence having potential). But under Muste it was "a by-product of the crisis and disintegration of official Communism in America . . . a product of the CP's [Communist party's] 'Third Period' policy, a home for political renegades." Unfortunately Muste pretended to shape a movement between the right and the left, in the process stultifying the "rebellious instincts of the workers" and arresting their progress "on the path of struggle for a class movement," because he failed to jettison his capitalist ideology.[16] Trotskyists therefore labeled the CPLA a "progressive movement," simply the left wing of the social democracy; nevertheless its growth was "a sign of great significance for the revolutionary party."[17]

Did the CPLA actually do anything? Its members claimed it figured prominently in textile and mine strikes from Illinois to North Carolina and in building unions in textile and public utility firms. When the CPLA at its December 1933 convention in Pittsburgh agreed to build an "American Workers Party as a revolutionary expression of the American masses," what Trotskyists had perceived in 1931 as the latent potential of this grouping began to unfold.

The American Workers party would "convince the decisive sections of the American people that it can run society"; increase its influence among industrial workers; lead "immediate struggles," strikes, demonstrations, and the like; analyze capitalist propaganda to undermine confidence in the capitalist state; work among "potentially revolutionary" farmers, Negroes, and other oppressed groups, showing "how racial differences are used by the capitalist dictatorship to drive down the standard of living of all workers and to keep workers and producers from uniting"; work among the professional classes to overcome their "hesitancy . . . to take part in social and political activity"; work with the unemployed which "may be the army in the next war, it may be the party of fascism"; join the antiwar movement with the goal of overthrowing the capitalist system; aid struggles of subject nations; work in elections as a means to "give the party opportunities to appear openly before the people of the country, to present its aims and its programs, to cut through the sham issues to the real issues that face us and must be solved." And—the American Workers party would shun "American exceptionalism."[18]

Keeping to the theme of Americanism, Salutsky-Hardman advised the labor movement to reject "canonized truth and canned reasoning" and "the tutelage of political puppets maniuplated from a distance of seven thousand miles" if it hoped to be "realistically aggressive."[19] Budenz suggested the slogans "Advance America" and "Win America" to promote an amendment to the Constitution to ban the profit system.[20] Muste later recalled that Budenz was "enthralled by the American revolution . . . [and] thought of himself as a combination of Patrick Henry and a Minute Man, carrying the American Revolution into the twentieth century."[21] Sidney Hook advised amalgamating the principles of the Declaration of Independence with American socialist philosophy, rightfully reclaiming the ideas from Rotary, the American Legion, and boards of education who monopolized and twisted them to their own uses.[22]

Meantime, the Communist League of America in December 1933 announced an "action program" to give direction to united front relations with other radicals and soliciting memberships on a "broader basis than before."[23] It was only a matter of time before the two organizations would meet for serious talks.

In a political committee meeting, Shachtman recalled, he proposed to investigate the Musteites and their program, print a series of articles "in friendly criticism," then plan negotiations on the subject of union. Cannon agreed completely and the rest of the committee voted in favor.[24] Accordingly, the League initiated contact. In January 1934 the national committee sent a formal invitation to the American Workers party to "join hands" to construct the sorely needed revolutionary association and, because both groups shunned the Communist party, "repelled by Stalinist bureaucracy," to exchange opinions and clarify the ambiguities in the American Workers programs. They might perhaps effect a fusion.[25] Remembering the political oscillations of the CPLA, Trotskyist spokesmen made four stipulations. First, they insisted on a true communist program, no petty bourgeois class collaborationist socialism. Second, they would maintain their keen interest in European and Russian events, thus remaining internationalist as real Marxists must do. The new party and a fourth international were inseparable. You cannot build parties first, then the international: that "is Utopian, not to say non-Marxist," declared Cannon. Comrades must subject all events, any party program, warned Shachtman, "to the pitiless fire of Marxian criticism."[26] An inviolable principle was attachment to the world party, the fourth international.

Linked with internationalism were the third and fourth special concerns: questions of terminology and the character of the Moscow-based Communist party. When it rejected the Communist party as "sectarian" and labeled Marxist phrases alien "factional jargon . . . represented by Union Square" and "Jabberwocky," the American Workers party betrayed its reformist past, its incomprehension of the fifteen years of Communist party history, its overconcern with superficiality. However, the Communist party had suffered defeat after defeat, the blame should fall on its lack of "revolutionary analysis" and its fixation with "socialism in one country," not on "sectarianism." The new party could not, of course, turn its back on American language, traditions, and experiences and still win members. Not incompatible entities, internationalism and American traditions had to be compounded in the party. Naturally, Trotskyists hoped for fusion with the American Workers party on these bases.[27]

The American Workers party's errors were rooted in its centrist character; it would be hopeless were it not so sizable, and it did seem to be "moving in a leftward direction." Let the two come to terms on a program, then merge, advised a League circular; but do not anticipate a "peaceful and unperturbed existence" because a struggle against centrism would begin. Since a major plank in the League platform instructed capturing "leftward-moving forces" and turning them toward the correct revolutionary path, Trotskyists should go ahead with the merger. As if already probing future possibilities, the memo concluded "We should possibly give much attention to the Socialist Party and we have *not.*"[28]

While the League sent its most persuasive speakers to Canada, New England, and the Midwest to publicize fusion, the American Workers party, clearly on the defensive, in extraordinary session considered the criticisms of its program. Next, Muste, Budenz, Hook, Calverton, and Burnham met with Cannon, Shachtman, and Swabeck to explore merger and "immediate collaboration in practical tasks." Swabeck reported to Trotsky that the Musteites had made significant concessions. They agreed to join the fourth international, accepted the League's characterization of the Socialist and Communist parties, stood firmly but critically behind Russia as the first and only workers' state, and subscribed to democratic centralism as the basis for discipline. The two would work together to form a left wing in the trade unions and to create a labor defense division, and the League would simply move into the big Musteite Unemployed League. Hook recalled much later that the terminology question seemed settled too:

> After the first meeting when the Trotskyists trotted out all their Leninist nonsense about the dictatorship of the proletariat [exercised?] through the party I reported back that their position hardly differed from the official Communist view. I was then besieged by my friends among the Trotsky group who told me they really didn't mean it, etc. In later sessions the Trotskyists dropped all their offensive ideological doctrine . . . .[29]

Shachtman reminisced,

> We met with them; we were as affable as we could be; as reasonable as we could be; we didn't insist upon the letter of the law from the Marxist and Leninist standpoint; we were amenable to using language in our program that they were more accustomed to and not the specific jargon in which we felt so much at home.[30]

Hook remarked, "The theoretical basis of the merger was really the program of the Am. Workers Party," and in fact Hook's group did have the upper hand.[31] Musteites, especially Budenz and Hardman, continued to view suspiciously the league's "dogmatic attitude toward all fundamental problems" yet were flattered because the League relentlessly through 1934 pressed its suit for union.[32]

The Minneapolis and Toledo strikes in 1934 increased the respect each bore for the other and without question militated toward merger. But events in France that summer made merger seem even more irresistible to the Trotskyists who would accordingly not rest until it was accomplished.

The French Turn: France

France was troubled by government instability and resultant polarization of her people in the period 1932-1934. After Britain and the United

States devalued their currencies, French prices remained too high to be competitive; every successful French government, whether left or right, tried by deflationary policies to bring prices in line with the world market but without success, for the French had a mystic affection for the franc and its value. Production diminished, income slumped, a surtax even brought the cost of living down but general discontent turned gradually more violent. The middle classes joined fascist leagues such as the "Cross of Fire" supporting full repression particularly during the general strike of February 12, 1934, for which the Communist party took full credit.

Trotsky felt dismay at the French Trotskyists' inaction. The workers were ready, he lamented, but invariably the inept Communist or Socialist leadership "applied the brakes." The same thing had occurred in Germany. "The German proletariat was not smashed by the enemy in battle. It was crushed by the cowardice, baseness, perfidy of its own parties."[33] Numbering only about 100, his French followers published *Truth* and distributed it to a surprisingly wide readership of 3,000. Socialists in France could choose between two groupings, the reformist General Confederation of Labor (CGT) and the left-wing French Section of the Workers International (SFIO), led by Léon Blum. Trotsky thought the SFIO was promising. Scolding his handful of French followers as "muddleheads," "arrogant," "philistine," "petty-bourgeois," he commanded them to join at once down to the last man the militant socialists of the SFIO and win for bolshevism "tens and hundreds of thousands of Communist and Socialist militants." Only a big "real movement" impelled by correct ideas could "smash fascism" as a small propaganda group however correct its ideas could not, Trotsky argued. Duty dictated that the small group, blessed with the proper perspective, should seize the helm.

Why did Trotsky choose the SFIO rather than the French Communist party? He explained that in France in 1934 the Communist party through a united front yielded to centrists on every issue. The Communist international moved from third period militance to united front mushiness like an "acrobatic flip flop," showing no principle; it was hopeless.[34] As Shachtman later noted, a Trotskyist simply could not function in the Communist party for, as Stalinists were conditioned to hostility against them, Trotskyists could not utter a word at a meeting without being physically ejected.[35]

The Communist League of France must penetrate that united front. Keeping its separate identity with its own organ all the while, it must enter and point the way inside the SFIO. Trotskyists could debate and agitate for their program. In the crisis of bourgeois democracy, fascism impending, "democratic" politicians would cease tolerating labor and reform movements and would expel their spokesmen from the state machinery, forcing the moderate left to lose confidence in the state. Left-wing forces would launch an inept attack, doomed without proper revolutionary leadership. Within the SFIO, Trotskyists could lead the groundswell, even luring away Stalinists. All of this was "a positively grandiose idea," observed Shachtman thirty years later.[36]

How could Trotskyists accomplish all this and remain devoted followers of Lenin who had insisted on severing ties with reformist groups? Trotsky distinguished between events surrounding Lenin's 1914 decision to break with the "social-patriots" and the events of this hour in 1934, adding ". . . while preserving absolute irreconcilability insofar as our principles are concerned, organizationally we must be very resourceful, very spry, very supple and very enterprising. Otherwise we will decay even with the very best ideas." Marxism, "the liveliest theory," should not be made into "a sectarian faith under cover of which to be able to remain passive instead of intervening with all . . . force and determination in the stream of the living labor movement." Dismissing opponents of the "turn" as dogmatists, he continued, "as Marxists, we cannot be pettifogging doctrinaires, pedants. We always analyze the living stream and adapt ourselves to every new situation without losing our identity. Therein lies the whole secret of revolutionary success. . . ." "He who does not seek and does not find the road to the masses is not a fighter but a dead weight to the party."[37]

Identity was the key. The French League under Pierre Naville and Marceau Pivert entered the SFIO in October 1934 as the "*Truth* faction," "openly under our own banner." Entrism, nevertheless, bred its opposition: Max Geltman in the New York branch; Hugo Oehler, who introduced a motion at a plenum to condemn the "turn;" in France, J. Thulier who argued against it in the *Internal Bulletin.*[38] But it was done. Eight months later, Trotsky assayed the results, concluding, "The correctness of our entry into the SFIO is now proved by objective facts. Our section, thanks to the entry, has changed from a propaganda group into a revolutionary factor of the first order." In fact, he exhorted all sections to emulate Naville's French section. After one year in the SFIO (but only because Trotsky's directives to his faction laid the groundwork), on October 1, 1935, the SFIO expelled the Trotskyists.[39]

Negotiating Fusion

In the United States, 1934 seemed a propitious year for the Communist League of America to enter the social democratic movement. The comrades in September endorsed the French turn for France and wherever Trotsky ordered it, but it did not occur to them to merge with the Norman Thomas Socialists; instead they read the new policy to mean merger with the American Workers party, a course already practically decided. Indeed the American Trotskyists were assured they would not be making a French turn, but it was a promise soon broken.

Because the reaction of rank-and-file comrades was unpredictable (Oehler and others might win them over), the national committee publicized fusion in the *Militant*.[40] The leadership believed haste "desirable and necessary." Cannon recalled that the Stalinists had "fully intended to absorb the Muste organization," yet "the despised little 'sectarian' group of Trotskyists" had beaten them to the draw, and "were deep in the unity negotiations . . . before the Stalinists realized what was going on."[41] Once they caught on, warnings to the Musteites appeared in the *Daily Worker*. Alexander Bittelman cautioned that a trap was being laid for them, "the trap of counter-revolutionary Trotskyism," and he alerted, too, misguided Trotskyists. Your leaders, he warned, "are leading you into unity with Muste, the champion of bourgeois nationalism." Why not, if both are so corrupted, throw them both together in one sack? asked Cannon.[42]

On September 9 a general membership meeting steered by the zealous Shachtman voted unanimously to endorse fusion.[43] The American Workers party met at Valencia, Pennsylvania, to draft an appropriate response. While leaders hammered out the all-important "program," settled organizational problems, and collaborated on practical matters, together they showed up at labor and party meetings. Trotskyists spared no effort to win the nonideological Muste to their habits and for a time seemed to succeed. By the end of 1934 Muste was speaking the jargon of a seasoned Bolshevik. The first public meeting held under joint

League-American Workers party auspices drew 300 silk workers and supporters to hear Muste and Cannon denounce the Lovestoneite conduct of a recent strike and praise the coming Musteite-Trotskyist unity. Although some cat-calling and a Communist party exodus marred the occasion, the event dramatized the birth of the new party for which so much was hoped.[44]

Meantime, the League's organizational proposals were approved, possibly because Trotskyists could claim more dues-paying members; but Cannon thought the "obvious fairness, even generosity" made them acceptable too.[45] The League recommended "a fifty-fifty arrangement all up and down the line": Muste would be national secretary and Cannon, editor of the paper. A propaganda group would naturally carry its habits over into a fresh association, so the League preferred the editorship to titular premiership. Similarly, the League wished to appoint one of its own as "educational director," leaving labor concerns in capable Musteite hands. Ernest Rice McKinney, one of the rare blacks in the party, came from Pittsburgh to New York in February 1935 to work on the political committee. Both parties would have equal representation on the twenty-two member national committee, and they would settle further organizational problems on a parity basis.

The program was harder to define, but after several drafts one was forged which even Trotsky blessed as "rigidly principled." Hook remembered that in negotiating for the American Workers party "the theoretical basis of the merger was really the program of the American Workers Party."[46] Such agreement between radicals was rare. It was signal in that each of the two parties had attracted different kinds of radicals—the American Workers party drawing those opposed to the dogmatism endemic in leftist groups, people active in the labor movement but not in left-wing politics, while the League comrades were theoretical Marxists, Bolsheviks. It was a delightful courtship and honeymoon. But their respective (and different) pasts were to rise up, haunt, and bit by bit sunder them.

In October 1934 Cannon traveled to Paris to the plenum of the International Communist League, the meeting that sanctioned the French turn. From there, he went to Grenoble and a conference with Trotsky, his first since Trotsky's exile. The French press demanded Trotsky's ouster. Accordingly, Daladier revoked his visa but no country would as yet receive him. His existence was one of slipping in the cover of night from one friend's house to another. Trotsky's current host drove Cannon and Trotsky up to a secluded spot in the French Alps, and in this rarefied atmosphere they discussed the projected fusion. "The Old Man approved everything we had done. . . . He was fully in favor of it, and he also was greatly interested in the personality of Muste, asked me questions about him and entertained some hopes that Muste would develop into a real bolshevik later." Shachtman remembered too that "Trotsky was entirely in favor of what we did at every single stage" in the matter of merger.[47]

Reassured, Cannon returned prepared to fight Oehler's resistance to the French turn. The Oehlerites yielded this time, but their tendency eventually hardened into a faction that produced a split the following year. But in late 1934, despite Oehler, fusion was consummated.

In November 1934 in New York City fifty League delegates from twenty cities convened for four days to thrash out details and ratify the declaration of principles. Nearby the American Workers party members met simultaneously for the same purpose. Then, in joint session on December 1 and 2, the two formally fused into the Workers party of the United States. On December 8 the freshly united party press announced the "Launch Workers Party of the U.S.," its job the "overthrow of capitalist rule in America and the creation of a workers' state," and reminded the reader that "Minneapolis and Toledo . . . were the stars that presided over its birth." With the combined membership roster of the parent parties, the new one numbered between "a few more than 1,000" and about 1,500 members counting those in Unemployed Leagues, according to Hook and Burnham. Budenz from his sickbed reinforced in the faithful their sense of mission: the New Deal had promised the masses figs and gave them only thistles.[48] The infant party bore on its shoulders an awesome responsibility.

The Workers Party: First Months

Was merger with the Musteites the biggest mistake the Trotskyists made? Max Shachtman almost forty years later believed it was. "Muste was never really with us—never *really,*" he reasoned. In 1976, remembering the fusion, Arne Swabeck still thought it a "progressive" step. Certainly great cooperation characterized the first year of unity.

The main task set forth in the declaration of principles was to mobilize the American masses for struggle against capitalism. To gather in the unaffiliated forces waiting for their movement to crystallize into a party, Muste and Cannon left on a coast-to-coast speaking tour. Such tours became a regular feature of party activity, although Shachtman, "a scintillating and masterful speaker," traveled most often as party spokesman.[49] Completing details, the national committee merged *Labor Action* and the *Militant* to form the *New Militant,* its first issue heralding party fusion. The *New International,* theoretical organ of the Trotskyists edited by Shachtman, would serve the Workers party now; but Shachtman would share editorial responsibilities with James Burnham, a New York University philosophy professor who had been with Muste in the CPLA. Finally, the Workers party drafted an eleven-year program. The party hoped to double membership in six months, raise a $50,000 party fund in sixty days, build the paid circulation of *New Militant* to 10,000, of *New International* to 6,000, and publish "at least one popular agitational pamphlet per month." It pledged to organize actively, aiming to unite labor with the jobless in a massive pressure grouping and stage huge demonstrations, guided by appointed district organizers in five centers plus New York, part of an elaborate national and local party structure. It approved an education program under Hugo Oehler's directorship for which the International Workers School was speedily established. A multifaceted operation, the education program would function parallel with the party at all levels and include district schools with Marxist and labor studies, a national training school in New York to coach leaders in organizing and guiding demonstrations "for progressive measures," and even a research department. The new party lost no time in trying to implement its plans.

While Muste and Cannon were on tour, the Workers party moved its district office and national headquarters to a high-rent suite in New York City. The suite served many purposes. For instance, classes began there in mid-February. Then, that necessary appendage to a thriving radical operation, the bookstore, opened in the suite. Comrades soon had the place humming as they planned New York district functions such as marches and rallies, and as they debated invited antagonists in the meeting room. Headquarters rang late into the night with strident declamation and Marxist bombast.[50]

When Trotskyists joined A. J. Muste they enjoyed an entrée, albeit a brief one, into the elite of liberal intellectual circles. At Muste's testimonial dinner on January 9, 1935, on the eve of his speaking tour, Trotskyists sat down with Stuart Chase, Roger Baldwin, George B. Counts, John Haynes Holmes, Reinhold Niebuhr, James Rorty, Freda Kirchwey, George Soule, Oswald Garrison Villard and others of that civil libertarian coterie. But by degrees Muste's wealthy patrons stopped contributing to his causes (including his party) after fusion and after they met the Trotskyists. Cannon observed that, for these persons, "Trotskyism is entirely too serious a matter"; they discovered that "the Trotskyists mean business."[51] In fact, after only six months, funding and membership gains not proving as impressive as anticipated, the Workers party was evicted from its commodious headquarters for non-payment of rent. From there the party moved to "a rather unprepossessing old loft." Nor were the grandiose education schemes realized. An initial flurry of enthusiasm dwindled to declining enrollments and nonattendance, forcing the suspension of one-third of the classes and inability to begin branch classes. One report lamented that instructors were even tardy and inefficient.[52]

Still, the party did generate interest among radicals. It began to recruit, but it suffered early losses too. Sidney Hook recollected that Salutsky-Hardman "who knew that Trotskyists better than I dropped out."[53] Louis Budenz, hero of Toledo, and Arnold Johnson, national secretary of the Unemployed League, both shining stars in the labor movement, resigned in June and October, respectively. Budenz had been talking about an amendment to the U.S. Constitution abolishing capitalism and wage slavery; the Workers party branded it a "retreat to parliamentarism." Obviously uneasy outside an ideological home and very uneasy about fusion, Budenz while still ostensibly a member of the Workers party in early 1935 secretly joined the Communist party where he stayed ten years, rising to editorship of the *Daily Worker*. Johnson joined the Communist party in 1936.[54] When they left, the Workers party lost two energetic, talented radicals, but in the general optimism the loss did not seem serious. Then a party directive threatened to limit recruitment potential. The ruling forbade foreign language federations: "full participation in party activity in the U.S. is possible only to those familiar with the language of the country." Complaints flooded

the national office, forcing leaders to modify the rule and allow local
executive committees to authorize equal-status branches of foreign-
speaking members.[55]

Some "dissident elements from the Communist party—one or two
here, half a dozen elsewhere," came into the Workers party. In December 1934 Joseph Zack, a Communist party founder, joined, as did W. W.
Norris, a leading member of the Socialist party's Revolutionary Policy
Committee, along with nine previously unaffiliated people.[56] In January 1935 three Akron Communists joined, and in February, one Socialist; then Weisbord's tiny Communist League of Struggle which had had
an on-again, off-again courtship with the Trotskyists since its formation
in 1931 entered the Workers party for a short stay. In March the *New
Militant* boasted that five left the Communist party to join the Workers
Spartacus Youth League, and then a week later, two more entered who
were disgruntled over the poor defense effort for leaders of the Cannery
and Agricultural Workers Industrial Union indicted on charges of criminal syndicalism. After three months, Workers party membership had
risen "40 percent" to about 200 according to the *New Militant.* Sidney
Hook remembered that the Unemployed Leagues, active in the South,
brought in sizable numbers from that section, especially Texas. April
brought five orange belt Californians and twelve from the Buffalo, New
York, Young People's Socialist League (YPSL). The pattern continued
through the summer of 1935, appearing to validate Cannon's and
Trotsky's buoyant predictions.[57]

In admitting Zack (party name of Joseph Kornfeder), a founding
father of American Communism and before his expulsion secretary of
the Trade Union Unity League, the Workers party unwittingly added a
new voice to the Oehler faction. As Zack had found Stalinist discipline
difficult, so he would find intolerable the democratic centralism of the
Workers party. Clearly a bolshevik system for party decision-making is
as susceptible to one-man or clique control as is another arrangement,
and Zack simply joined the factional chorus against Cannon's strong,
brusquely asserted influence in the political committee—an influence
that had provoked Shachtman's ire earlier. Though Shachtman was no
factionalist, he had come perilously close when in 1932 together with
Arne Swabeck, Karl Skoglund, and Albert Glotzer he had considered
the feasibility of expelling Cannon from the League for trying to silence
the youth leadership.[58]

Zack's trouble erupted after Oehler and his crony, Tom Stamm, lost patience with Cannon and Shachtman who (they believed) dragged their feet in guiding the politically naive, non-New York Musteites to a genuine Marxist outlook. Oehler agitated to "bolshevize" the Workers party: to train the new comrades by an intensified educational program in Trotskyist theory, but Shachtman and Cannon squashed the plan noting that a stepped-up attack would repel these people, not yet fully won over. The Musteites "would just simply drop away from the movement, and . . . in no time at all we would be left with the people we had brought into the unity—namely, ourselves—with perhaps one, two, a dozen, a score or so of the AWPers. The unity would be frittered away," for they were in no mood to be bolshevized. "Professional ultra-leftist" Zack allied with Oehler and Stamm to fight the French turn, and when rumor circulated that Cannon was thinking of entry into the American Socialist party, the matter never yet raised at an official meeting, newcomer Zack openly attacked Cannon for leaning toward social democracy. He jumped to his feet at a New York meeting, "contradicted a party representative" (so the charge read) and labeled the French turn "a plot to capitulate to the Socialist Party." He then distributed, without approval, a four-page manifesto for a new labor organization which proclaimed, "Joseph Zack, prominent advocate of independent unionism, will be the chief collaborator," and asserted that the bureaucrats in the radical parties declined to sponsor the new union because it conflicted with their special interests. Finally, in April 1935 when Dan Tobin had revoked the Teamster charter of Local 574 and the political committee was trying to contrive a policy to meet the crisis, Zack wrote to Vincent Ray Dunne in Minneapolis advising him, "If you are weak then take Cannon's policy. It provides for a respectable retreat with Tobin coming out on top."[59] What Zack had failed to absorb in his short time in the Workers party was that in the Trotskyist party (and without question the Trotskyists had taken command in the merged group) one did not openly buck Trotsky or his henchman, Cannon, and escape expulsion; at the least, the challenger's name would be tarnished and his future chances for party promotion or influence nil.

Zack's case went first to his Bronx, New York, branch, which exonerated him, but at last in early June after a special plenum and a plea for no laxity and "discipline for all members," the party expelled him. Naturally, Oehler and Stamm believed the expulsion unjust, conceding

that Zack had acted rashly—although "driven to it by the Cannon caucus"; but under like circumstances, they asked, why is not Lore thrown
out? Or Budenz? Both were anti-Marxist. They concluded that the
purpose of expulsion was to "annihilate all who oppose the Cannon
line or orientation on the social democracy."[60] After expulsion, Zack
moved into syndicalism briefly, forming a One Big Union club and an
Equalitarian Society. But Cannon reported that later still Zack, paradoxically, became a contributor to the *New Leader,* publication of the
Socialist party's right-wing splinter, the Social Democratic Federation.[61]
Party policy toward Zack, a relative newcomer, presaged that finally
pursued toward Oehler, whose voice mounted during the summer and
fall of 1935 after Zack's expulsion.

As planned, Workers party members joined strike actions as part of
the established union movement. Swabeck had selected the auto industry as a focal point for concerted effort, and in March 1935 as
Toledo Chevrolet workers struck, Worker party members in the Lucas
County Unemployed League demonstrated in sympathy, suggested strategy, and lectured to enlist support for the strikers. Soon workers struck
all the same Toledo plants affected in 1934, and this time milk drivers,
government workers, building tradesmen, and grocery employees left
their posts too. Other cities felt labor disruptions. Rubber employees
struck Goodyear in Akron and the Workers party published their *Gum-
Miner* for them. Workers party members were involved in several strikes:
Musteites were present when Barberton, Ohio, chemical workers in a
Mellon-owned plant staged one of the first sit-down strikes; in August
Trotskyists picketed with Minneapolis iron workers and hosiery mill
workers. The Workers party was concerned with the jobless movement
as well. The Unemployed League scheduled an October caravan from
Ohio to Washington, D.C., to present Frances Perkins, secretary of
labor, a workers' security bill asking for a thirty-hour week, a $10
billion public works program, unemployment insurance, and cash relief. The Musteite Unemployment League published a weekly paper
and claimed 1,000 branches in twenty-two states were committed to
the proposition that all persons have the duty and right to employment.[62]

The most crucial labor problem occurred as a continuation of the
work begun in 1934 in the Teamsters' Minneapolis Local 574. In the fall
of 1934 the Minneapolis local sent Miles Dunne to Fargo, North Dakota's
Local 173 to teach militance to workers there. Gaining publicity first

by winning collective bargaining, seniority, and other rights for milk truck drivers, Dunne soon had coal and transport workers enrolled in the union, expecting to extract a favorable contract from employers. When in January 1935 the employers organized the Associated Industries of Fargo-Moorhead and refused a contract, drivers struck demanding union recognition, a uniform wage scale, and no discrimination against strikers. Vigilantes attacked the Fargo strikers with clubs and ax handles; thirty-two arrests and sixteen "riot" convictions resulted. Despite harassment, the strike persisted; morale stayed high and spirits were boosted by a *Special Strike Bulletin.* Police raided the union hall and arrested ninety-four more strikers. When the Minneapolis local volunteered to send reinforcements for the depleted picket line, the North Dakota governor reportedly said he "would meet outsiders sent into the Fargo strike three to one," and the Fargo paper quoted one citizen's comment: "Miles Dunne should be taken out on the prairie, stripped to his underwear, and made to walk barefoot back to Minneapolis." The resultant trials of strike leaders held in mid-February brought verdicts of guilty; the American Civil Liberties Union and the Nonpartisan Labor Defense stepped in to take an appeal to the state supreme court.[63]

Dan Tobin dealt the crowning blow when he prompted the Teamsters to revoke in March the charter of the Fargo local severing it formally from the larger labor movement. Two weeks later he revoked the charter of the Minneapolis local on a spurious charge of nonpayment of per capita tax. The *New Militant* noted that the union leaders were "too militant, too dangerous" and the workers "clamoring for industrial unionism" only too happy to follow them.[64] When the Zack issue raised its head, the Workers party was responding to this crisis, while Zack was demanding that the party fight for the reinstatement of both locals. But a decision had been made that part of the Worker party policy for the months after fusion must be to steer clear of "explosive, divisive issues" in order to enhance its appeal and facilitate recruitment, a new, uncharacteristic, and short-lived tactic for the Trotskyists, adopted purely for expediency. Moreover, consistent with its bid for popularity (but also uncharacteristically) the party would, as a "special decision" and "no precedent for future campaigns" support the farmer-labor party candidates in a forthcoming election.[65] Local 173 in Fargo henceforth went the way of an independent union.

The Minneapolis Central Labor Union appointed a committee of three to investigate Tobin's charge, discovered it unfounded, and voted unanimously for the local's reinstatement. Tobin replied with demands which would center union control in his hands and exclude the troublesome radicals. A new charter would permit him to approve all activities and applications for membership, and expel all present officers and active members in Local 574. The officers were, of course, the Trotskyists who had guided the local through the strikes. In October, fifteen locals of the International Brotherhood of Teamsters voted to rush a resolution for reinstatement to Tobin and to William Green, head of the AFL. Both men had wanted to purge the radicals but could not persuade the AFL rank and file to agree. Green sent Meyer Lewis to Minneapolis in early November to wrestle with the situation and to assure employer groups of full union cooperation in educating union members about the menace of Communist leadership, and, hopefully, by this means to inspire the workers themselves to repudiate the radicals.[66]

William Brown, head of Local 574, pointed out that the Citizens' Alliance, unable to keep its accustomed control over Minneapolis since the drivers' strike of 1934, now turned to the AFL. Vincent Ray Dunne spoke of the groundswell for industrial unionism brought out into the open first by John L. Lewis, and its threat to William Green and Matthew Woll. The Farm Holiday Association, the Farmer-Labor party, the Central Labor Union, and the University of Minnesota's *Minnesota Daily* repudiated Meyer Lewis, so in late November, thwarted in his attempt to purge the radicals, he left the community. In a last-ditch stand the Minneapolis mayor in January 1936 recommended to businessmen that employers "compel" their men to join the AFL, but industrial unionism had made too much headway; on February 12 many Minneapolis unions voted to join John L. Lewis's Committee for Industrial Organization.[67] The Trotskyist-led Local 574 nevertheless remained independent although affiliated with Farrell Dobbs's General Drivers Union until 1938 when Tobin, noting the successes Dobbs had realized in piecing together the eleven-state Central Drivers' Council, made overtures to the union to recapture it (and Dobbs's organizing genius) for his IBT-AFL. But a final showdown between Tobin and the Trotskyists was to occur in 1941 when Tobin, a loyal Democrat cooperating with Roosevelt's war effort, aided the administration in removing the disruptive radicals from his union, paving the way for their prosecution under the Smith Act of 1940.

Hoping to contain their own labor militants, citizens' committees in other cities campaigned in lecture halls and newspapers for action against "reds" in local unions. The Nonpartisan Labor Defense (NPLD) organized in League years by George Novack, Felix Morrow, and Herbert Solow served the united party as it had the League, attracting in addition the support of the Socialist Lawyers' Association.[68]

The NPLD got the North Dakota Supreme Court to reverse the convictions of three drivers' union leaders. In California it went wholly into the defense of the eighteen organizers of the Communist party's "dual union," the Cannery and Agricultural Workers Industrial Union. In 1934 while the League and the American Workers party negotiated fusion terms a young radical named Norman Mini who had left the Communist party and become a Musteite was arrested in Sacramento and jailed for vagrancy, then kept in jail for trial on criminal syndicalism charges. His trial (and others similarly arrested) opened in Sacramento as the Workers party opened its first year; and on April 4, 1935, eight were convicted, one of them Mini. He refused the probation offered him and so through 1935 he languished in San Quentin Prison while the NPLD prepared the appeal, fought for it against local obstructionists who delayed in releasing the trial record, and made it a national issue.[69]

Each party in the merger kept its prefusion commitments, now functioning with added strength because working together, the cooperation symbolized by the Sacramento case. Mini, a Musteite and former Stalinist, who ran afoul of authorities while organizing workers in a "dual union" received the full panoply of Trotskyist defense from attorneys to publicity.

The First Year: A Tally and a Portent

The party organ kept its format but showed fresh features. New names appeared. "Comments on Life, Liberty and the Pursuit of Happiness" by Bill Reich pointed up with irony the contrasts between poverty and plenty: relief payments, heiresses' daily allowances; good will remarks by preachers, lists of church investment properties; medi-

cal association boasting, medical statistics; and the like, a forerunner of
Harry Ring's "Great Society" column in the *Militant* of the late 1960s.
Trotsky's regular length theoretical articles disappeared for eight months.
So too did the *New Militant's* page devoted to international news. Ar-
ticles by James Burnham under the pen name "John West" focused on
the American revolutionary period. Muste wrote a series entitled "An
American Approach."[70] But the Workers party was not the only radical
party stressing the American heritage at this time.

In keeping with the popular front, Earl Browder instructed Communists to proselytize inside liberal and radical groups. The Communist party also drew upon the rhetoric of history, quoting the founding
fathers, plunging the Moscow-directed party into the American mainstream. Trotsky labeled the new line, clearly calculated to lure friends
for a Soviet Union facing possible invasion, "another vacillation," another "unprincipled zig-zag" as swiftly imposed as the order to halt
third-party collaboration in 1924, as the dumping of Lovestone in 1929,
as the launching of the third period. But the Communist party line
seemed likely to enhance the Communist appeal and gave another
reason, beside the commitment to an "American approach, for the
fusion party to stick to historical themes even at the expense of international coverage. The series "Our Revolutionary Heritage" ran almost
to the end of the Workers party's first year.[71]

In addition to pillorying the capitalist America for its contradictions,
New Militant editorials bombarded dragons strictly in the New Deal
camp. Roosevelt's measures were reformist sops, reinforcing concentration of wealth instead of alleviating poverty, hunger, and unemployment. The Agricultural Adjustment Act, passed in May 1933, a program providing subsidies to farmers and funded from special taxes levied
against processors of agricultural products (subsequently declared unconstitutional by the U.S. Supreme Court) was "lunatic." The National
Recovery Administration, set up by an act passed in June 1933 with the
aim of reviving industry by halting cutthroat competition, discouraging
overproduction, inflating prices, and supposedly giving labor a fair
shake, all to be done through voluntary cooperation by businessmen
themselves, was contemptuously labeled "the blue buzzard." (Cooperating firms displayed stickers with the NRA insignia, a solid blue eagle, in
their windows.) Still worse, the president "under the cloak of liberalism pursue[d] the ends of imperialism" as he militarized the Pacific and

fostered for future use the development of chemical warfare horrors. Nor were American fringe movements immune. The Townsend Plan was "the Panacea of a Quack Doctor," failing to strike at the root of economic ills, private ownership of the means of production. Father Coughlin was the "Pope's Fake Liberalism," and Huey Long, "Tammany Hall Rising from the South," both of them "homegrown fascists" and therefore targets for *New Militant* bombast.[72]

In its first year, the Workers party took two turns of importance. Gradually the international orientation was reestablished, and Trotsky's theoretical articles reappeared, doubtless because foreign questions commanded increasing attention from all sides. When in October 1935 the Workers party prepared resolutions for its second convention to be held in March 1936, eleven resolutions constituted the party's "Statement on the War Crisis" and included reactions to Italy's "imperialist invasion of Africa"; the League of Nations' "sanctions" (cover-ups to assure control by capitalist powers); the USSR's treacherous undermining of the workers' state with diplomatic deals; and the sham of neutrality legislation. Resolutions reaffirmed that "the struggle against war is part of the class conflict of our day," and pledged to stand solidly with the parties of the fourth international.[73] Trotskyist views had come to prevail over Musteite views; pacifism was submerged altogether, and the "American Approach" was on the wane as the *New Militant* more and more resembled the old *Militant* of the prefusion period.

The second significant turn came at the national committee plenum of June 1935, called by Cannon "outstanding in the history of our party," and about which he minced no words. "We came organized and determined, prepared with resolutions, to make the plenum discussions the springboard for an open fight in the party which would clarify the issue and educate the membership" for a fresh look at the Norman Thomas Socialist party. Cannon recalled that the question of the Socialist party loomed uppermost at the plenum, that the Cannon-Shachtman wing in the Workers party determined then to "establish close relations with the Left Wing in the SP, aim to fuse with them," to "send in a group—30 or 40 members— to join the Socialist Party and work inside it in the interests of the Bolshevik education of the Left Wing." Plenum minutes revealed plans to "build up a left wing in the SP and the YPSL," and instructions to take action in the "most responsible and confidential manner."[74]

Yet a rumor making the rounds that the national committee contemplated a flirtation with the Socialist party was vigorously denied. The *New Militant* protested that such gossip was "absolutely without foundation, that no leaders or members of the Workers party advocate or have advocated any such program," and repeated the standard nostrum that the Socialist party was hopelessly reformist. Despite denials at the plenum something drew Muste, a firm opponent of an American French turn, Abern, and McKinney to Oehler in an informal bloc.[75] Shortly after, its proponents labeled "sectarian" those who fought this further step into the broader movement, and the battle was on.

At the end of the first year, the Workers party had not expanded as predicted. But leaders boasted that they had achieved much in practical pursuits—organizing, strikes, the jobless movement, legal defense. "Fusion is a success," Muste concluded in November 1935.[76] Cannon agreed in his reflections years later, and others who remained Trotskyists into the 1970s viewed it as a step well taken. Still others, also participants in the merger, evaluating fusion with the perspective of nearly forty years described it as "as waste," "stillborn," and recalled that fusion brought in capable labor leaders like Ernest Rice McKinney, but portentously, brought in as well Sylvia Agelof who would in 1940 unwittingly and innocently introduce to Trotsky his future assassin.[77]

Of course the Workers party had expected an increased following, people looking for a truly native revolutionary party. It had not attracted them. The Socialist party, even though wracked by internal convulsions, was luring "hundreds and thousands of new young radicals." Naturally the pragmatic Trotskyist leadership began to eye carefully the recently moribund, but now growing, Socialist party.[78]

6

Making the French Turn

The Workers party did not fulfill its members' high hopes but remained a sect as its parent parties had done. The Communist party's fortunes rose as a result of the popular front, or coalition, policy which enjoined open support for President Franklin D. Roosevelt and the new "Americanism" tack "to combat fascism" taken by Earl Browder on Comintern instructions. The Workers party remained a sect compared to the Socialist party, too, which in 1934 and 1935 drew many young people, radicalized by depression, unemployment, and the specter of European fascism.[1] Accordingly, the national committee set its compass for the French turn, abandoning promises made to hesitant Musteites before fusion of the Workers party. Depleted by departure of some of its most influential members such as Arnold Johnson, Louis Budenz, and J. B. Salutsky-Hardman, the Muste group proved powerless to prevent it, particularly as "the Trotskyists took over the merged organization bag, kit, and boodle."[2]

The French Turn in France: Postscript

On August 28, 1935, the French Section of the Workers International (SFIO) demanded excommunication of the Trotskyist faction inside the party. Their paper, *Truth,* "no longer an organ of the Socialist Party," engaged in divisive tactics, indulged in "outrageous criticism" of Socialist leaders, and talked of a fourth international. Already the Socialist youth had expelled the Trotskyist youth leaders. So on October 1, French Socialists duly ousted the rest of the Bolshevik-Leninists.[3]

Trotsky claimed he had engineered the episode: "No one thought we'd be linked to the SFIO indefinitely." When the SFIO decided on common cause with the French Communists, Trotsky told his followers to provoke Paul Faure, SFIO national secretary, to demand expulsion. One of the two French Trotskyist leaders, Marceau Pivert, at this point went over to popular frontism and stayed in the SFIO supporting the new coalition government of Léon Blum. On their own again, Trotskyists launched on June 2, 1936, the Party of International Workers (POI). The front page of the first issue (June 12) of its organ, *Workers' Struggle,* shouted "Into the factories and into the streets . . . . Power to the Workers—Permanent Workers' Councils—Armed Workers' Militia"; the Blum government ordered all copies seized.[4]

In spite of the difficulties accompanying expulsion, Trotsky judged the entrist policy as a whole salutary, even necessary. He claimed that his followers graduated from a propaganda sect of 200 members to a "revolutionary factor" influencing the working-class movement of France, presenting Trotskyist views to a far larger audience, bringing into the SFIO 6,000 to 7,000 new members, acquiring "precious practical experience," yet all the while remaining under control of the International Communist League. In the future, he said, Trotskyists inside a reformist party should establish good rapport with its worker-members to instruct them in language they understand. As in France, they should concentrate on youth, always keeping firm ideological cohesion. On the basis of the French experience which he saw as so great a success, Trotsky advised immediate entry for American Trotskyists: "Personally in favor of entry"; "Act quickly . . . . Pay no attention to European criticism . . . Use 'entry' to become stronger . . . . Time presses."[5] Thus the issue debated for several months somewhat surreptitiously now surfaced as Cannon and Shachtman, backed by instructions from Trotsky himself, proceeded to rally the Workers party for entry into the Socialist party of America.

Fissure in the Socialist Party

Socialist party history shows continual tugging from several sides: the impossibilists with a maximum program geared to their millennial aspirations; the trade unionists caught up in periodic battles for immediate demands; the so-called sewer socialists, involved in municipal reform and election campaigning; and other ad hoc factions that coalesced from time to time. Noting that this large party of around 24,000 members (figures vary) was wasting valuable energies in intraparty disputes and believing that bolshevik discipline could harness this energy to the service of the Kremlin and the third international, Earl Browder harangued all through the mid-1930s for a united front with the Socialist party. Norman Thomas, Socialist leader and presidential candidate, presented a major obstacle to Browder's scheme because he found unpalatable what he considered Russia's perfidy to socialism. He particularly objected to Stalin's trade and security agreements with capitalist powers.[6]

While fascist governments consolidated their regimes in Europe, demagogic appeals caught the attentions of despairing Americans, and as the New Deal reached its apex, tensions among the disparate factions in the Socialist party tightened, then snapped. The crack that later became a chasm appeared first in 1932 at the Socialist party's convention in Milwaukee. Because of the economic crisis, the party swelled with new members. Among them were young militant midwesterners from the municipal reform leagues, Paul Porter as an example. Intelligent, aggressive, ambitious, they collided in the contests for leadership with the long-term gradualist-socialist comrades of the Old Guard. These old-timers, associated with the Rand School and possibly the *Jewish Daily Forward,* had followed the leadership of Morris Hillquit; some had come from the foreign-language federations. Many of the Old Guard were European-born, self-educated, and dedicated to keeping a working-class character for the Socialist party. They have been called "conservative" radicals; they were, in fact, very cautious Marxists. The Militants, youths whose numbers had doubled the Socialist party membership in four years, wanted a "drive for political power." The polarity crystallized with some of the Militants steered by a Lovestoneite infiltrator, Irving Brown, sent in to capture the Socialist party for bolshevism forming the Revolutionary Policy Committee (RPC), and naming as chair-

man a former Methodist missionary and Musteite, J. B. Matthews. After
the Austrian putsch of 1934 the RPC drafted a Marxist program for the
1934 convention.[7] At that stormy meeting the RPC embodied its call
for greater militancy in a hotly debated declaration of principles. It
was "a call to revolution," "a fantastic Bolshevik program," "an an-
archic, illegal, and communistic doctrine," complained attorney Louis
Waldman.[8] Right-wing Socialists led by Waldman pulled away when a
majority adopted the revolutionary declaration by a vote of 99 to 47,
heralding a turning point in party development. Encouraged, ex-Com-
munists such as Benjamin Gitlow and Herbert Zam applied for membership in the new-look Socialist party and were accepted. In 1935
the right wing, fuming over the leftward turn and even stooping to
charge the Militants with "communism" in the capitalist press, was
virtually purged. At the national executive committee meeting in
1936 the Socialist party revoked the 1901 charter of the Old Guard
and gave it to the Militants. In May at the Cleveland convention the
Old Guard made its formal exit from the official party, followed by
several eastern state branches, thus diminishing membership by 30
percent.

Less restricted in its leftward movement now, Militants at the convention reaffirmed the Detroit declaration, incorporating planks and
slogans that could only please the Trotskyists: "Every party member a
trade unionist"; "turn the imperialist war into a civil war"; "defend the
U.S.S.R. as the first workers' country against all capitalist attacks."
Waldman recorded in disgust that the convention was stage-managed by
Militants "with all the totalitarian showmanship of a Hitler demonstration," the hall hung with red bunting, "the clenched fist salute . . .
fervently observed," and the band playing *Solidarity*.[9]

The Old Guard became the Social Democratic Federation, continuing to publish what had become its faction organ, *The New Leader*.
James P. Cannon and Max Shachtman scrutinized with keen interest the
people who remained in the Socialist party, concluding that they were a
core of embryonic revolutionaries still confused, muddled, undisciplined.
These babes in the woods needed only Trotskyist guidance to find the
correct revolutionary path. Moreover, they fairly invited capture by a
disciplined Bolshevik party, for Norman Thomas, hoping to make his
party the haven for all non-Stalinist radicals, had announced a new
"all-inclusive" policy.

Exceedingly skeptical at first about the convulsions in the Socialist party, Workers party Trotskyists disdained any thought of finding common cause with the Militants. After all, they reasoned, the militant wing sprouted from a fundamentally reformist grouping. Militants only "blow into the Socialist party some radical phrases and make it more presentable for conditions of crisis." Their talk of workers capturing power was like shooting the capitalist to death with paper bullets, sneered Hugo Oehler after the Socialist convention of 1932. The Detroit declaration two years later attracted no more confidence. It was a "typical centrist document" reflecting the Militants' "lack of theoretical clarity" said V. F. Calverton, briefly a member of the Musteite American Workers party, who had opened his opinion journal, *Modern Monthly,* to Trotskyists and other anti-Stalinists.[10] The Socialist party's recovery program was geared to helping capitalists recover from their crisis. In fact, doomed by its liberal-pacifist-clerical constituency, drawing from "young professionals on the make, shopkeepers, and the YWCA," the Socialist party was still hopeless. It had all the vices and none of the virtues of the European social democracy: Socialists exercised no influence in the trade unions; they maintained no respectable press of their own; no Socialist sat in Congress; they were "ridiculously weak—torn at this moment by internal dissensions."[11]

Elaborating further, an official statement on the fresh developments in the Socialist party proclaimed that the Militant group was

> Shot through with treachery, deception, reformism whose objective (and often enough subjective) aim is to preserve social democracy from the too-compromising Right wing and a too-embarrassing left wing . . . .

and continued,

> The greatest and most dangerous enemy in the revolutionary development of the Left wing workers in the American Socialist movement is the Militant group. Its victory at the Detroit convention and the formal adoption of its "declaration of principles" placed the American socialist party definitely in the camp of Centrism . . . . [It] aims to fulfill one function: to save social democracy from Communism.[12]

The statement, undated but evidently written in late 1934, was equally unflattering to the RPC: "shot through with Centrism, confusion, in-experience, cowardice, but expressing to a considerable degree the striving toward a Marxist position of the young and revolutionary ele-ments in the party and the YPSL." A final sentence instructed: "We must try to centralize all Marxist groups within the SP—some SPers are sympathetic to Trotskyism; very likely these elements can help build the Fourth International."[13]

Once that corner was turned, and the above undated statement likely came out on the eve of the Musteite-Trotskyist fusion, about November 1934, the way lay unobstructed to the controversial plenum held in June 1935 when the question of the Socialist party was debated night and day for three days.

Making the French Turn: The United States

When by December 1933 a "united front" with the Comintern which the Labor and Socialist (second) international proposed had failed to materialize, Norman Thomas seemed moderately receptive to a united front with people whom he construed to be Trotskyists: Weis-bord's Communist League of Struggle. (Thomas had known Weisbord since 1926 when he worked on Weisbord's Passaic strike committee.) On December 30, 1933, Thomas wrote Clarence Senior at the Socialist party's national office that "Trotskyists" had visited him "in earnest," anxious for a united front, suggesting a joint hunger march on Wash-ington, D.C., to be followed by a national general strike. Senior, re-sponding, called the scheme "poppycock" and nothing came of it, but Thomas had been impressed. Again, soon after the 1934 Detroit meeting, Thomas greeted warmly the idea of cooperation with Trotsky-ists. Paul Porter at that time proposed that a committee of militants invite the IWW, "the Lovestoneite and Trotskyist Communists," and the American Workers party to consider entering the Socialist party en masse to "help the Militants make a radical organization," conform-able to the ideal of an all-inclusive party. Although no such mass entries took place Gitlow, Zam, and others joined as individuals.[14] Al Gold-man did so in November 1934, coming from the Musteite American Workers party on the eve of its fusion with the League, and founded in

Chicago with YPSL leader Ernest Erber the *Socialist Appeal* to present a Trotskyist orientation.

Cannon and Shachtman, increasingly convinced that their small size, in 1935 about 2,000 members, was "a real problem the Workers Party had to face" and surely must correct, found the invitations issued by the Socialist party Militants especially attractive. Confronted by growing factional opposition in the Workers party but bolstered by Trotsky's personal appeal and the fact that entry into a mass party affiliate of the reformist second international now had sanction from the International Communist League and had become part of the movement's history, and content that as "official" policy entrism could not be excoriated in the party press, the Trotskyist leadership pushed on. What they saw as a continued leftward movement in the Socialist party served as added spur.[15] Initially they thought to orient the Militants toward the Workers party, believing the Old Guard would prevail and throw out the new left wing. The plenum resolutions of June and October 1935 never explicitly stated who would join whom. After the Socialist party rupture of the winter and spring of 1936 with the reverse result (the Militants threw out the Old Guard), and with Goldman's *Socialist Appeal* in Chicago urging that "realistic revolutionaries rejecting Stalinism"—especially those in the Workers party—"must come into the party," the die was cast.[16]

Cannon's promotional campaign had succeeded. Shortly after the fusion, with help from Trotsky in Norway, he waged a relentless campaign—branding dissidents "sick sectarians," expelling a faction here, winning over a faction there—and by mid-January 1936, he had the result of a national branch referendum: unanimous for entry. Cannon explained his method: "A party cannot be maneuvered; it must be educated—that is, if you have in mind the building of a revolutionary party . . . . If you believe in something, the thing to do is to begin propagandizing it right away . . . ."[17] Meantime, the Cannon-Shachtman faction prepared the way to enter the Socialist party "while it remained in a state of flux, before a new bureaucracy would have time to crystallize." At the subsequent political committee meeting a majority present signed the motion for entry, and the issue at last came out into the open. The resolution on the Socialist party read at the second Workers party conference stated that recent developments in the Socialist party were of first importance for the revolutionary movement in the

United States; the reformist Old Guard was "ossified and reactionary"; the otherwise promising left wing failed to produce a bolshevik program. From Chicago came the report that Cannon, emboldened by the vote for entry, began an address in March, "We are advancing with seven league boots . . . . We are going to take over the party."[18] Burnham attacked the Old Guard and praised the leftward direction of the Militants; then while the Socialist party members met in Cleveland in May, he and Shachtman printed a daily, dated report in the *New Militant*. They smugly noted the defeats handed to Louis Waldman, James Oneal, and the rest of the right wing, and applauded the triumphs of the Militants, who got majorities on committees, persuaded the convention to reject reformist planks and slogans, and secured another nomination for Militant ally Norman Thomas as presidential candidate.[19] Vistas seemed brighter than ever, well worth the year of preparation.

Cannon remembered of the negotiations, "It was a difficult and sticky job . . . a long, involved and tortuous process."[20] In his judgment Trotskyists gained from differences among Socialist party members who could not adhere to an established line and therefore bickered. Some Socialists disliked Stalinism and permitted Trotskyist entry in order to stave off Stalinist influence, but some feared communists might be right in seeing Trotskyists as counterrevolutionaries in disguise and "wreckers." Socialists in Reading, Pennsylvania, cautioned their comrades, reminding them of Trotsky's alleged destructive activities in Russia. Some Socialists feared that Trotskyists only entered to recruit and would create "a sect of starry-eyed believers" from which the others would split, making an even bigger rift.[21]

When negotiations bogged down, Sidney Hook met separately with Thomas, and the Militants at last agreed to admit the Workers party. Thomas pressed for this, "a mistake he was soon to rue," according to one biographer.[22] The terms hardly justified Cannon's boast that Trotskyists turned Socialist disagreements to their own advantage. Violating the party tradition but having learned from experience in that the *Socialist Call* had begun as a factional organ, the Socialists expected the *New Militant* and *New International* to cease publication. Moreover, the Socialist party refused to admit the Workers party as a body, but stipulated that each comrade had to apply individually. Cannon said this was contrived to make it appear that the new members enlisted humbly as pupils of the Militants, but Shachtman correctly saw it as a screen to hide from the public the news that "dreaded" Trotskyists had entered. Even though the Socialists were evasive and the terms irritating, Cannon and Shachtman, dead set on the appointed course, persisted. At last on June 6, 1936, the *New Militant's* last issue announced "Workers Party Calls All Revolutionary Workers to Join the Socialist Party," and explained that the national committee had dissolved the eighteen-month-old Workers party and was suspending *New Militant.* A youth group merger had been part of the entry design since its inception. The *New Militant* told the young comrades in the Spartacus League to join the Young People's Socialist League (YPSL).

Trotskyists did not at first feel the loss of their press except insofar as the termination marred their collective dignity. *Socialist Appeal,* already coming off the press in Chicago, was bolshevik and pro-Trotskyist. Editors Erber and Goldman had promoted entrism and after June 6 kept *Socialist Appeal's* pages open for matter that would have appeared in the *New Militant.* But Trotskyists did feel deeply their diminution in status. Some were veterans of years of radical leadership; now they were relegated, virtually, to rank-and-file membership. Cannon and Shachtman grumbled that they were never treated as equals. "Not one of the leaders of our party was offered so much as a post as branch organizer by these cheapskates—not one." They consoled themselves by remembering that their program was bound to win because, keeping factional identity and discipline as ordered by Trotsky, they could propagate bolshevik ideas from a solid front. Moreover, their faith in the future kept them going. "These world-conquering ideas were once again on the march." Dimly they foresaw that either Socialist party rightists would get rid of them or vice versa, but in either case, Trotskyists would emergy as a larger revolutionary group.[23] Such opportunities more than compensated for temporary slights and wounded feelings.

The Fragmentation Process

Certain questions have provoked the fragmentation of radical parties more persistently than others. Among them in the 1930s were the political nature of the Soviet state, the Spanish civil war, the alleged errors of other groups, and correct strategy and tactics for the American scene. Clearly the last of these loomed largest for the Workers party in 1935 and 1936. Noting a mounting impetus toward a French turn in the party, Musteites early began complaining. They had built their American Workers party on the principle of ignoring Communists and Socialists while creating a fresh native American movement, and desired to carry this over into the fusion organization. Muste had personally regretted the French League entry into the SFIO, and he opposed a Workers party entry into the Socialist party. But his was neither the first nor the loudest voice raised.

Hugo Oehler came into the Communist League of America in 1930 with a brilliant record as trade union organizer in both southern textile mills and Colorado mines, as Communist party organizer for the Kansas district, and, finally, as budding left oppositionist. At the Communist party's seventh convention in 1930 he had made several controversial demands, one of them that Trotskyists be readmitted into the party. He could hardly remain welcome any longer in that regime. Once in the League he shot into the limelight during the 1934 New York hotel strike. He next distinguished himself by casting the lone vote at the October 1934 plenum against the national committee "statement" endorsing French League entry into the SFIO. Defending his unpopular decision, he said he understood the intent of entrism was organic unity with the host party, that is, submerging factional identity and not functioning as a caucus. He knew an "organic unity" group that functioned within the ICL, he said, and he disapproved it as a tactic. In fact, French, Belgium, and British entrism were disasters because of excessive organic unity, virtual capitulation. At all costs, Trotskyist identity must be preserved, preferably as an autonomous bolshevik party.[24]

While the League was pondering fusion with the Musteites, Oehler began to associate with Tom Stamm, former Cleveland organizer.[25] In subsequent months Oehler and Stamm archly resisted each merger the Trotskyists effected. Opposing the fusion declaration of principles as "centrist," reminding the League that it had called Musteites "opportunists" since 1933, Oehler voted first against negotiating at all with Musteites, then withheld his vote at the prefusion conference of November 19, 1934. When merger was accomplished, the Oehlerite wing was still intact, first pressuring to bolshevize the Musteites, then attacking entrism in principle.

The Cannon group suggested expelling the Oehlerites for threatening to paralyze the party. Moreover, Cannon and Shachtman refused to allow Oehler and Stamm to present their views in the party press. Muste agreed with Oehler in opposing entrism, but felt more strongly that a comrade's right to full discussion must not be abridged; and Trotsky, not so intransigent as Cannon, though as eager to set aside obstructionists as was Cannon, concurred that expulsion should not take place until the whole party understood the substantive basis of difference.[26]

Over the plenum of June 1935 hung the pall of Zack's impending ouster and Oehler's disapproval of "French turns." From June until the October plenum Oehler and Stamm propagandized with leaflets for a hard Leninist line to save the fourth international from "irresponsible adventurism." National secretary A. J. Muste argued defiantly their right to propagandize because official organs refused to consider debatable the now historic policy of entrism.[27] Over the summer hostilities deepened and by October the party was forced to consider the problem. Belatedly party leaders accorded Oehler and Stamm "full discussion rights," probably because they had the support of Muste, seconded by Trotsky himself. But at the same time leaders cited them for breaking discipline, because denied *New Militant* or *Internal Bulletin* coverage they had in October printed independently two issues of *International News* to present their position.

Oehler and Stamm feared that the Marxist program would be diluted if organic unity took place and degenerate into armchair bolshevism and practical reformism. They were afraid that to liquidate factional identity would be to destroy their program or reason for being.[28] But the plenum rejected Oehler's motion condemning French League entry into the SFIO.[29]

Invectives flew. However, the plenum vote revealed that (in Cannon's colorful language) "The body of the party had been cured and was in good health." The vote should have alerted Oehler that the party would take action, and indeed the political committee on October 29 suspended him with Stamm and Louis Basky from committee and party, denied them further rights of membership, and forbade members to collaborate with the "splitters."[30]

Suspension, described as a "voluntary walkout" in the *New Militant,* took place before the promised free full discussion could be held. Cannon continued his metaphor: "The tip of the little finger remained infected and began to turn gangrenous, so we just chopped it off."[31] From Honefoss, Norway, as usual relying on Cannon's and Shachtman's appraisals, Trotsky scolded Oehler for refusing discipline, and for "slanders."[32] His reaction made it simpler to justify the suspension. Patently, the compass was set for the French turn.

Oehler soon set up the Revolutionary Workers League, a stronghold from which to batter Trotskyists and invite disgruntled Trotskyists to "break with Cannon and re-unite with us." Shachtman said they "hammered away at us for years and years afterward." Calling the Oehler splinter an ultraleftist impediment to serious revolutionary work, Stamm left it to found another Revolutionary Workers League, and according to Emanuel Geltman in 1972, "may still have a group." In 1941 the Oehlerites were yet intact, continuing to shed splinters and harping on revolutionary defeatism as the war crisis deepened in Europe.[33] Gitlow carped, "The louder these righteous groups called for unity the more they split." Even the tiny Weisbord group split "when one of its members sold the communal mimeograph machine." Noting that all the sects were born in dissidence, critic journalist Dwight Macdonald quipped, "The splinter groups looked on us Trotskyists as we looked on the Communists, as opportunists who had sacrificed principle for popularity." He continued, "Thus each sect is a group of vestal virgins jealously guarding a flame that may some day ignite the Revolution. Weisbord is sure *his* flame is the destined one. And so is Gitlow and so is Cannon and so is Lovestone and so is Browder." Shachtman found the spectacle of fragmentation depressing: "All of them marched resolutely into early oblivion, together with their program, their polemics, and their periodicals, which thereafter became the rarest of collector's items for specialized students of political anthropology."[34]

Some who left or were expelled simply abandoned the Marxist movement. Leaving his Marxist commitment when he left the party, Harry Roskolenko twitted the remaining faithful: "The grim garbage buckets of socialism, Russian style, had overflowed the theoretical kitchens, and the most sensitive thing any of us could do . . . was to shove all the soup, all the theories, and the whole kitchen down some incinerator—and walk away."[35]

A. J. Muste's Departure

With the Oehlerites gone, others began to denounce the French turn. Within the Workers party, Larry Cohen and others formed in January

1936 a "Marxist Action Group," propagandizing with broadsides to "keep the Workers Party pure and not drag it through the swamp" of a centrist or reformist party, a tactic "untenable for Marxists," "unwise, unnecessary, opportunistic, and adventuristic." The Cohen faction reluctantly went along with the decision, nevertheless. Cannon and Shachtman would not even brook hesitation on the French turn issue in the spring of 1936. When Bessie Shapiro applied for Workers party membership at this crucial time but failed to clarify her stand on entrism to Cannon's satisfaction, or to condemn Oehler roundly enough to please him, she was not admitted.[36]

The Trotskyists had pledged no French turn for the United States for three solid reasons. There was no big Socialist party here like the SFIO or the British Labour party. There was no "advanced revolutionary crisis." The Workers party carried a "clean banner" as a new section of the fourth international, and would not sully it by dragging it into class collaborationism. After fusion, they raised the question anyway and prepared for entry. Muste concluded that the "turn" in France had influenced their thinking, so in July 1935 he joined his voice to Oehler's charging "liquidationism." By August he still saw little redeeming virtue in the Thomas party, but thought that discussions with Socialist party Militants might be permissible if intended to persuade them to study the Workers party program; later, perhaps, fusion might take place—on Workers party terms. Muste was relenting. But he had already attacked "Cannon-Shachtman bureaucratism," a "politburo" meeting regularly in the Workers party. Moreover, he had defended first Zack's, then Oehler's, right to air their views. Both actions had muddied the water, and he and his faction supporters, Abern, McKinney, and J. R. "Jimmy" Johnson (party name for C. L. R. James) were labeled everything from sectarians and splitters for daring to resist "established" policy to cowards for not showing the courage Oehler and Stamm had shown in building a separate organization.[37]

In the political committee the defiant Muste refused to vote for entry. A quarrel erupted in the Musteite Workers group at Allentown, Pennsylvania, bringing the argument over the French turn to a head. The Allentown leaders, contrary to discipline, were appearing on speakers' platforms with Communists and had been officially suspended from the Workers party, but remained full members because the branch defied the suspension order.[38] In the heat of this disagreement, to

silence the debate (about which Cannon kept him informed) Trotsky
cabled to his leaders and to Muste, "Unanimous prompt entry seems
best way." Armed with this dictum, Cannon and Shachtman forced
the March plenum vote: two-thirds in favor of entry.[39]

The cable triggered Muste's disillusionment with bolshevism and
spurred his growing doubts. He confessed he knew at that time that
"Trotsky was quite as much a dictator as Stalin in the Communist
party."[40] Quixotically looking for universal peace and brotherhood, as
proletarian minister and labor leader Muste had tried to find ways to
solve the perennial problems of poverty and human exploitation ever
since he had left theological seminary. He turned to revolutionary politics only because he had despaired of change toward a more humane
world within a fundamentally conservative system. During his short
alliance with bolshevism, he turned his back on religion as Marxists are
supposed to do. "Religious institutions are the bulwark of the existing
order. We must break the hold on men of religious ideas and symbols,"
he had said. But in a Bolshevik organization he was astonished to find
that the party demanded full surrender every bit as much as the church.
In the movement, he later reflected, the party (instrument of historic
destiny) cannot err, just as among Christians the church (instrument of
God) is infallible. To either of these institutions an individual is called;
if he accepts he must give total obedience. "Discipline" in the Bolshevik
parties is, after all, drawn from "disciple." Muste found a parallel, too,
in the symbolism of color: the red of revolution is also the red in the
saving blood of the Lamb.[41]

Philosophically he found he disagreed with bolshevism as he earlier
disagreed with the church. A part of him "just never did accept Marxism-
Leninism" with its implications of violence, he admitted in the early
1950s. Already by June 1936 he had expressed disapproval of bolshevik tactics. He was dismayed at the ruthless manner in which Trotskyists schemed to cannibalize other parties and after entry into the Socialist party at the way in which they maneuvered behind closed doors.

Although continuing to doubt his own elected course of action and
the propriety of entry into the Socialist party, Muste yielded. In June
1936 he visited Trotsky, who sensed his wavering and tried to persuade
him to stay in the party saying, "Perhaps an American version of the
'French turn' was not the right tactic, but it *has* been done and you
should not let it drive you out of the party. You have too much to

give."[42] Following that visit, on Trotsky's orders he talked with Sneevliet, Trotskyist leader in Amsterdam, then did Trotsky's bidding and, together with Shachtman representing the American section, took part in an executive meeting of the nascent fourth international near Paris. But the Paris interlude presaged a dramatic change in Muste's life. He experienced reconversion while stopping in Notre Dame cathedral. Subsequently Muste withdrew from the Trotskyist movement. In a sixteen-page letter he informed the party of his return to religion, and allowed his membership to lapse. Generally he kept silent about Cannon's and Shachtman's "surreptitious activities" inside the Socialist party.[43]

B. J. Widick believed that somehow Muste was alienated during the visit with Trotsky. The details remain a mystery. The upshot was that once again he became a Christian pacifist. Five years later he wrote ". . . only the Christianity of Jesus—only religious pacifism—can build a movement which goes to the root of evil in man and in society, a movement which men will trust . . . ." Retaining certain elements of his earlier Marxism, he declared that Christianity was the one measure by which the capitalist system stood condemned; and amalgamating the Christian impulse with labor activism again, he assumed in August 1937 the directorship of the Labor Temple of the Presbytery of New York.[44]

Sidney Hook recalled that Muste's departure surprised him. "He became more fanatical than the Trotskyists, attacked Trotsky for the French turn, and then after a visit to Trotsky returned to God."[45] Shachtman after personally promoting fusion in the first place had become aware that Muste was never really "with" the Trotskyists, and noted, "Members of Muste's movement all went out to liberalism, to right-wingism, only E. R. McKinney staying with us as a Trotskyist."[46] "Muste was the last chance and the best chance," James P. Cannon lamented, "and even he, the best prospect of all, couldn't come through in the end because of that terrible background of the church, which had marred him in his formative years."[47] If Muste's assertion is correct, that pacifism was his most enduring and fundamental credo obscured only briefly during his flirtation with Marxist politics, then indeed an insurmountable incompatability prevented his ever being "with" the Trotskyists. Pacifism, in Burnham's words, was a "subtle and dangerous enemy" which socialists must oppose.[48]

The fusion of a party of intellectual labor leaders with a corps of disciplined Marxist theoreticians was bound to result in domination by the Marxists. The Trotskyists, Hook observed, asserted leadership right after fusion. In retrospect, Muste thought fusion failed. Cannon welcomed the memberships that Musteites contributed and proclaimed fusion to have achieved everything hoped for: it had broadened the party and strengthened it for the French turn ahead.

7

In the Socialist Party

Initial Accord

The initial prognoses for the union of Trotskyists and Socialists were optimistic. But constant and protracted contact caused differences to surface. First, in joining the Socialist party Trotskyists, paradoxically, also had enlisted in the Labor and Socialist (second) international. Yet they were already pledged to reject the first three and to rally "under the banner of the fourth international." The Socialists would in a few months come to realize that a party could not serve two "international" masters at once, one reformist, one Bolshevik. Second, right away Trotskyists circumvented the stricture against a faction press and freely expressed their views in the Chicago-based *Socialist Appeal* and in a West Coast paper. Third, they circumvented the command to dissolve their faction. Meeting in private caucus every two weeks, they developed positions for which to press on principal issues confronting radicals generally.[1] Although on some points their stand paralleled that of "native" Socialists, on others their attitudes were at variance. But all appeared to pull together at the outset. As Communist demands that Socialists expel the Trotskyists increased in tempo, Norman Thomas, Clarence Senior, and Devere Allen showed defiantly their support of the new comrades by cabling to Norway protesting Trotsky's impending

123

ouster from that country.[2] Socialists and Trotskyists with few exceptions agreed on war policy, how to regard pacifism, support of the CIO
rather than the AFL, trade union activism, rejection of the popular
front, defense of Russia as the first workers' state, and the election
goals and strategies of the 1936 campaign.

James Cannon went to Tijunga, California, to publish a "workingman's paper," *Labor Action,* aided by Glen Trimble who led the left
wing in the West, and by Charles Curtis, Paul Montauk, Bill Morgan,
and Sam Meyers. *Labor Action's* purpose was to attract western Socialists to the Trotskyists' point of view and it did so remarkably successfully. Cannon reported regularly on progress in this business to Al
Goldman in Chicago and to James Burnham and Max Shachtman in
New York. Cannon, Burnham, Shachtman, Goldman, and perhaps
Joe Carter, the Trotskyists' leading intellectuals, were more than a
match for the Socialist party's New York intelligentsia; and *Socialist
Appeal* in the first year came to exert much influence "far beyond the
confines of the Trotskyites," complained one of the Militants.[3]

After the Old Guard left the Socialist party to found the Social
Democratic Federation and the Workers party entered the Socialist
party, new cleavages appeared among the Militants. The newcomers
forced polarization on the degree to which the party must assume a
bolshevik orientation. Hard-line Communist jargon filled the press,
provoking the Communist party and the ousted right wing to label the
Socialist party as "Thomas-Trotskyist" and antagonizing some of the
Militants. The Militants and left-wing YPSLs had formed a short-lived
Revolutionary Socialist Education Society with the Trotskyist "immigrants." Leading Militants like Robert Delson, Murry Gross, and Sam
Baron sundered it by the fall of 1936, at which time the Trotskyists
with the left YPSLs had become the "Appeal caucus."

Jack Altman, secretary of the New York local and a "good faction
fighter," and Paul Porter, Socialist intellectual from Kenosha, Wisconsin,
emerged as spokesmen for a new right wing comprising about fifty,
"Altmanites" who wanted a mass labor party and were dead set against
bolshevization. Aiming their fire at the Appeal group, the Altmanites
presented a facade of such solidarity that the budding left wing was reluctant to align with the Appeal caucus programmatically. The Altmanites accused the Appeal group and former Militants who were not
standing behind Altman of rabid anti-Stalinism, reviving an old third

period epithet, "social-fascists." They attacked the Appeal faction as "sectarian" for resisting any possible fresh farmer-labor party and for scorning the AFL bureaucracy.[4]

Left of this faction stood the remainder of the Militants, some Revolutionary Policy Committee members, and assorted leftists, about a hundred comrades in all. This contingent took the name "Clarity caucus." Its members used Bolshevik rhetoric proficiently and often, first in the *Socialist Call,* the official party paper edited by Gus Tyler, then, after the Altmanites seized control of the *Call* in late 1937, in the *American Socialist Monthly.* Herbert Zam, former Lovestoneite, and Tyler led the Clarity caucus; Norman Thomas sometimes identified with it too, although on the whole he stood above the clamor. On most questions the Clarityites agreed with the Trotskyist Appeal group, but they could not bring themselves to render the fealty and unquestioning obedience to Trotsky to which the Appeal caucus was committed (and which in effect was its adhesive). Moreover, at meetings Clarityites invariably modified their language to get resolutions passed and to avoid incurring the enmity of the Altman right wing. For example, they had on principle opposed a farmer-labor party as class collaborationist, yet when Jack Altman proposed one, they compliantly seconded him. On one question Clarityites sounded more revolutionary than the Appeal group: at every faction conference and convention they demanded a statement on the road to power.[5]

With good reason Zam courted Altman's favor. It fell to the lot of Clarity to hold the party together. Some Clarityites, Zam for instance, had come into the Socialist party from the Lovestoneite splinter and did not relish seeing their adoptive party degenerate into a puny sect. Appeal Trotskyists called over and over for unity of left-wing forces under Trotskyist direction. Clarity preferred unity with the original Socialist Militants.[6]

In spite of disagreements, all three factions worked together in the 1936 elections. The Trotskyists knew electoral activity permitted the party to reach many people and so increase membership, to apprize workers of the program through speeches and political literature which the public receives more willingly during election campaigns, and to demonstrate to the public through strikes, antiwar rallies, and the like the link "between their employer and the state." Even Harry W. Laidler, a reformist Socialist and New York state chairman in 1936, cer-

tainly advanced a similar rationale for running candidates and campaigning. And Gus Tyler admonished, "Press a class point of view; propose
militant action" during the campaign, sounding exactly like the Trotskyists.[7]

Norman Thomas as presidential candidate had to contend with a
groundswell for President Roosevelt's reelection. In 1936 the Communist party's fresh slogan "Communism Is Twentieth Century Americanism" directed its popular front fire at Alf M. Landon, the Republican candidate, at Father Charles Coughlin's Union party, and at the
Socialists. Although Earl Browder ran for the presidency, the Communist party obliquely urged Americans to vote for Roosevelt, not
Browder. The United States might have to take up arms against fascist
powers encircling the Soviet Union. Labor's Nonpartisan League, too,
backed reelection. Stopping short of actual endorsement but adding
his voice to the chorus, John L. Lewis, president of the United Mine
Workers and chairman of the CIO, advised workingmen to vote for
Roosevelt, "this great humanitarian," sponsor of remarkable social and
labor legislation. Lewis observed that big business used every resource,
capital, propaganda, and front groups (such as the Liberty League, the
National Association of Manufacturers, the U.S. Chamber of Commerce)
to defeat the incumbent.[8] To compete with this powerful surge for reelection, Thomas pointed to Roosevelt's essential conservatism and to
the oncoming conflict portended by billion-dollar-a-year military and
naval establishments that would bring fascism, introduced not by Liberty
League fanatics but by Roosevelt himself.[9]

His overtures bore little fruit. For example, in New York although
Socialists drew more votes than the Communists, Thomas had only
86,000 cast for him while Roosevelt and his running mate, John Nance
Garner, with support from the Social Democratic Federation and New
York's American Labor Party, drew 238,000. In the small city of
Reading, Pennsylvania, long a Socialist bailiwick, Thomas got a mere
4.7 percent of the vote, the lowest total for the Socialist party since
1908. California Socialists campaigned hard, reported Cannon, but
had lost ground to the End Poverty in California (EPIC) party which
backed Roosevelt nationally.[10] The national 1936 tally, showing that
Thomas attracted 187,720 votes, may have reflected in part that for the
first time since 1929 the Socialist party experienced a sharp net loss in
memberships; but it principally reflected Roosevelt's massive appeal.

The national tally showed him carrying all states but two, with nearly 28,000,000 votes. Garnering the support of radicals and labor people who saw in him "a chance to get half-a-loaf instead of pie-in-the-sky," Roosevelt simply added them to the liberal and farmer vote and the traditional backing of powerful members of the financial-industrial community and the South.[11]

The Socialist party never again polled even as many as it had in 1936. With the stated aim of electoral activity chiefly educative, however, the vote hardly represented failure and it did guarantee a forum, but, importantly, it provided the last real opportunity the several intraparty factions would have to suppress their differences and unite in a common cause. In the next year's New York mayoralty contest they were poles apart.

Deepening Enmity

In the wake of the election, rival radical parties and factions looked ahead to a special Socialist convention "to be held secretly in Chicago the last week of March 1937," its goal, taking the first steps to reorganize the party and "to recruit a new mass base." Such secrecy was unprecedented. Clearly the national executive committee had seen the dismal returns as failure. Once again, Appeal and Clarity caucuses appeared to converge positionally, both publishing in their factional organs blueprints for restructuring the party, both promoting "tightening up the apparatus" through centralization and discipline. Trotskyists urged turning to a real Marxist program. Clarity spokesmen agreed that Socialists must adopt a party line on issues by taking clear stands, promoting them, expecting members to assimilate them down to the tiniest local, and appointing comrades able both to organize and to impose discipline effectively.[12]

Meantime, Communists pelted the Socialist party membership with pamphlets and letters-to-the-editor begging them to expel the "Trotsky-ite wreckers" who were in truth fascist agents serving the German Gestapo and had reduced the Socialist party to "a maze of warring cliques." Norman Thomas in late 1936 himself questioned the wisdom of admitting Trotskyists into the party. To Altman in December he confessed "the things which disgust us have been enormously intensified since the admission of these comrades . . . . I for one . . . want a party, not a sect." In a postscript he added, "It is a problem of an attitude, a frame of mind, a manner of speech, a way of conducting meetings, a failure to understand what things are essential and vital and what are of secondary importance." A month later he wrote Clarence Senior, "I must confess that increasing experience with the Trotskyists, or most of them in America, makes me realize how sectarian they are." The Altmanites, not conceding any Appeal connection with the Gestapo, began to find reason in the argument that they should be expelled for disruptive tactics. In time Altmanites agitated fervently for expulsion, even setting up a "committee of correspondence" to press this measure. At yet another level, Trotskyists hotly defended their actions. They were charged with taking up valuable time and stirring up hostilities in branch meetings by raising national and international issues to argue for the Trotskyist line, by proposing resolutions and trying to put them to a vote.[13] In retaliation, Trotskyists leveled their own charges. They chided the Clarity caucus for standing so resolutely in the center, thereby aiding Altman, who in their judgment was "playing into the hands of the Stalinist campaign to destroy the party."[14]

Trotskyists under mounting attack inside the party believed it necessary to bring the comrades to a sharp bolshevik turn now, or it could never be done. Since November 1936 they had tried to negotiate with Zam for a united Socialist party left wing, a fusion of Appeal, Clarity, and uncommitted co-believers, recommending a conference to devise convention strategy. In December 1936 Zam and Tyler rejected the plan; Frank Trager proposed instead an invitational "left-wing leadership conference," which Goldman rejected. As a consequence, the "Appeal Association of Chicago," an ad hoc group led by Goldman and Al Glotzer, called an Appeal institute for that city to be held February 20-22.[15]

The Appeal institute in Chicago attracted ninety-three delegates, seventy-eight of whom came from outside the city, and represented twelve states. Even though Clarity sent Zam and Trager, the institute was plainly a Trotskyist meeting, its roll of participants reminiscent of the early days of the Workers party: Glotzer gave the greeting; Abern chaired the credentials committee; Goldman, Burnham, Vincent Ray Dunne, and B. J. Widick served on the resolutions committee; Shachtman delivered the opening address; Burnham and Goldman engaged Zam and

Trager in debate on the Trotskyist platform. Obviously planning to
meet regularly, the delegates formed a national committee to serve as
an ongoing caucus to "coordinate branch work" and "formulate Appeal
policies," with Dunne, Goldman, Shachtman, Richard Babb Whitten,
and Francis Heisler (an NPLD attorney in Chicago) as committee members. Statements on unity and on the desirability of democratic "freedom of discussion" were approved, the latter consistently demanded by
Trotskyists when a minority faction in an umbrella group but reluctantly (if ever) accorded dissidents in a Trotskyist party.[16]

Zam and Trager attacked the Appeal platform for omitting a statement on the road to power and for opposing "working class parties."
To include a dissertation on the road to power in this inner-party left-
wing platform, argued Goldman, "would have been the height of scholas-
ticism." As for a labor party, working-class parties by no means assured
virtue and breadth; the Communist party was a working-class party,
Burnham reminded the Clarityites. Burnham attacked the labor and
Socialist (second) international, an issue inevitably surfacing at this
juncture, and wanted the Socialist party to break with it and affiliate
with the fourth international. On the Appeal platform, seventy-six
voted in favor, two abstained.[17]

Then the conference adopted three resolutions, and Goldman pontifi-
cated, "Every basic principle enunciated in the resolutions is considered
essential by the appeal group as a basis for any left wing." A person
could join the Appeal caucus and try to change them, but until such
change was effected, he must be bound by them. One resolution was
the labor party statement, not unequivocally opposing a labor party
as previous Appeal utterances had done, and as Zam and Trager had
charged, but giving limited approval to support for one "in local situa-
tions." The second was an expected declaration in favor of the CIO:
"the direction of advance for the labor movement."[18] The third concerned the civil war in Spain, a question looming larger and larger in
intraparty debate and one which with two other important issues would
at last provoke formal division.

The Militant right wing led by Altman favored the Spanish Loyalists
of the Popular Front government in their struggle against General Francisco Franco. At that time Largo Caballero headed the republican
government representing resistance to European fascism generally, for
Franco drew direct aid from Germany and Italy. Norman Thomas spoke

publicly and engaged in fund-raising drives to send a "Debs Column" to Spain to help sustain Caballero.[19] For two reasons Trotskyists shied away from enlisting in the Loyalist cause. First, the Communist party similarly blessed and aided the Caballero government, dispatching to the Loyalists its "Abraham Lincoln Brigade," whose soldiers, Trotskyists charged, battled Trotskyists in the midst of the civil war. Second, a key principle in Trotsky's theoretical structure was resistance to popular front governments. Accordingly, the Appeal caucus took a more radical view and cheered the tiny Workers' party of Marxist Unification (POUM), the Iberian Anarchist Federation (FAI), and the anarcho-syndicalists in the National Confederation of Labor (CNT), whose combined peoples' militia in Catalonia won localized victories in 1936 and 1937 and immediately began to experiment with collective farming, and to set up councils to run industrial and communications facilities.[20]

Communists branded these anti-Stalinist left groups "Trotskyite" agents of Franco and Hitler and their efforts to seize power and to impose collectivization "infantile ultra-leftism." Captivated by the popular front idea of unity American liberals tended to second the Communist party, and when the Altmanites did also, the Clarity caucus in the interest of unity over this, "the hottest issue before the party at that time" as Shachtman remembered it, refused to endorse the Appeal institute's resolution on Spain in support of the POUM.[21]

Increasingly relations between Militants and Trotskyists, who had no desire at this time to leave the Socialist party, grew strained and hostile. In his position as party leader, Norman Thomas was beleaguered by all to break the impasse. As promoter of an "all-inclusive party," he did not wish a split. "His whole political and personal and moral make-up is alien to the idea of splits or of expulsions," Shachtman observed, but he could see the party tearing end to end. "We could . . . content ourselves by simply asking for the same right that everybody else had . . . the right to put forward our point of view."[22] Moreover, the Trotskyists were recruiting successfully for the Socialist party as a whole. Clarity too opposed expulsions. At the Appeal institute, Frank Trager actually favored a bloc with the Appeal group, an institute aim, but as Zam rejected it, Clarity continued in the center.[23] During the remaining month before the Socialist convention Clarity was in the enviable position of having both sides bargain for its favors, as Trotskyists accused the right wing of pro-Stalinism and popular frontism, and as the right wing demanded expulsion of the Trotskyists for narrow sectarian behavior.

To try to stave off a showdown, Vincent Ray Dunne and James Cannon arrived in New York to confer with Thomas, Tyler, Altman, and Murry Baron. Debates on Spain and the Moscow trials ringing into the wee hours at branch meetings had been charged against *Appeal.* Cannon and Dunne would use their influence to restrain this annoying practice. In return, Thomas vouchsafed no restrictions on the *Socialist Appeal,* pledging for the upcoming convention no resolves to halt factional organs.[24]

At the March convention in Chicago the Trotskyist Appeal group showed considerable strength and exerted influence virtually as a party within a party. Still, no Appeal faction member present had the status of delegate (although Vincent Ray Dunne and Al Goldman served on committees), and Cannon reported that their purpose in being there was to delay the issue of a split. Certain Socialist party leaders came to check what they feared was a drive to seize the party. Thomas, conceiving the party to be primarily political and educative rather than revolutionary, disagreed with the Trotskyists that it "had to have a correct theory for the past, present, and future."[25] Presenting his convention plan, Laidler wrote that the party must remain adapted to the American scene, not abroad, and must not "let an aggressive, articulate, thoroughly disciplined group" capture the convention.[26]

In a prepared statement, Jack Altman sought to win Clarity support and to shear them finally away from the Trotskyists:

> The acid test today is the question of cooperation with the power caucus within the party formed by members of the former Workers Party. We consider this group to base itself upon reactionary sectarianism and feel its ideology and general perspective to be injurious to the best welfare of the party . . . it has stamped itself within the party as a Communist opposition rather than as a Socialist group . . . . We have no intention of helping the party to become an anti-Communist anti-Soviet League. Therefore we have declared that a condition of unity [with the Zam-Tyler group] must be a refusal to make political deals with this power caucus . . . . [for] left-wing unity by our United Group without the Trotskyites.[27]

Reports described a businesslike conference "unmarred by political hysterics" but glowing with accord on the slate of resolutions. Two issues produced minor friction. The question of support for a possible labor party arose again. Thomas's favorable resolution was approved, but only after a verbal duel between the Wisconsin delegation, which wanted an endorsement of the (Wisconsin) Farmer-Labor Progressive Federation, and California delegate Glen Trimble, who said endorsement would violate party purity. Then Dan Hoan of Wisconsin resigned from the executive committee rather than endorse the CIO, a resolution which nevertheless passed. Curiously, despite the fact that the notion of ousting the Trotskyists was being widely discussed because of Altman's and Paul Porter's campaign to expel them, not one voice put the question before the assembly. But to appease the anti-Trotskyists, Norman Thomas violated his pre-convention pledge and proposed by resolution to abolish all factional organs, a move unprecedented in party history. Even some "native" Socialists cried out against this but the resolution passed.[28]

Another followed, the "Resolution on No More Resolutions," called the "gag law," reputedly the work of Gus Tyler of the *Call.* Stipulating that no resolutions on disputed questions would be permitted henceforth at branch meetings, the gag law severely hampered the Trotskyists in their drive for party acceptance of clear stands on problems such as Spain and the Moscow trials.[29]

Its wings temporarily clipped, Appeal met afterward in caucus in New York where it adopted enthusiastically Cannon's slogan, "Deeper into the Socialist Party."[30] Soon "caucus letters" went out regularly but confidentially to a select list supplying "information and guidance" and replacing the banned *Socialist Appeal.* Dedicated as always to the enlargement of their little band, Trotskyists had grown adept at committed and continued faction fighting. On his arrival in California right after the entry into the Socialist party, Cannon allegedly had asked an astounded Travers Clement, "How long do you think it will take us to take over the Socialist party?"[31] With this goal in mind, the Appeal caucus could hardly allow the official suppression of their organ to deter or distract them.

The Trotsky Defense Committee

Three factors brought eventual expulsion of the Trotskyists from the
Socialist party. The first was divergence between official Socialist and
Trotskyist positions on issues, the second was the determination of the
Altman Militants to oust this faction which they rightly perceived to be
unassimilable, and the third was Trotsky's own decision to orient toward
break with the party.

Two of the controverted questions were global in scope and at the
convention of March 27 received scant attention and weak resolutions.
As noted, one concerned factional support in the Spanish civil conflict.
The other was the validity of the Moscow trials. By the spring of 1937
two of the show trials had already been staged. Leon Trotsky's allies
and, paradoxically, some of his enemies, were tried and convicted in
absentia in the Kremlin Military Collegium on charges of working for
the espionage services of England, Germany, France, and Japan; of
collusion with the Gestapo and Japanese agents to cede slices of Soviet
territory to Germany and Japan; and of plotting with them to assassinate
Stalin and other high Soviet officials. There were four trials from August 1936 to March 1938, and although scores of old Bolsheviks and Red
Army generals were convicted, Trotsky was principal defendant in
these proceedings.

The prosecutor, Andrei Yanuaryvich Vyshinsky, accused Trotskyists
of plotting to restore capitalism and to sabotage railroad operations and
construction in Russia, and of international conspiracies. From exile in
Norway Trotsky issued emotion-laden denials and invective-filled
counter accusations. He hoped Soviet authorities would try to have him
extradited. The extradition process would necessitate a hearing before a
Norwegian tribunal where Soviet accusations could be aired and the defense position stated for the international press. Instead, for three
months and twenty days, August 28 to December 8, 1936, Trotsky
claimed he was kept under house arrest at Sundby, Norway so he could
not declaim publicly against the head of the Soviet state with whom the
Norwegian government wanted peaceful relations. On orders issued by
the Norwegian Labor party's minister of justice, Trygvie Lie, he was
then deported.[32] Nation after nation refused Leon and Natalya Trotsky
asylum. Catalonian Loyalist forces were threatened with an end to
Soviet military aid if they admitted the Trotskys. At last under en-

treaty by prominent liberals and intellectuals in the United States such as James T. Farrell (who organized the "Committee to Obtain Right of Asylum for Trotsky"), Norman Thomas, Edmund Wilson, Bertram D. Wolfe, Joseph Wood Krutch, John Chamberlain, and Louis Hacker, and Diego Rivera in Mexico, the president of Mexico admitted them. The committee's first public meeting in New York drew a crowd of 3,500 and collected $1,000. A succession of notable personalities exhorted the audience in Trotsky's behalf, including some who disagreed with each other on almost all political questions except Trotsky's international plight. As Norman Thomas said, the issues surrounding Trotsky's situation were "clear and unambiguous." Bertram D. Wolfe, no longer a Lovestoneite, warned at the meeting, "The Russian purge and the methods it employs concern the very life of the labor movement. . . . Anyone who fails to raise his voice unequivocally on this question makes himself a guilty accomplice by his silence."[33]

Shachtman and the young secretary of the NPLD, George Novack, welcomed the Trotskys on their arrival at Tampico in January 1937, and traveled with them by special train to Mexico City where they remained as Diego Rivera's and Frida Kahlo's house guests in Avenida Londres for several months. Trotsky then purchased a secluded, fortress-like, and picturesque residence in Coyoacan.[34]

All the while under these severe pressures, Trotsky persistently demanded an impartial investigation commission to reveal to the world his innocence. The committee that found him asylum now became the Trotsky Defense Committee, its duty to uncover further information and send a subcommission down to Coyoacan to give him his day in court. The committee's work to publicize Trotsky's cause attracted the sympathies of some unaffiliated radical intellectuals. One was Dwight Macdonald, who had just left an editorial post on *Fortune* when he wrote a letter taking Trotsky's side; he was asked to join the committee and accepted. The defense committee was called the Dewey Commission of Inquiry because of John Dewey's leading role on it. Sidney Hook prevailed upon Dewey, his mentor at Columbia University (against Dewey's family's objections), to serve as chairman lending the committee considerable prestige.[35] Others beside Dewey appointed to go to Coyoacan as subcommission were Otto Ruehle, biographer of Karl Marx, who with Karl Liebknecht in the Reichstag had voted against war credits in 1914; Benjamin Stolberg, labor historian; Suzanne

LaFollette, journalist and editor; Carleton Beals, Latin American affairs specialist (who resigned); Mauritz Hallgren, journalist (who also resigned); and Alfred Rosmer, former member of the executive committee of the Comintern. George Novack accompanied the group as secretary. John Finerty, veteran of the Mooney-Billings and Sacco-Vanzetti trials, was legal counsel for the Trotsky Defense Committee, and Al Goldman of *Socialist Appeal* and the NPLD was Trotsky's personal attorney. Having endorsed the Farrell Committee seeking asylum for Trotsky and having pledged cooperation with "any responsible commission of inquiry which may be established to investigate the facts regarding the charges made against Trotsky and his answer thereto," the national executive committee of the Socialist party planned the March emergency convention even as these appointments were being made.[36]

The Moscow trials became one more divisive issue. It is not insignificant to question a major government's conduct of a judicial affair of world interest. The Trotskyists condemned the proceedings and at first the Clarity caucus echoed them. The Altman group, by now drawing closer to the Communist party, disapproved of the implied attack on the Soviet judicial system and were joined by much of the liberal intellectual community, at least until the third trial in June 1937.[37] The make-up of the defense committee and the moral support it attracted, however, proved that sizable numbers doubted the propriety and legitimacy of the Soviet processes. Cannon later reflected that the Trotskyists were fortunate at that time in being part of the Socialist party with its myriad connections in academia and journalism to rally behind a hearing for Trotsky: "We conducted a terrific campaign to expose the trials and defend Trotsky." Shachtman observed, "Our campaign against the Moscow Trials was the most successful in the entire world—far more than that achieved by any of the other Trotskyist groups." On the validity of these trials, the radical intellectual world split wide open, and "we got our first big collection of sympathizers."[38]

The sudden broad attraction of Trotsky's cause stemmed first from the appeal of Russian communism in the face of depression in the capitalist world. Intellectuals exulted that planned production replaced the anarchy of the marketplace. Fascism in Europe appeared as a double menace with its suppression both of democratic exchange and of the labor movement, and its big militarization programs. The Communist party popular front policy, embraced in 1935, was viewed as part of the fight for democracy and peace, the highest form of democracy being the Soviet system itself. It attracted all varieties of intellectuals to rush to the Communist banner, to join, or simply to cheer on the sidelines, for they contrasted the economic agony of the United States with a rosy vision of a bolshevik paradise. But the purges of the old Bolsheviks (Trotsky alone was out of reach) brought disenchantment, then disgust, and finally departures. Trotsky emerged as a tragic, maligned figure. He tried to read his statement charging a frame-up, *I Stake My Life,* over the telephone from Mexico City to be broadcast in New York, but when the telephone wires were snipped, allegedly by Stalinists, Novack read it at midnight on February 9, 1937.[39]

The story had another side. Many radical intellectuals believed the Moscow defendants guilty. They may have been troubled by the star chamber procedures but they nonetheless believed the defendants had conspired against the Soviet Union. This group of Americans tried to discredit the commission of inquiry, even stooping to personal attacks on John Dewey's integrity and competence. Hallgren, resigning from his post, grumbled that "the present liberal movement" to win justice for Trotsky "is nothing more than a Trotskyite maneuver against the Soviet Union."[40] Dewey was called "senile," a "red baiter," a "Trotsky-ite." Those who defended Trotsky or sought a fair hearing were branded "Hitlero-Trotskyites." Dewey was, of course, not a Trotskyist at all, holding serious disagreements with Trotsky on philosophical grounds.[41]

Writers in *New Republic* saw no reason to question Soviet justice, or to doubt that Trotsky had been guilty of plotting against Stalin. Freda Kirchwey's *Nation* similarly kept its faith in Russian judicial fairness, viewing the trials as part of the forward march of democracy in Russia. Walter Duranty, Moscow correspondent for the *New York Times,* pronounced the trials completely aboveboard. Like Philip Rahv and William Phillips in *Partisan Review,* Calverton in *Modern Monthly* after the first show trial expressed sympathy for the old revolutionist in exile, noting that the trials represented Stalin's effort to destroy Trotsky's influence; but a symposium on the question of his guilt printed in the journal five months later evidenced much wavering—three votes of "guilty," six of "frame-up," and three of bafflement.[42]

On September 21, 1937, the subcommission found Trotsky and his son, Leon Sedov (also charged although deceased) "not guilty." It concluded that the conspiratorial letters allegedly written by Trotsky never existed, reports of them having been lies; Trotsky, a consistent opponent of terrorism, never instructed any assassinations nor did he order "sabotage, wrecking, and diversion," but only the advancement of Soviet industry and agriculture; he never conspired with fascists or any foreign powers against Russia; and he did not foster the restoration of capitalism in Russia. Indeed, the "prosecutor fantastically falsified Trotsky's role, before, during, and after the October revolution." Because the logical structure of the first three trials rested on eight defendants who alleged they had been intermediaries between the "Trotskyite-Terrorist Center" and others, yet because all proof brought forward appeared to show that communications between themselves and Trotsky were impossible, "not guilty" was the only realistic verdict.[43] Sidney Hook said in a New York radio talk on March 22, 1938, that the story of the whole affair made the *Arabian Nights* seem as dull as a grocer's bill.[44] Quite expectedly, the Communist party and others found the "proofs" unconvincing, particularly since Trotsky's own writings abound in calls to world revolution, illegal activity, and a new regime for the Soviet Union. But for many, the old man had been exculpated.[45]

Expulsion from the Socialist Party

Countering Cannon's admonition to go "deeper into the Socialist Party," Trotsky himself sent word to the Appeal caucus to break with the right wing and the centrists. Patently the Trotskyists had failed to win the left-wing Socialists in Clarity to their position, Clarity choosing to keep the old "native" Socialists together with them even at the expense of concessions. Trotsky recommended that Appeal focus on the disagreement on the Spanish question to provoke quick expulsion, Cannon of course concurring; but Burnham and Shachtman decided it would be wiser to prolong the matter, and that the superior tactic was to seize on a local American issue, germane to this country, rather than Spain or the Moscow trials. The forthcoming mayoralty election in New York City could propel the split orientation toward climax.[46]

The Social Democratic Federation, the Communist party, and the American Labor party endorsed Republican candidate Fiorello LaGuardia for the November 1937 mayoralty contest. It was an unusual endorsement, but LaGuardia was an unusual candidate. Professing many politi-

cal beliefs cherished also by Socialists, in Howard Zinn's words a "pragmatic radical," LaGuardia remained a favorite of the Progressives too
and successfully transcended party lines. But for all that, to Trotskyists
he was a "bourgeois candidate," and the mounting prospect of Socialist
party endorsement was anathema. They harped on this theme and the
Altmanites found the development most welcome—left wing and right
wing were seeing eye-to-eye on a possible split.

In support of LaGuardia, Socialists warned that if the masses (who
seemed to embrace LaGuardia warmly) were ignored, it would alienate
the Socialist party from them. Additionally, Socialists should uphold a
labor party, in this instance the American Labor party which had thrown
its weight behind LaGuardia, to help break the masses' ties with capitalist parties. Finally, Socialists reminded themselves of the small vote
Thomas had attracted in 1936.[47] The Clarity caucus, at first proclaiming that backing LaGuardia constituted a betrayal of socialism, gradually
relented under national executive committee prodding. All the while
Trotskyists issued reminders of LaGuardia's links with J. P. Morgan
and the New York Police Department, sure badges of basic capitalist priorities.[48]

Simultaneously, the Altmanites were succeeding in winning over
Clarity leaders who now echoed the epithets flung at Appeal by the
right wing: ". . . no sane working class party could possibly make the
trials its most important activity"; ". . . they believe a revolutionary
party can't exist without one current, a Trotskyite current"; they have
faith in nothing "except their pure selves." As different branches around
the nation through the spring of 1937 agitated to throw out the Trotskyists, Thomas, returning from Spain, began also to see the matter
from the Altmanites' point of view. He had reached the entirely justified conclusion that Trotskyists had enrolled in the Socialist party not
to help build a stronger, more united party, but to capture it for Leon
Trotsky. On June 19 the national executive committee met in New
York facing demands from all quarters to eject the sectarians.[49]

Meantime, the Socialist party's backing of LaGuardia became increasingly certain. Trotskyists on orders from Coyoacan to provoke their
own expulsion stepped up their charges of "capitulation" and "class
collaborationism," challenged official Socialist support of the Spanish
Loyalists, remonstrated against Stalin and Moscow for the trials, and
urgently pressed for Trotsky's vindication by the Dewey Commission of

Inquiry. On June 24 and 25 the national action committee of the Appeal caucus held an emergency meeting, vowing by near unanimous vote tighter local organization of the "left unity opposition to LaGuardia," and to reestablish *Socialist Appeal*.[50] The campaign produced the expected result in two months. A rump meeting of the central committee of Local New York led by Jack Altman on August 9 started the ball rolling, expelling by a vote of forty-eight to two (with eighteen abstentions) fifty-two New York Trotskyists, and ordering seventy more brought before a "grievance committee" to hear charges.[51] Of the hearing, Shachtman remembered, "We were in effect given a mock trial, and we were unceremoniously kicked out of the party," finding balm in the knowledge that they had deliberately courted their own ouster at the behest of Trotsky in Mexico and predicting that the purge would bring many "sympathy departures."[52]

Altman stated the charges in the *Call* on August 21. First, the Trotskyists had tried to undermine the Socialist party. Second, they wrongfully rendered their prime allegiance to the fourth international. Third, they refused to heed the discipline of the Socialist party national convention, the national executive committee, and the central committee of Local New York.[53] Except for the initial charge which was imprecise and therefore meant little, the accusations were true enough. But an all-inclusive party, if not a contradiction in terms, should be prepared to harbor and accommodate all manner of ideas and behavior. Actually, the French turn experience revealed that an all-inclusive party was a pipedream. A broadly based, left-wing consensus party still cannot digest uncompromising agitational groups.

Shortly afterward, the national executive committee suspended the California Socialist party's charter on the advice of the state central committee where Lillian Symes and Travers Clement, centrists, had strong influence and where Glen Trimble, at first a left Socialist, had now swung over to the majority.[54] Cannon, editing *Labor Action* in Tijunga, had focused on these branches for about nine months; consequently the Californians had immediate experience with Trotskyist pressure tactics. On August 20 the national executive committee expelled the left YPSLs. In response, Trotskyists called a second emergency meeting for August 28, this time of the expelled New York branches, which by then were said to number "over twenty." Resolutions charged illegality in the expulsions and renamed the group "Local

New York Socialist Party (Left-Wing Branches)" reminiscent of the defiant label assumed by the expelled Trotskyists in the winter of 1928.[55] Some branches protested the ouster. Shachtman said, "We raised a hue and cry" but were not unhappy.[56] After all, that all-important organ had already resumed publication: *Socialist Appeal* reappeared on August 14. When over the Labor Day weekend the party's national executive committee met and formally and unanimously approved the Altman-Thomas motion ordering "the mass expulsion of every revolutionist from the party," the news generated no alarm whatever in Trotskyist quarters, despite a bit of blustering.[57]

The French turn was a violent emetic. Entering with about 1,000, the Trotskyists made their exit with 1,000 added to their number. In Harry Roskolenko's pithy terms,

> In less than a year with the Spanish Civil War still raging, we destroyed the Socialist Party's courteous liberalism and its old-maid political practices, then we charged, bull-like, out of their now-dismembered china shop . . . . Our gain was almost one thousand gullible young socialists . . . .[58]

Daniel Bell called it cannibalism. Roskolenko called it colonization. Shachtman recollected that in one country after another, Trotskyists raided a Socialist organization, plucked out people, and started over again. In fact, 66 percent of the 1934 membership left the party, principally due to the appeal of Roosevelt "establishment" politics and trade unionism, but the Trotskyist raiding added the crowning blow.[59] Figures show 11,922 members in 1936 and only 6,488 at the end of 1937. Muste hinted later in an interview that the whole American left deteriorated on account of this episode, but his evaluation, shared by James Oneal and so many others of the Old Guard, is too dire. Communist party spokesmen carped that for one-and-a-half years, Socialists were prisoners of "Trotskyite" fascists, wreckers, pariahs.[60] Manny Geltman rued the wasted hours of internal struggle that should have gone into the labor movement: "While the big movement was going on to organize workers in the CIO we were arguing 'til three a.m. about the French turn." Too many in the Socialist party came to look to Russian authority, to Russian tradition, to Russian example, it was said. Little benefit accrued to the Socialist party except in an educational sense: Social-

ists learned to fear and distrust Bolsheviks and to abandon the idea of
an "all-inclusive party."

In retrospect one former Trotskyist believed the French turn had
been "a stupid maneuver; it is self-defeating if you can't make it on
your own as a party to have to go in and capture another broader
party."[61] Some former members held that Trotskyists should have remained inside the party, forestalling ouster, building within, and continuing to propagandize but with greater subtlety.[62] The French turn
in fact proved a windfall for the Trotskyists. By December 31 when
the expelled branches and locals allied at a convention in Chicago to
found the "Socialist Workers party," the American section was the
strongest one in the world movement and New York virtually the center of world Trotskyism, Isaac Deutscher noted.[63] "Our activities in the
Socialist party were an almost unqualified success from the standpoint
of the Trotskyists," commented Shachtman pragmatically, with the
warning that if they were to remain narrow followers of Trotsky and
exegetists of his scribblings, they deceived themselves that they would
ever be more than a propaganda sect, and certainly they would not be
a significant political movement. They could not deliver a recordable
vote. Although they may discuss politics all day and all night, they
could not do anything about politics. "Theory has to be tested in the
crucible of events," he remonstrated.[64]

Clearly Shachtman gave the turn a strong vote of confidence, but not
wholeheartedly the method of its execution. If all small radical groupings had followed the technique of entrism seriously, not

> running in on Monday, convincing one or two people on Tuesday,
> and walking out on Wednesday to form a new little propaganda
> movement, a new little sect, but remaining in and trying to influ-
> ence that section of the working-class movement which was Social-
> ist, which had already acquired sufficient political consciousness
> to be Socialist of one kind or another, I think the prospect for a
> left-wing tendency or a Marxian tendency inside the broader move-
> ment would have been vastly enhanced.

But, he added, Trotsky brought the French turn to an abrupt end. All
over, Trotskyists plucked a few out only to begin again as a little
sect.[65]

Cannon exulted that when the Socialists expelled the Trotskyists, they expelled the heart of their party; Trotsky had won over all the serious young activists, leaving only a dead husk: ". . . we . . . demolished the opportunist party of Thomas and Co."[66] Ben Gitlow knew that "the Trotskyists were too much for the S.P. to digest without getting the most violent cramps . . . ." The Socialist party "succumbed to the Communist virus, eating at its vitals."[67] From the perspective of the 1970s, a Socialist Workers party comrade on the *Militant* staff, Harry Ring, believed the Trotskyists, like the Socialists, reaped educational rewards: they drew on the French turn experience at the time of Nikita Khrushchev's Twentieth Congress revelations. Because of it they "knew how rapidly to gather in leftward-moving forces."[68]

From Coyoacan, Trotsky commented,

> I for my part believe that the passage through the Socialist party was a salutary action for the whole development of our party and that the "regime" (or the leadership) which assured this passage was correct against the opposition which at that time represented the tendency of stagnation.[69]

So very successful was entrism in his judgment that he issued fresh directives to his French section, now the International Workers party, to enter the new French social democratic organization, the Socialist party of Proletarian Workers, in April 1939! They obeyed.[70] But much truth lay in Bert Cochran's arguments that entrism, immediately triumphant, was in the long run self-defeating. Into the Trotskyist sect in 1936 and 1937 came scores of middle-class youth and intellectuals—many "sympathy departures" too, as predicted. Dramatic political changes overseas were soon to create a polarization between the persistent division in the group, the intellectual wing (now broadened and considerably stronger) and the proletarian-oriented wing. During the French turn disputes began to come into focus that would in 1939 and 1940 wrack the party and usher in a real crisis, disputes over political principles, organizational and propaganda methods, and attitudes toward national and international questions. This polarity, growing into a fissure, would in 1940 split the party down the middle bringing to completion the breach that had been incipient since 1928.

8
Trotskyists in Crisis

A. SEEDS OF SCHISM

Expulsions from the Norman Thomas party ushered in the next period for American Trotskyists. Just three months later, another of the many small splits that afflicted the group took place. The lines of the quarrel that in November 1937 prompted twelve comrades to walk out were prophetic.

The "Political Question"

James Burnham in 1936 had begun to doubt a cardinal Trotskyist principle: that the Soviet Union remained a workers' state, although degenerated. To elaborate, property was still in the hands of the people, but an unscrupulous bureaucracy had usurped control. As the only existing workers' state the Soviet Union still merited unconditional defense if at war with capitalist powers. But Burnham doubted that it warranted defense. Speaking at the Socialist party convention in 1936, he said the USSR had become through its alliance system a dupe of imperialism.[1] Now Burnham was bold indeed to question the party line, and it brought him into conflict with the bolshevik theory of party organization. To doubt was to violate discipline. The seeds of dispute, crisis, and schism were thus sown.

In the fall of 1937, Joe Carter and Burnham questioned the entire official analysis. Soviet property relations (they found) were not those of a workers' state because the proletariat did not manage or control the means of production. The state, after all, is the sum of the tools for social and political coercion—army, police, courts, prisons, and bureaucracy—to aid those who did manage or control. As the big bourgeoisie benefited from these tools under German and Italian fascism, so in Russia the bureaucracy, a new ruling class, reaped the rewards of the state. "Within the last two or three years it has completed that divorce from the proletariat; and consequently, the state is no longer a workers' state." Nor was it a bourgeois state, and to defend it "unconditionally" would do nothing to restore the revolutionary ideal.

The challenges spurred Trotsky, who exercised great authority in determining the stand on international questions, to write heated rebuttals from Coyoacan. The bureaucracy could not be called a class, he said; rather, it was a "clique," as class was determined by relationship to the means of production. Property remained in state hands; the bureaucracy simply had illegal but temporary control. Accordingly, the cause of world revolution demanded a continued pledge of unconditional defense.[2]

When the issues were articulated at the Chicago conference of the expelled branches in November 1937, a group of young comrades agreed with mavericks Burnham and Carter and came under Arne Swabeck's sharp rebuke:

> . . . all of you must give up your anti-working class views regarding the workers' fatherland, the Soviet Union, if you wish to remain here. As long as private property and the means of production and exchange are still nationalized, the Soviet Union . . . must be defended.

While Cannon berated Burnham for mongrelization of theory, twelve members, including Harry Roskolenko, Max Geltman, and Max Eastman's son Dan, led by the artist Attilio Salemme, walked out into the night.[3] Relieved, Roskolenko recalled, "I was out of it all at last." Within two-and-a-half years, half the party would have left, in part over the same question, the culmination of a process reaching back not merely to 1936 but to 1932.[4]

Founding the Socialist Workers Party and the Fourth International

On December 31, 1937, and January 1, 1938, a reported 100 delegates gathered in Chicago at an "emergency convention" and heard Al Goldman open the meeting, then cheered addresses by such party regulars as Cannon, Shachtman, and Dunne. Young People's Socialist League delegates met at the same time; but since 90 percent of the younger Socialist party members had left during the expulsions, efforts to revive the YPSL within the party failed. Both conventions roundly (and ritualistically) denounced the popular front and class collaborationist support for LaGuardia in the New York mayoralty contest, then pledged loyalty to their own Socialist Workers party and its declaration of principles.

Standard declaimers were trotted out in the declaration. Fascism mobilized desperate middle classes in the interest of big capital. Because the United States shuddered "in the final throes of capitalism" the only road away from war and repression was to eliminate capitalism. Through overthrow by means of "class organs like Soviets" bolshevik-leninists could take power and inaugurate the workers' state, "a temporary political instrument" needed to defend the revolution against class enemies, aiming to abolish "the necessity of state coercion, that is, to do away with itself, with any form of state whatever." Finally, these efforts would bring in a socialist society with planned production, a labor force of free producers, and the disappearance of "socially useless classes."

The declaration then scrutinized radical parties for their potential to lead world revolution, finding all but one useless for the task. That one was the Socialist Workers party, instrument of world salvation because the only collection of true revolutionaries.[5]

Then, because the goal was "to mobilize the American masses for struggle against American capitalism and for its overthrow," the Socialist Workers party would have to devise ways to recruit among the middle classes, "Negroes and other oppressed racial groups," unemployed youth, trade unionists, and "colonial peoples." The comrades would have to show each group that its best interest lay in endorsing Trotskyist positions on such global issues as the clash of democracy with fascism, "imperalist war," and (of major significance) the Soviet Union. On the Russian question despite Burnham's and Carter's outburst the declaration plainly stated that the workers' state survived and all workers had the duty to defend Russia unconditionally.

But the seeds of doubt planted by Burnham and Carter had begun to germinate. The "Resolution on the Soviet Union" failed to reaffirm Trotsky's uncompromising stand. It introduced a modification. Since the bureaucracy was not a class, nor were the Stakhonovites, the pace-setting production workers on which the bureaucracy relied, a class, "both contain[ed] elements of a new, i.e., a capitalist class." The Soviet system was neither socialism nor capitalism. (Burnham had said that it was neither a workers' nor a bourgeois state.) The resolution neverthe-less commanded "unconditional defense" as "the imperative duty of the international proletariat" to forestall capitalist restoration. But clearly Burnham and Carter had made inroads.

The Socialist Workers party viewed European war as inevitable and United States intervention "to maintain its own power and profits" as certain; therefore it opposed any involvement pitting the United States against the Soviet Union.[6] The Trotskyist "revolutionary defensist" argument seemed intact, but a fresh class analysis had almost surfaced. A renewed commitment to democratic centralism phrased in the reso-lution on party organization ensured loyalty to defensism, if future conventions voted that policy.

With the birth of the new "pure" party came a desire to found for-mally the fourth international. For the September 1938 founding con-ference, Trotsky wrote the "transition program" under the sweeping title, *The Death Agony of Capitalism and the Tasks of the Fourth In-ternational.* It restated the party line and beckoned workers everywhere to rally for future triumph "under the banner of the fourth interna-tional." At the spring plenum in 1938 the comrades discussed, approved, and adopted Trotsky's blueprint.[7] If Burnham and Carter had objections, they kept silent.

Prognoses of war were not ill-founded. Axis powers were on the move. In March 1938, the last of the Moscow trials was under way. Mussolini had invaded Ethiopia, Japanese forces had occupied Man-churia, and that month Hitler moved into Austria. In the United States the House of Representatives debated and barely rejected the Ludlow

Amendment which would have mandated a national referendum before Congress could declare war, except in case of invasion. Opposing it, President Roosevelt and Secretary of State Cordell Hull talked of world responsibilities and commended collective security to deter military aggression. In the spirit of the popular front, Earl Browder endorsed collective security to save the world from "catastrophe."[8]

Trotskyists believed approval of Roosevelt's collective security anomalous for revolutionists. What a calamity that the requirements of Soviet foreign policy had prompted American Communists to turn their backs on class struggle for the sake of national unity. Collective security was simply a design to defend Anglo-American imperialism. Answering historian Charles A. Beard, who recommended that the United States stay aloof from European and Asian entanglements, Burnham observed that America's intricate and permanent bonds with the world market system and commitment to uphold world capitalism made isolation impossible. War would erupt and the United States would intervene.[9]

In this atmosphere bristling with the amassing of armaments, the whetting of nationalist fervor, and the stoking of international hatreds, Trotskyists founded the fourth international. Delegates from eleven countries met in Paris at Alfred Rosmer's home (publicly reported as "somewhere in Switzerland") September 3, 1938, for a one-day session over which Max Shachtman presided. Little debate occurred; Pierre Naville gave the main report, then delegates merely adopted Trotsky's "transition program." They quarreled briefly over the pretentious ring of the term "international" for so small a movement, then with Trotsky's admonition in mind, kept the term and rejected an alternate label, "movement for the fourth international" in favor of "the fourth international." The little group optimistically appointed an "international secretariat" and a subsecretariat, and talked grandly of centralizing operations. In high hopes they adjourned, dedicated (in Shachtman's words) to "go ahead under the banner of the Fourth International, with our old convictions, our tested principles, and with no doubts as to the final outcome."[10]

Shachtman said the congress climaxed fifteen years of struggle. Five years before, Trotsky called for a new international and four years earlier the "pact of four" delegates had met. The nascent organization had even boasted a "secretary," Rudolph Klement, who allegedly fell victim to the GPU (Soviet secret police) in mid-summer 1938. *Socialist*

Appeal melodramatically reported that Klement was "kidnapped from Paris at midnight," taken to Spain and murdered, his headless and legless body found there later, a sure sign (Trotskyists believed) the Comintern thought the fourth international was a real threat.[11]

Reviewing party history to this climax, Trotsky noted three stages. The first had been the propaganda sect period (1928-1934); the second, that of fusion politics and trying to make reformist parties the vehicle for revolutionary activities (1934-mid-1938). The third stage began in September 1938 with the founding of the fourth international, deemed mandatory after massive expulsions from Socialist parties (including the second international).[12] His millennial vision would remain a mirage because, as Trotsky could not foresee, the congress portended a significant event. Sylvia Agelof of the New York branch came and was introduced by Ruby Weil (a former Musteite) to Trotsky's future assassin, for whom she would in all innocence gain access to Trotsky's private quarters in Coyoacan.

The fourth international amounted to little. Isaac Deutscher called it a "stillbirth," for "there was no revolutionary movement to breathe life into it." It was "unreal." Another scholar believed it failed to grow because Trotsky floundered as leader, did nothing to ensure succession, and so "doomed the Fourth International as an effective organization." "Trotsky was admirably suited to attaining power," the argument ran, "but not to holding it," so the matter of succession was never even raised.[13] Trotsky lived exactly two years after the founding conference, and those years were in exile. His loyal followers were no substitute for the personal leadership he might have exercised by his presence at conferences. But even had this been possible, Marxist revolutionary movements were doomed in the period immediately ahead. Stalin dissolved the Comintern in 1943 and the Socialist international remained ineffective, too, as demands of World War II, Soviet military expansionism, and nationalist revolutions in developing nations channeled energies.

The Charge of Party Conservatism

Had the party grown conservative? In its eleven years a specific style of leadership had evolved to which members were now habituated. Initially the support comrades gave a strong leader seemed justified in terms of bolshevik discipline. But instead of the will of the membership through majorities taken at annual conventions, *democratic centralism,* over time forceful, even domineering personalities came to exert excessive sway over policies.[14] A kind of enforced consensus reflecting powerful leaders' views emerged in place of democratic centralism; and, as a result, new faces, new ideas, and new leadership talent were shut out. Perhaps factionalism and the leadership cult are endemic in radical politics, but plainly reform was in order by 1939.

World events indirectly commanded a decision on reform. What seemed capitulation of the workers' state to a national socialist regime in the Nazi-Soviet pact of August 22, 1939, added to the German invasion of Poland signaling the onset of World War II, forced American radicals to review their official "lines" on European governments. In the process of review the Trotskyists' long-festering hostilities burst open and the need for party reform was vigorously debated. So it happened that with centripetal force personal antipathies, need for reform, and world events precipitated the crisis of 1940.

Two interrelated but distinct issues opened the quarrel. The political question involved the party line (dictated by Trotsky) on the Soviet Union. Did Russia still merit the "unconditional defense" of Marxists? The other issue centered on the right (or lack of it) within bolshevik form of comrades to question publicly a party stand, even though the "stand" might have been taken after factional intrigue and bullying. This was the organizational question. Burnham had of course already raised both issues in 1937; now world events shoved them once more into mid-arena. The debate was on and Trotsky intruded at every turn, writing under a variety of pseudonyms: "Lund," "Crux," "W. Rork," "V. T. O'Brien," even "Your Old Man." The resolution of both questions would decide the fate of party reform.

At a plenum before the July 1939 convention Shachtman volunteered organizational suggestions and reported on party leadership in order to provoke intraparty discussions that might lead to needed reforms. First, he wished to see the power of the bureaucracy reduced. Second, he wished to see Marxist *praxis* implemented: "revolutionary ideas tested in the crucible of action," significant roles going to young people rather than "hallowed leaders." Loyal Cannon supporters distrusted Shachtman's motives and viewed his proposals as an attack on Cannon. So the national committee rejected them on the spurious grounds that such matters had to be decided locally.[15] Cannon's undisputed leadership had long rankled in Shachtman's breast. So too had Cannon's special, favored relationship with Trotsky, who appreciated Cannon's unassailable proletarian, syndicalist, and Communist background, particularly since the membership comprised only one-sixth industrial workers. This "working-class party" had its greatest strength in its city intellectual and student radical contingents, and Trotsky, yearning to reverse this, catered to Cannon.

Quarreling between Cannon and Shachtman over admission of younger forces into leadership stemmed from 1932. Already by June 1932 Abern, Glotzer, and Shachtman noted an "ingrowing conservatism" in the leadership, and recommended that the tiny Communist League of America "refresh the ranks—with new forces [and] transform our N.C. [national committee] into a working body, alive and energetic." Citing Cannon for four evidences of poor leadership they noted that after October 1928 Cannon "began to 'droop' " and let others do his work, saying "it was 'a protracted up-hill struggle so cool off, hot heads,' a rationale for conservatism and drift." Second, Cannon resisted any challenge to his entrenched position from new faces and concocted what Abern, Glotzer, and Shachtman labeled the "gestation theoy," or, "the legend of the historic left." Calculated to convince comrades to accord "a special privileged significance to those who once had formed a part of the Cannon group in the party," Cannon commanded deference through "repeated reference to his remarkable qualifications," his proletarian, IWW, and Communist party background. Third, Cannon took long absences from duty in 1929-1930 due to "personal difficulties" [undefined], leaving affairs in the hands of trusted cohorts; and last, when present he finagled to keep criticism of his leadership and views not in accord with his own out of the party press. Although the 1932 quarrel which briefly threatened split resolved itself later in pledges of unity, lines had been drawn.[16] Thereafter Shachtman was found on the side of innovation and collective leadership whether through envy and a wish to see Cannon displaced, or through true respect for youthful ability and eagerness for fresh approaches; and Cannon just as consistently opposed reform whether he dreaded loss of status in the party or whether, as dedicated revolutionist, he sincerely wanted to preclude dilution of doctrine.

Neither Cannon nor Shachtman reported the early quarrel in their memoirs, but the alignments carried faithfully over the years into the crisis of 1939 and 1940 and tended to reflect and perpetuate the age-old division within radical movements between the intelligentsia and the working-class element.*

Crisis in First Phase

Ignoring the national committee ruling, Shachtman raised both the organizational and the political questions at the July 1939 convention. He stood and read his slate for a new national committee to include for stability and continuity a core of old leaders but adding "new blood" through a large draft from the YPSL. This, he argued, would check growing "routinism and conservatism." Then he recommended a new post, that of "organization secretary," a kind of ombudsman, to be established within a new "organizational department." Furious, Cannon assailed the innovations as a plot to overthrow him, an attack on his leadership. Cannon then in parliamentary style called for a vote of confidence by announcing his term as national secretary had ended and that he would not run for relection. In this way he whipped his faction, "a clique of Cannon hand-raisers" (in Shachtman's words) into line. The structural change was dropped from consideration, and Cannon did not withdraw from service as national secretary.[17] Political committee records showed repeated instances of such leadership cult politicking. Certainly this time his threat put the organizational question into cold storage.

---

*Shachtman kept with him the "city intellectuals": Carter, Emanuel Geltman, Glotzer, Abern, Burnham, C. L. R. James, Dwight Macdonald, Isadore Bern, E. R. McKinney, B. J. Widick, the literary figures who dabbled briefly in revolutionary politics such as Leslie Fiedler, Irving Howe, and Saul Bellow, and of course the youth whom he championed. Cannon's support in fact largely came from trade union circles, Minneapolis being a particular stronghold and contributing Vincent Ray Dunne, Dobbs, Skoglund, and university professor Grace Carlson. Swabeck backed Cannon, as did George Clarke, Bert Cochran, Charles Curtis, Murry Weiss, Sam Gordon, Al Russel, the two "city intellectuals" Felix Morrow of New York and Al Goldman of Chicago, and the budding theoretician who would one day take the position Shachtman had held in the American section, George Novack. Last but not least Leon Trotsky was found regularly on the side of Cannon.

Next Shachtman and C. L. R. James addressed international matters—the political question of the party's position on Stalin's demand
for the right to "guarantee" Poland and the Baltic states against German
attack. They also wanted the party to take a stand on any possible pacts
(predicted by Trotsky) between Hitler and Stalin and on the war. But
the delegates did not tackle these thorny problems.[18] Procrastination
was hardly possible in August when the Nazi-Soviet pact became a reality, followed by dual invasion and division of Poland. The existing
loose alignment of Socialist Workers party forces polarized, then crystallized.

Through September 1939, the political committee met biweekly and
Shachtman, Abern, Johnson, Widick, and others called repeatedly for a
plenum to consider questions raised by war. Burnham on September 5
after almost two years of silence again spoke out asking that the fourth
international renounce unconditional defense of the Soviet Union. Under present circumstances "unconditional defense" was counterrevolutionary, therefore "social-patriotic." Supporting Burnham, Shachtman
now branded Russia as "imperialist."[19] But from Coyoacan, Trotsky
rejoined, "Our house must be kept clean . . . . We have no reason at the
present time for changing our principled position in relation to the
USSR," Cannon naturally seconding him and urging that the pact "is
new only in the sense that an old policy of Stalin on the field of foreign
policy . . . has reached diplomatic realization through the agreement of
Hitler." Because the economic structure of the Soviet Union had undergone no change, "For my part I am not willing to revise the well-
considered decisions of our party convention." Although Cannon insisted that organizational and political questions stay separate, he himself linked them when he said: "individual editors at their whim" had
refuted decisions taken at convention, plainly a matter of discipline and
so, connected in the closest way to the organizational question.[20]

With the issue joined, now even rank-and-file members chose sides
and argued "defensism or defeatism," "workers' state or new class,"
"collective security or no entangling alliances with capitalist powers."
On the issue of war, for example, would the Socialist Worker party uphold a "defensive" war if the "democracies"—Britain, France, the United
States, and Russia—were called into battle? Was Russia now an imperialist power or was Stalin simply an agent of imperialism?[21] Burnham,
Abern, and Shachtman became the antiwar faction, insisting "the war

is an imperialist war on both sides," so the revolutionists, as a "third camp," should stand aloof from battle while Axis and Allies (including Russia) fought it out, spurning "unconditional or any other kind of defense of the Soviet Union." This faction gradually drew in students and others from the YPSL who found its stand compelling. George Weissman remembered that as Trotskyist leader at Harvard University he tried to soft-pedal the quarreling because students were choosing sides and of course party spirit declined. "I was very naive about it and the group that called themselves Shachtmanites went to work on them and the next thing I knew most of the new ones were converted to that position."[22]

The first verbal matches were on a high plane. Resolutions on the Russian question at the October plenum set forth the contrasting "lines" and Trotsky gave his side in two eloquent articles, "Again and Once More Again on the Nature of the USSR" and "The USSR in War."[23] Burnham hoped the comrades would adopt his and Shachtman's viewpoint by majority vote at the convention in the spring of 1940. The organization question was raised briefly first when Burnham at the plenum asked for a referendum on the war issue. The majority said no, and Trotsky with tortuous logic sided with them in the name of democratic centralism. Whoever favored a referendum favored mandates, he wrote; every local under that system could dictate the vote of its representatives at convention. Whoever recognized such mandates disdained "the highest organ of the party," the convention. "The party as a centralized whole disappears." A referendum would subject the party to "the influence of the least experienced, backward sections, etc."[24]

Because Cannon's positions received majorities in the national committee meeting, the plenum reorganized the political committee to give Cannon a majority. The alignment still had not solidly formed. Abern and McKinney supported both Cannon's and Shachtman's motions, and Goldman, after having made one motion himself, later stood by Cannon. To keep his majority Cannon summoned the influential Farrell Dobbs, trade unionist Bert Cochran, and Goldman to the plenum. The Cannon group then placated the other side by appointing Widick, Carter, and Abern to noninfluential party posts, and sent Cannonite Joseph Hansen to Mexico so Trotsky could hear the quarrel from the "proper" perspective.[25] Buttressing his side, Burnham convinced the Trotskyist sympathizer Dwight Macdonald, brilliant young writer for *Partisan Review,* that he should formally join the Socialist Worker party.[26] In November the Cannon majority pleading "financial exigency" voted one editor on *Socialist Appeal,* named Cannonite Felix Morrow to the office, and kept Shachtman as "consultant." Somehow Shachtman and Burnham managed to remain editors of *New International.* Unanimously adopted at the political committee meeting of November 7 was a "statement on party unity," pledging democratic process for clarifying issues at the next national convention, and no expulsions or withdrawals even if the antagonists failed to agree. The "statement" provided for a commission of four, two from each side, to investigate grievances or violations of discipline. Meanwhile both factions would go right on collaborating in duties and jointly editing the *Internal Bulletin.* Based on the unity resolution, prospects for a compromise seemed bright in November; but even then partisans rallied forces for battle, Cannon often prating of the "line-up," the theater of operation national headquarters in New York.[27]

B. THE SCHISM

Crisis in Second Phase

The organization question precipitated the acrimonious second phase. Burnham asked to have pages of *Socialist Appeal* and *New International* opened to full discussion of the issues from both points of view. The national committee majority turned down the request. Accordingly, on December 13, Abern, Burnham, Shachtman, and Isadore Bern drafted for the political committee minority a devastating portrayal of the Socialist Workers party as a party corrupted with inner-circle rule, a betrayal of democratic centralism, and a party stagnant with do-nothing policies oblivious of shifts in world politics. Borrowing from the term "bureaucratic collectivism" used by an Italian ex-Trotskyist, Bruno Rizzi, the minority branded the Cannon regime "bureaucratic conservatism." The indictment, written by Burnham, traced party history to prove Cannon's obsession with personal status and power, a fixation that caused him to place "the organizational question" first even while insisting the political question was paramount. Cannon encouraged a "cult of the leader" and accepted, robot-like, Trotsky's political line recapitulating it for equally blind acceptance by his clique.[28] In short, Burnham's "War and Bureaucratic Conservatism" summarized the dispute smoldering for nine years.

The thrusts and parries of the ensuing debate unveiled Trotsky's peculiar position. Faithful party members "voluntarily and enthusiastically accepted" his total authority—a relationship unduplicated in other radical movements. A chasm in prestige and authority separated "Trotsky at the top and the most prominent of his followers," with Trotsky gladly receiving the awesome responsibility that as the "last representative of Marxist internationalism" he was the "link between yesterday and tomorrow." For Shachtman it was no surprise when he or Burnham wrote articles that Cannon or Goldman never were first to reply: the initial responses setting forth the line of rebuttal always came from Trotsky. "He was our opponent, period."[29]

Trotsky's reply to "War and Bureaucratic Conservatism" was not so temperate. The *Internal Bulletin* must suffice as the vehicle for rebuttal. The debate was to be kept from any "public" press. "Under such conditions for the opposition to have their own public paper or magazine is a means not to convince the party but to appeal against the party to the external world." Perhaps then one issue of *New International* could be given over to the discussion, but the arrangement must give the last word to the majority. After all, said Trotsky, the Burnham group had a primitive argument and could not win in a theoretical fight. Did they seek publicity, perhaps, "to justify themselves before democratic public opinion, to shout to all the Eastmans, Hooks, and the others that they . . . are not so bad as we?" The charge of bureaucratic conservatism incensed him, and in a final crescendo Trotsky exhumed the old epithet "petty bourgeois" to pitch at Burnham, Shachtman, Abern, and the rest, adding in a furious postscript to one of his letters: "It is absolutely sure that the Stalinist agents are working in our midst with the purpose to sharpen the discussion and provoke a split."[30]

Before the July 1939 convention Trotsky had written Cannon that the superabundance of middle-class elements in the large cities, especially New York, spent too much time discussing among themselves and too little time recruiting. From time to time he had reminded his followers that petty bourgeois comrades should be outnumbered by proletarians, for their tendency to scorn discipline and follow individual whimsy posed a danger to a "combat party."[31] On December 13, Trotsky answered with a major article focusing on philosophical incompatibilities, pragmatism pitted against dialectical materialism. It was a reply to an earlier essay by Burnham and Shachtman, "Intellectuals in Retreat," in which both had revealed their growing doubts about the relevance of the dialectic. Trotsky bared his anti-intellectualism, astonishing in a man characterized by friend and foe alike as an intellectual of high caliber and who at no time, except during school-boy odd jobs, had lived a working class life. A proletarian could only think dialectically, Trotsky was sure, whereas a petty bourgeois, prejudiced toward pragmatism, was reinforced in academia, the whole process leading him farther and farther away from a revolutionary analysis and from usefulness to a combat party. The dialectic, the only truly scientific mode of thought, made obsolete Aristotelian logic with its static view of reality. Hegel and Marx had displaced Aristotle. Similarly, Darwin's dynamic description of biological unfolding supplanted Linnaeus' static "immutability of species." A motor force propels human society, slow growth periodically precipitating conflict of opposites (revolutions) as shells of older social systems explode.

Having defined and defended his philosophical base, Trotsky addressed the organizational question. The dialectic was at work inside the Socialist Workers party itself causing the intraparty quarrel, he claimed. Shachtman and Burnham, petty bourgeois eclectics, had shifted from a correct position to a regressive one "with its tinge of academic pedantry and journalistic impressionism." Of course Abern too had assailed "unconditional defense," but after all (said Trotsky) Abern's struggle against Cannon was the oldest struggle in the party. Abern's was a "propagandist group, petty-bourgeois in its social composition," clashing with the progressive proletarian party and now joined by Burnham and Shachtman. Comrades should "reject the anti-Marxian novelties of the opposition and guarantee party unity," for "if the party as a whole should take the road of the opposition it could suffer complete destruction."[32]

Trotsky's second article, "From a Scratch—to the Danger of Gangrene," thrashed the theoretical enemy with physiological metaphor as his scornful rhetoric mounted. In December when he invited Shachtman to Coyoacan to try to effect a meeting of minds, Shachtman declined; consequently Trotsky initiated a campaign of vilification that further revealed his anti-intellectualism and anti-Semitism. He cast "Jew," "petty bourgeois," and "city intellectual" in one hat and pleaded that "the Jewish petty-bourgeois elements be shifted from their habitual conservative milieu and dissolved in the real movement," a persistent theme in the debate lending credence to subsequent accusations of anti-Semitism. How did this old revolutionist answer the charge of conservatism? He said Burnham and company were the real conservatives: they rejected Marxism itself. Moreover Shachtman's "philosophic bloc against Marxism" was compounded of "intellectuals disillusioned with Bolshevism"; his views were "weak-kneed and capricious," "the economics of the declassed petty-bourgeoisie" based on "arbitrary, not thought out and downright false" historical instances.[33] When the inevitable collapse should come, it would hurt both sides.

Defending Cannon against allegations of clique leadership, Trotsky (cued by Cannonite Hansen in Mexico) harped on the "Abern faction" which had "existed uninterruptedly, statically if not 'dynamically,' " concerned chiefly in "combinations at the top," a phrase left unexplained.[34]

Actually Abern had impeccable credentials which were hard to attack. In battling with Abern, Trotsky fought one of the three members of the Communist central committee who staked their party fortunes on his defense in 1928. Abern could boast as solidly American a background as Cannon's. In addition, his leftist political opinions had gotten him in hot water; a civil liberties lawyer once saved him from deportation. In Chicago in the 1920s he served as a district leader in the Communist party, and in New York in the mid-1930s he was the Bronx branch organizer.[35] Briefly he allied with Muste, McKinney, and others in questioning the wisdom of the French turn, but he stayed loyal to the party and set aside his doubts. Now, coached by Hansen, Trotsky insulted Abern for raising with Shachtman the "Russian question." No evidence, only accusation, of a Martin Abern clique appeared in party records.

Trotsky painted a picture of a party in real peril: Burnham sowed seeds of doubt about the lynchpin of party theoretical structure, the dialectic: the "eclectic" unprincipled Shachtman falsified party history; the "dangerous" Abern led a clique; and all conspired to obstruct bolshevik discipline and frustrate the true Marxian party.

Both sides set to work in January 1940 to rally the vote for their resolutions at the spring convention, slated for March. But since the combatants needed time to defend their cases at various branches and locals, an appeal to the national committee got the convention postponed to April. Vigorous campaigning was begun. Cannon boasted that in February alone he had made forty-three speeches, and a total of sixty by April. He debated Shachtman again and again in meetings. "In debating with Shachtman I crawl on my belly in the mud for the sake of the Fourth International," Cannon wrote.[36] By February 20, the mimeograph machine had churned out eleven special *Internal Bulletins* and would print four more by April 5, the opening date of the convention. To win the California locals the national committee launched Murray Weiss on a western tour. C. L. R. James left New York for Los Angeles (without official authorization) to present the minority viewpoint to western comrades. Shachtman toured the Midwest. All the while heated letters-to-branches poured from Cannon's pen.[37] Received cordially at other branches, Shachtman was rebuffed in the Twin Cities because the local was solidly with the majority from the beginning. Cannon wrote to Trotsky, "the Minneapolis comrades remain unmoved. They have read and studied all the bulletins and discussed them in meeting after meeting; they know Shachtman; and they don't want to hear any more from Shachtman."[38]

The right to equal press coverage seemed basic; the minority pointed out that bolshevik tradition permitted a free press. For instance, Carter remembered that Lenin allowed Bukharin a factional organ, and Trotsky had demanded a public press to state his position in the 1920s. Even Cannon just two years earlier had demanded of the Socialist party's national executive committee the right to an organ to present Appeal caucus views. Because Trotsky insisted, the Cannonites finally compromised: on the editorial board of *New International* the opposition could keep the two seats it already had out of the five. But *Socialist Appeal* was closed to them.[39] By the time this tiny token was offered, the fissure had grown too wide.

The minority managed to keep the initiative they had grasped and to pick each patch of ground for skirmish. But Trotsky and Cannon ingeniously seized the political epithets thrown at them—"bureaucrats," "conservative," "factionalists"—and aimed these back at the minority. Small incidents now loomed large, igniting flares of temperament and evoking volleys of name-calling. "Traitors," "splitters," "liars," were heard with increasing frequency.

As an example of an insignificant episode ridiculously inflated, when one of Trotsky's dispatches was read aloud at a January meeting Martin Abern cried out, "This means split," then muttered that Trotsky treated the minority as "second-class citizens." What ensued was a four-corner exchange involving Abern's denial, then Cannon's and Goldman's heated affirmations. Finally Trotsky stepped in, vouched for Cannon's reliability, retorted that in labeling them "the Cannon clique" the minority made "second-class citizens" of the majority, and scolded Abern for threatening split: "a dispicable betrayal of the Fourth International."[40] Abern was not adept at writing the theoretical treatises so integral to the radical movement and to the present debate. But Trotsky had upbraided him. He struck back, first defending Burnham's "bureaucratic conservatism," next dismissing the charge of an Abernite clique as "just palaver uttered by those who demonstrate a totalitarian concept of leadership."[41]

Burnham, Shachtman, and newcomer Macdonald, skilled in polemical exchange, lost no time in parrying Trotsky's blows. Accused of forming a bloc, Shachtman attacked on the historical front. Trotsky had himself belonged to factions having allied with opposition groupings in 1923, 1926, and 1927. He had said whoever rejected the dialectic was not a revolutionist and should not be in a combat party; in reply Shachtman quoted Lenin (May 26, 1909): "A political party cannot examine its members to see if there are any contradictions between the philosophy and the political program," reminding Trotsky that Lenin had worked in a bloc with a philosopher who rejected Marx and that both had simply excluded philosophy as a neutral field. True, Burnham shunned dialectical materialism. Still, after the manner of Lenin, Trotsky and the American party had for five years worked with him, even calling on him to employ his talents to write important party documents.[42]

Dwight Macdonald, a neophyte in the party but ardently pro-minority, attacked on the political front. Having had three articles rejected by the *Internal Bulletin* (in his experience a harder publication to break into than *Fortune, Harper's,* the *Nation, New Yorker,* or even *New International*), he thrust a mimeographed tract, "Shamefaced Defensism," into intraparty circulation to prick Trotsky's balloon of "principle." Trotsky's position on Russia was two-faced, he found. Outside the party to keep his intelligent readership he parlayed an anti-Stalinist line, yet in the *Internal Bulletin* "for the unscrupulous and hypocritical sheep in the Cannon camp" he championed Stalinism, or seemed to.[43] Macdonald's claim had truth, especially in the thick of this battle. In the party Trotsky argued manfully for defense of a system he excoriated as degenerate and despotic outside it. Hansen called Macdonald's remarks "slander." Trotsky called them "guerrilla warfare," and Macdonald, amused, recalled that "the article roused the majority to fury, not because of its arguments, which they paid no attention to, but simply because a new boy had talked back to the principal."[44]

Wheeling out the biggest guns in the minority arsenal, James Burnham signed his name on February 1 to a scathing attack on the philosophic front, like schrapnel aimed in all directions. "Science and Style" accused Trotsky of confusing his followers and throwing a smokescreen over the two central issues, "the strategical orientation of the Fourth International in the present phase of the second World War" and "the question of the regime in the Socialist Workers Party." Trotsky used witty, flashing rhetoric and stentorian phrases such as "the logic of events" and "the historic course of the struggle" to cloud an altogether unscientific analysis devoid of evidence—and why?—because the threads of his arguments simply did not connect logically. As for Trotsky's displacing Aristotelian logic with Hegelian dialectic, Burnham sneered that Hegel, thrown out by modern scientists and mathematicians except Russian ones, was "the century-dead arch-muddler of human thought" whose dialectics had "nothing whatever to do with science" and whose "vision of a block universe" was totalitarian. After all, every faction from Oehler through Abern and Shachtman to Stalin swore by the dialectic. The clincher should be that dialectics bore no relation to the questions at issue.

Trotsky was also conservative, Burnham continued. The founding fathers of Marxism were sacrosanct to him. Like church authorities and state despots, Trotsky spoke of the dialectic as a "fundamental question," and liberally used capitalized abstractions like "Freedom," "God," and "Truth": an obscurantist and reactionary ploy, a "red herring to divert attention from the political issues at stake." Analysis, not the dialectic, is the tool of modern science, and analysis insists on rigorous criticism of belief. There were two political "fundamental questions" in the present struggle. What is our goal? How do we reach it? The antagonists agreed on the first question, but disagreed on the second. Cannonite idols had feet of clay. Hegel provided only words, and Trotsky resurrected hoary dogmas to solve modern problems.

Burnham's assault grew more pointed when he confronted Trotsky's tactical blunders and personality failings. The old man pandered to "backward provincialism," to prejudices against Jews and professors to win and hold his tenuous trade-union following. As for the Trotsky-Cannon "anything goes" method sanctioned for these tugs-of-war, "lies and disloyalty and slander," Burnham explained that socialism, a moral ideal, cannot be attained by means that corrupt. If the majority branded him "petty-bourgeois" for this, he cared not a whit.[45]

To the devastating dissection of his methods Trotsky had nothing substantive to say, only more name-calling. Burnham was "an intellectual snob," a "strutting pedant," one of the "common swindlers in the field of politics." Burnham, Abern, and Shachtman were "bankrupt" purveyors of "ideological charlatanism" and "pompous phraseology." He hurled abuse too at former European supporters in scattered references.[46] Trotsky plumbed the depths of his reservoir of invectives becoming ridiculous as he flailed wildly at the American opposition.

The April Convention

While the war of words raged the minority leaders met in Cleveland on February 24 and 25. Trotsky in desperation wrote Al Goldman to urge unity. He honestly wished to avoid rupture but would make only organizational, not political, concessions. Obediently, Cannon wired the conferees that the majority, desirous of unity, would oppose any expulsions if after votes were taken they remained a majority. Moreover, they would make reasonable concessions. And if after the vote they became the new minority, they would "maintain unity and discipline." Cannon requested a like pledge from the conferees, but none came.[47] Instead the Burnham group prepared a resolution restating the issues from the minority viewpoint and granting each irreconcilable tendency the right to publicize its views. Trotsky and Cannon were certain now the minority fully intended to split formally. "To impose a factional organ on us is to impose a Norman Thomas all-inclusive party on us, a

perpetual talk-shop, which they know we can't allow," said the Can-
nonites. Through March each side arched its back and declared that
the other prepared a split. Because they were refused equal space in
New International and *Socialist Appeal,* then censored from the *Internal
Bulletin* and now denied a factional organ, the minority "knew" the
Cannonites intended rupture.[48]

Since July 1939 Cannon had prevented discussion. When the pressure of events forced it on him, he hoped to confine debate to one
meeting of the New York local, and supposedly succeeded in damping
controversy in the Minnesota, Michigan, and Ohio locals. The correspondence showed that he labored for a month to prepare his faction
psychologically for split. Unlike Trotsky who wanted to give limited
concessions to keep the party intact, Cannon felt no aversion to separation. Shachtman claimed that Cannon was reconciled to split from
the beginning of the quarrel. "Let's have a cold split, Max," Cannon
reportedly said in the fall of 1939 in a "friendly, cynical, personal discussion between him and one of his comrades on one side in his office
and Burnham and me on the other side." Reluctant to incur the dis-
pleasure of Trotsky, who wanted unity, Cannon later tried to explain
the incident away by saying he was joking, but Shachtman insisted that
on the basis of his twenty-year acquaintance with Cannon he knew
Cannon was serious.

As Shachtman recalled it, because the minority not only challenged
Trotsky's political stand but also challenged the organizational status
quo, Cannon reasoned that his own position would stay secure if they
would go ahead and leave the party. Outside, they would be a minor
nuisance. Inside, they would be "an unendurable thorn in his side."
So he did nothing to avert a split.[49] On the eve of the convention, Cannon circulated his bitterest diatribe.

"The Struggle for a Proletarian Party" recapitulated the events connected with the dispute in the manner in which "War and Bureaucratic
Conservatism" had done this for the minority. By now "petty bourgeois intellectual," "cliquism," "bureaucratism," "conservatism," the
"leader cult," and the rest of the repertory were too familiar phrases,
but Cannon trotted them out again describing "intellectualist insurrection" in a tiresome eighty-two-page recital calculated (in case letters,
speeches, and the *Internal Bulletin* had failed) to win the last hesitant
few to his position.[50]

The minority leaders participated fully in the April convention, watching their resolution for a factional organ go down in defeat. In the final session four resolutions passed. One, a lengthy document contrived to instruct the dissenters, reaffirmed democratic centralism and set forth membership duties: to yield loyalty, labor, and material resources to the party's ongoing task. Final paragraphs proclaimed the right to regimentation of party discussions and prescribed expulsion for anyone reviving a matter closed by majority decision. A second resolution warned that the factional organ demanded by the minority would make the Socialist Worker party an all-inclusive party. The Cannonites must keep the helm or the party would go under, pulled down by enemy agents and infiltrators. Commands followed threats. The particularly corruptible student comrades must be proletarianized. Members must get jobs at once in factories and mills and integrate themselves into "unions and workers' mass organizations and unemployed leagues." Such orders revealed the hysterical majority's incredible naïveté, one source of the incurable frailty of radical movements in America, for, continuing, the resolution explained that these actions were mandatory because "the working class is the only class in modern society that is progressive and truly revolutionary. Only the working class is capable of saving humanity from barbarism." After making this sweeping sociological pronouncement, the resolution offered dissenters either the carrot of revolutionary camaraderie or the stick of expulsion.

A third resolution rejected "the attempt of the petty-bourgeois minority to impose its will" in the matter of a factional publication, and ordered expulsion of members caught violating the decision, even expulsion of entire units ignoring the order to eject disobedient individuals. A final one reiterated the pledge Cannon had wired to the minority conference, offering seats on the political committee, space in *New International,* and joint editorship of the *Internal Bulletin,* all concessions for party harmony. As a last admonition (assuming the "carrot" would be declined) the resolution officially "closed" the discussion on organization and warned members to honor strictest discipline. The vote upheld the majority, 55-31. As Cannon phrased it, the minority was forced to accept the decisions "or go on their way and unfurl their own banner."[51]

The convention over, Shachtman, Burnham, and Abern still remained in the party. No one had so much as raised the Russian, or "political," question. No one debated the validity of the "third camp" idea, or the existence of a new bureaucratic class in Russia, or whether or not Russia was imperialist. The political issues had been totally eclipsed by this, the question of leadership power versus membership rights. Yet the nature of Russia and the onset of war had triggered the crisis. The Russian question had simply forced the subterranean currents of discontent to the surface. Cannon said the minority had succumbed to the bourgeois environment. He may have been right. Burnham believed he influenced the others and he had been first, after all, to question several hallowed tenets. Shachtman conceded that Burnham had swayed him, and George Novack, who remained with Cannon, reflected that Burnham unquestionably led the minority faction.[52] After half-a-year's dispute that rose to higher and higher levels of shrillness and sank to lower and lower levels of invective, the Socialist Workers party—veteran of five years out in the open political arena—now slowly turned around and began its retreat into the shell. The promise of party reform, a faint glow even in its ruddiest moments, flickered erratically from July through March and was at last snuffed out in April.

At a political committee meeting on April 16 the suspensions took place. Far more arbitrary was the majority against his faction, Shachtman recalled, than were the Lovestoneites against the Trotskyists in 1928, for the Lovestoneites allowed their adversaries to defend themselves against real charges at a real trial. Now there were no charges and no trial. The minority faced two short motions at the meeting. The first declared that if the minority did not vote for the two motions, all of them would be out of the party. The second motion ("fantastic," said Shachtman) provided that if the minority did not vote for the first motion, they would be out.

> We abstained from voting, and we were promptly expelled. I recall Cannon took a look at his watch, turned to his friends at that time and said, "Three minutes." He was proud of the fact that the whole split had taken only three minutes to carry through.[53]

Technically the minority remained in the party but under suspension until they should mend their ways. On April 20, 1940, in the *Socialist Appeal,* the national committee explained that the act was taken "to protect the party against disruption." *Fourth International* on May 19 endorsed suspension (repeating the official stand on the nature of the Soviet state and Bolshevik organization) and recommended a month's time for the suspended members to reconsider, signify acceptance of convention decisions, and be reinstated as party members in good standing. Otherwise, unconditional expulsion would be imposed. By September several faction members had taken that course, and more would return yet later. But the theoretical leaders had removed themselves even further from the Cannonites by that time, and so were expelled officially at the plenum held that month in Chicago.[54]

Cannon came perilously close to believing he and he alone had saved the proletarian party from ruin. It had been necessary to throw out the corrupting petty bourgeois intellectuals. And he engineered the ouster without the full sanction of Trotsky. Far from deciding terms from afar, when the issue was power in the American party Trotsky was a child in the hands of Cannon. C. L. R. James, expelled with the minority, agreed that Cannon played the decisive role. In James's estimation Trotsky was politically inept no matter with whom he tangled. In this instance Trotsky's authority and energy were unscrupulously used for an aim Trotsky did not have in mind. "When he recognized what was happening, it was too late," James ruminated.[55] Shachtman concurred. True, Cannon's criticism of the Burnham group came from Trotsky whose arguments he "repeated without change" when they concerned the Russian question. But on the organizational matter, Cannon had his own viewpoint founded in part on old antipathies and "he followed that point of view to the end," ignoring Trotsky who did not want the minority hounded out of the party. He "didn't want to drive [Shachtman] out of the Trotskyist movement, or Abern, or even Burnham."[56] But because Cannon was present and at the helm and Trotsky was miles away, Cannon's plans succeeded.

The Socialist Workers party split "right down the middle, fifty-fifty," the former minority faction taking 40 percent of the membership, including prominent intellectuals and 80 percent of the Young People's Socialist League. Before split, membership was variously reported as around 800 to 1,000 "hard core faithful." Afterward the saving remnant of the proletarian party was tiny indeed, even though Hansen recorded a 25 percent increase six months later.[57] In 1941 this minuscule band temporarily was to lose eighteen leaders, tried, convicted, and imprisoned under the Smith Act.

Shachtman and Burnham immediately formed the new "Workers party" and considered themselves Trotskyists despite the withdrawal of Trotsky's blessing. Cannonites scornfully branded them "a petty-bourgeois, semi-pacifist sect." For one of their organs they revived *Labor Action* and for the other, they merely continued publishing under the same title, *New International,* of which both had been editors anyway. Shachtman avoided explaining how this came about, but the Socialist Workers party national committee charged that they stole *New International,* usurped and appropriated it for revenge and made it a counterfeit sheet, devoid of the bolshevik-leninist stamp. Although the journal legally belonged with the Cannon party, because its name was sullied the Socialist Workers party washed its hands of it and embarked with a "clean banner." Fittingly, they chose the title *Fourth International.* For a time subscribers to *New International* received the two publications, because both circulation managers honored unexpired subscriptions.[58]

For eight years the Workers party kept going but without the presence of James Burnham who, one month after its founding, renounced Marxism altogether. Then, in 1948 concluding that to consider themselves a party was self-deception, the comrades renamed themselves the Independent Socialist League, keeping their fortnightly and their quarterly. In 1958 every one of the "Shachtmanites" joined the Socialist party, where, Shachtman reported in 1962, all "are to be found to this day."[59]

Loss of the Leader

As an exile for twelve years, Trotsky was hounded, despised, feared, and accused of collusion with the fascists by the Stalinist government to discredit him "in the eyes of the world proletariat." Before being granted asylum in Mexico, he shuttled from his native Russia through Turkestan, Turkey, France, and Norway.[60] Fate was to give Trotsky three and a half years in Mexico, but those would be no more serene than had been the preceding ones.[61]

He knew he was targeted for extermination. His son at age thirty-two died mysteriously in France in 1938. Infuriated, then saddened, at length mellowed by word of the death, he proceeded to transform his

living quarters into a veritable fortress manned around the clock by
sentries. It was in the line of this duty that twenty-year-old Joseph
Hansen came to Coyoacan in early 1940.[62] As a Cannonite, Hansen
doubtless described for Trotsky the crisis in the Socialist Workers party
skewed on the side of the majority and perhaps sparked Trotsky's bitter
diatribes against Burnham, Shachtman, and Abern. Hansen's personal
responsibility (if he bore any) for the ensuing rupture cannot be gauged.
But whatever his role in that affair, he performed the inestimable service
of recording in *Fourth International* the chonology of events leading to
the assassination leaving for posterity the only connected, continuous
account.

Communist papers campaigned to deport Trotsky as "an enemy of
Mexico," as an "espionage agent in their midst in the service of Wall
Street." Almost a recluse, he, Natalya, and his grandson made occasional
surreptitious motor tours of the Mexican countryside, but the pleasure
was marred by ever-present armed guards. One of his last letters, to
Charles Curtis in Los Angeles, mentioned that he had just received a
bullet-proof vest and a "wonderful siren."[63] Aside from a few diversions,
he eked out his days behind twenty-foot walls in political conversations
with a stream of carefully screened visitors and in writing, his chief labor.

One early morning in May 1940 this regimen was violently interrupted
when intruders scaled the wall and riddled his bedroom with bullets, then
bombed his grandson's bedroom. The Trotskys eluded death this time,
but they knew it would happen again. Police arrested the terrorists in
two weeks, with leads supplied by Trotsky. Two men on the staff of
the Communist journal *Future,* David Alfaro Siqueiros and Lombardo
Toledano, dressed as police, had led the raid. The sentry on duty,
Robert Sheldon Harte, had granted the disguised men their entry. Several days after their apprehension, police found Harte's body in a shal-
low grave near the home of Siqueiros's friend.

Did Harte entirely innocently open the gate to Siqueiros? Was an
organization behind his first assassination attempt? Was it self-assault
planned by Trotsky, as Toledano charged before his arrest? The Communist party denied complicity. One account protested that Harte, a
Communist turn-coat newly arrived from Russia, had been paid a fabu-
lous sum by an unknown malefactor to carry out the betrayal. Another
portrayed him as a disenchanted Trotskyist.[64] Neither bears scrutiny,
for a lone conspirator could hardly have gathered together twenty-five

men for the nefarious errand. Harte probably remained either a loyal Communist carrying out his assignment only to be disposed of ingloriously as potential tale bearer at its conclusion, or a loyal Trotskyist, a novitiate sentry opening the gate in all innocence.

The idea of Harte's complicity is interesting here for not only was he a member of the executive committee of Local New York but he was selected for guard duty in Mexico because of his trustworthiness. Only twenty-four years old and scion of a wealthy New York family, he said a rally against the German-American Bundists in Madison Square Garden first lured him to the Socialist Workers party. Trotsky hotly denied rumors that Harte secretly associated with Stalinists; despite rumors, indeed perhaps because of them and as if to prove them false, the Socialist Workers party sent him to Trotsky's side. Their official stand in the 1970s held absolutely to a belief in his fidelity and innocence. Trotsky affixed a plaque in Harte's memory in one of the fortified towers constructed to thwart a second assassination attempt. But police investigation suggested Harte's involvement. Later Natalya Trotsky talking with Shachtman showed that she had wavered and conceded Harte's likely collusion with Siqueiros, precisely for what reason she could not say in the absence of clear evidence.[65]

Danger lurked inside the Socialist Workers party but it was not (as Trotsky believed) the "petty-bourgeois minority." It was, and Trotsky suspected this too, infiltration by enemies bent on destroying its leader. Several years before, the Communist party patiently inaugurated action to that end quite apart from Siqueiros's scheme. Louis Budenz recorded the outline of events. First, the party "sent" a woman member into the Chicago branch of the Socialist party where she won the trust of her Trotskyist comrades. It then sent her to New York, obtaining a job for her with a Stalinist, a woman doctor, "to help her explain peculiar hours and regular income." Befriending Cannon's wife, Rose Karsner, she soon "had the full run of the Trotskyite offices" from which she supplied the Soviet secret police with copies of all correspondence with Trotsky in Mexico and with other Trotskyists throughout the world. The Communist party then placed Ruby Weil in the Trotskyist party to befriend and gain the confidence of the three Agelof sisters of New York. Ruth Agelof served as Trotsky's secretary in Mexico; Sylvia, a former social worker, was a courier to Trotskyists in Canada, Europe, and Mexico; Hilda, working in the New York local, was available for Weil's attentions.

Ruby Weil allegedly performed her errand ignorant of its full implications. Budenz claimed she thought her effort was to stop Trotskyist infiltration into Russia and thus prevent Stalin's assassination. Accompanying Sylvia Agelof to Paris to the founding conference of the fourth international in September 1938, Weil there introduced Agelof to a spurious "Count Jacques Mornard" (alias for Ramon Mercador). Mercador had been primed for his role.[66]

Agelof and Mercador traveled to Mexico together in late 1939, but now Mercador had a new alias, Frank Jacson. Jacson posed as a party sympathizer so, of course, Agelof gained him entry to Trotsky's household. Hansen recollected that he "appeared nervous, prematurely aged," and that he could not carry on a sustained political conversation. His interest in party affairs soared during the struggle that ended in schism in April 1940. After acquainting himself with the issues, Jacson scribbled out a rough draft for an article and gave it on August 17 to Trotsky for criticism. Hansen claimed Trotsky confided to Natalya and his comrades that it was poor, but he hated to discourage the man.[67]

Jacson (Mercador) returned on August 20 with the finished essay, "The Third Camp and the Popular Front." Shachtman noted, "It's really depressing to recall that the article was directed against us, the minority . . . denouncing us poor devils . . . ."[68] But these matters were still uppermost in Trotsky's mind; in fact, these final days he spent dictating an article in response to one by Dwight Macdonald. Arriving about 5 P.M., "very, very nervous," Natalya Trotsky recalled, Jacson (Mercador) met Trotsky and they entered the study. As Trotsky read the article, the assassin drew the woodsman's axe from his overcoat and with it struck Trotsky's skull, then his face.

At first the wounds appeared superficial. Actually Trotsky lived twenty-two hours, talking for two-and-a-half of them, admonishing that Jacson should be forced to "speak out." But the axe had destroyed much brain tissue. Trotsky dictated his last comments in a failing voice to Hansen: "I am sure of the victory of the Fourth International . . . . Go forward."[69] And if part of the account of the last hours slides over into apocrypha, it is perhaps unimportant, for the man has become something of a legend anyway.

On August 22 a funeral was held according to Mexican custom; Al Goldman, Grandizio Muniz, and another Spanish-speaking comrade delivered the eulogies. But the remains were not interred until August 27 pending the outcome of a request to the United States government to allow the body to be taken to New York for a funeral service. It was refused.

Mercador's trial stretched out over nearly two years, one ruse after another devised for delay. He first posed as a disillusioned Trotskyist, unhappy when ordered to Russia on a mission of sabotage and murder. He next pleaded self-defense, charging that the volatile Trotsky struck at him in a rage. But he was convicted, and Shachtman believed his connection with the Soviet secret police was substantiated because when released from prison after the Fidel Castro revolution in Cuba he proceeded to Havana by boat there to be met at the dock by Che Guevara, Fidel Castro's chief lieutenant.[70]

The details of assassination were included here for two reasons. First, members of the American Trotskyist unit were closely involved as sentries, guards, secretaries, even conspirators in Mexico, one being an unwitting accomplice of the assassin. The fact that conspirators and assassins' accomplices could proceed undetected reveals the very turbulent, hence vulnerable position of the movement during those years of fusion, fragmentation, and schism, and reveals Trotsky's pathetic yearning to hold fast to his small following and entice more into his fold.

Second, Trotsky's death brings the curtain down with finality on one phase of his movement in America. He believed the founding conference of the fourth international in 1938 had inaugurated a glorious new era for the Communist opposition. Instead it presaged by only two years its retreat, its step backward to become once more a propaganda sect, but a far less promising and interesting one than it had been from 1928 to 1934. Its writers, its theoretical leadership, most of those with a flair for political analysis, left the party in April 1940; then with Trotsky's assassination in August, the remaining core lost its principal touchstone, the arch-theoretician of the movement.

Trotsky of course anticipated the final blow. Apparently Stalin thought his existence was a growing menace to his regime in the face of European war. Trotsky simply knew too much. For one thing, the Dies Committee in October, 1939 had invited him to testify before it, and he had accepted. True, before the scheduled date of appearance,

November 12, because the state department refused Trotsky a visa the committee first postponed, then rescinded, the invitation. Nonetheless J. B. Matthews, chief investigator, planned a trip to Mexico to take a deposition from him, and of course Trotsky intended to disclose what he knew of the Soviet secret police's control of world Communist parties. For another thing, Trotsky was putting together his defense against libel charges brought by the Communist party of Mexico, a further opportunity to bring to light the collection of affidavits and other records he had collected for years on the secret police's operations. A third possible reason was his continuing labor, in its final stages, on a biography of Joseph Stalin—still another potential vehicle for revelations. Trotsky did literally die for his political views, remarked Mary McCarthy. His views, hated on both sides of the spectrum, coupled with his theoretical genius and magnetism, destined him for martyrdom. His very amiability and serenity came "as a last straw" to the killer.[71]

In 1976 a group of English Trotskyists in the London-based Workers Revolutionary League leveled charges against Joseph Hansen and George Novack ("desperate men") for laxity in defending Trotsky's person, and for likely complicity with Harte and the Soviet secret police. Hansen and Novack declined to answer the far-fetched indictment.[72] Probably for years ahead questions will be raised about Trotsky's death, for mystery still surrounds several details.

After August 20, 1940, the big question was whether Trotskyism would survive the death of Trotsky. Certainly the American Trotskyists had taken two stunning blows. Despite the stolidity and intransigence the Socialist Workers party displayed in weathering the Smith Act trial and convictions of 1941, and its flurries of trade union activity from 1942 to 1947, the theoretical sterility and blunting of political alertness that took place in 1940 was not made good until, perhaps, the late 1960s with the party's revived attraction and the emergence of a new theoretical generation. But that is another story.

9

Trotskyists and the Courts

Because they espoused opinions at odds with approved ideology, American Trotskyists found themselves tangled in the skeins of legalisms and courts over their right to free speech, press, and association. Constitutional rights plus the tenuous, imprecise "clear and present danger" doctrine were contravened in indictments founded on state and federal laws enacted to stifle dissent. Two cases in particular assumed sensational proportions. The first case was in California and involved charges brought under the Criminal Syndicalism Act of 1919. The second drew national notice because it was the first case brought against radicals under the federal Alien and Sedition Law (the Smith Act) of 1940. Both are germane to this essay for they brought Trotskyists and their attorneys face to face with contradictions in the American legal system, with "middle-American" attitudes, with financial-industrial communities intent on weeding out threats to the status quo, and in the second, with a presidential administration shoring up for worldwide military involvement.

For both, Trotskyists mustered all their legal resources even though in the California case only one Trotskyist among sixteen Communists was under indictment. The Nonpartisan Labor Defense publicized the cases with pamphlets and lectures condemning the judicial system, solicited funds through defense committees and rallies, and supplied bail monies and attorneys' fees. The indefatigible Al Goldman presented defense arguments based on Marxism-Leninism, leaving it to other attorneys to raise the "clear and present danger" and First Amendment issues. In both cases, Goldman fought counts of seditious conspiracy to overthrow the government and he argued vigorously, sometimes with cunning, but unsuccessfully. The public mood, manipulated to be sure, tipped the scales against radicals on trial. But then Goldman had essayed a socialist defense in capitalist courts, neglecting the very capitalist arguments devised to protect the right of dissent.

Trotskyists knew they needed a new legal defense organization when the Communist party's International Labor Defense (ILD)—which Cannon and Abern had served loyally—refused after 1929 to concern itself with their legal battles. The case which brought this truth into focus occurred in Philadelphia in 1931.

A 1931 summer issue of the *Militant* quoted the American Civil Liberties Union (ACLU) as noting that the previous year had been "a tough year for free speech under the stars and stripes," for there were six times more prosecutions in 1930 than in 1928.[1] The mood carried over into 1931. In Pennsylvania the Flynn Act made illegal any organization with a communist program, clearly proscribing the Communist League of America. Police booked two members, Bernard Morgenstern and Leon Goodman, early in 1931 for handing out tracts announcing a scheduled "Unemployment Day" demonstration, and the pair were indicted. Calling them "counterrevolutionists," the ILD denied them legal aid. An ACLU attorney defended them unsuccessfully, so Morgenstern and Goodman had to serve out their sentences.[2]

The progress (and failure) of the Morgenstern-Goodman case with the ILD rebuff proved that the CLA must produce its own defense arm and its own Trotskyist attorney. In 1933 the Nonpartisan Labor Defense (NPLD) began to function. A year later Al Goldman had joined the Muste party and was defending Musteite Norman Mini in the California criminal syndicalism case. By early 1935 and the trial opening, fusion between Musteites and Trotskyists had taken place. The Trotskyists had their lawyer.

The Norman Mini Case

Emboldened by New Deal legislation and smarting under the depression economy, radical labor organizers relentlessly recruited and called walkouts making 1934 a sensational year in labor annals. In the California agri-business fields, the Communist party in 1930 had created a dual union enrolling Mexicans, Filipinos, Puerto Ricans, Japanese, Chinese, and poor Southern whites. By 1934, flushed with successes won in strike actions from the Imperial to the Sacramento valleys, it had assumed a formal structure and the name, the Cannery and Agricultural Workers Industrial Union (CAWIU). Its leadership of idealistic youth, few of them field or cannery workers, showed considerable courage in facing up to the resistance tactics of American Legionnaires, local police, and vigilantes.[3] Raids and arrests took place periodically. Sometimes local labor boards intervened. To keep peace in the fields at harvest time, to assure their supply of cheap temporary labor, and to provide unity and strength in resisting strike leaders, growers organized in 1933 the "Associated Farmers," financial backing allegedly supplied by bankers, oilmen, and shippers who very well knew all business suffered when crops did not get harvested.[4] At their service as a tool to halt organization of itinerant workers and frustrate the IWW lay the Criminal Syndicalism Law of 1919 which made it a criminal offense to advocate or organize for syndicalist activities or to belong to a group with syndicalist aims. Other states passed similar laws. The "clear and present danger" doctrine was generally ignored in their phrasing; indeed, they modified "clear and present danger" by outlawing words and opinions with an assumed "bad tendency" apart from the overt act.

Important for the California law had been the resolution of the Anita Whitney case. California convicted Whitney in 1919 for aiding IWW workers and belonging to the Communist Labor party, and state courts twice upheld the conviction. In 1927 the U.S. Supreme Court upheld it, and maintained too the constitutionality of the California law, deciding it did not violate the due process and equal protection clauses of the Fourteenth Amendment. This law, then, validated arrests that removed "agitators" from the countryside at harvest time.[5]

During the commotion over the highly publicized San Francisco longshoremen's strike in late July 1934, police swooped down on Communist party headquarters in Sacramento arresting union leaders on vagrancy charges, and seized literature for "study." Arrested at the same time was Norman Mini, a former Communist party member and presently in the Musteite American Workers party. After the vagrancy trial, eighteen had criminal syndicalism charges entered against them, Mini still with the accused because he had been an active organizer in the fields.[6] By the time the trial opened in January 1935, the Musteites had merged with the Trotskyists; Mini therefore belonged to the new fusion "Workers party," the sole defendant not in the Communist party.

The NPLD supplied bail, formed a special defense committee, and sent Al Goldman out from Chicago to defend Mini. The Communist party attorney, the volatile Leo Gallagher, defended the remaining accused. Intending to make of the courtroom an arena for propaganda, Goldman tried when Mini took the stand to steer him into expounding communist doctrine. Despite state objections, during the course of the trial Mini was able to discuss "class struggle," insisting several times that Marxism does not advocate, it simply predicts, force and violence when the ruling class refuses to yield power peaceably.[7] A parade of defense witnesses followed Mini, saying essentially the same thing: communism predicts, it does not advocate. Strike leaders did not provoke violence. They sought to better the lot of the farm worker through strikes, and violence only occurred when police came to break up this lawful activity.[8]

Jeering and applause sometimes came from onlookers. Newsmen were constantly in evidence. Adding to the histrionics Gallagher and prosecuting attorney Neal McAllister shouted loudly at each other, with Gallagher often denouncing capitalist injustice and shaking his fist at the jury. Goldman tried to separate his defense from Gallagher's, aware that the ILD lawyer's behavior further alienated an already antagonistic white middle-class jury.[9] During the trial, rumor spread that Communists were camping in the hills near San Jose waiting for word from New York to march on Sacramento; and Max Eastman, in town briefly, addressed some clubwomen and in the course of his remarks expressed sympathy for the defendants, drawing the ire of the audience. To newsmen he lamented the hysteria gripping Sacramento.[10]

After 118 ballots, *Bee* headlines announced, "Eight Reds Are Convicted." Although the jury found all defendants not guilty of advocating criminal syndicalism, it found eight guilty of organizing and joining an organization put together "to advocate, teach, or aid and abet criminal syndicalism." The jury ignored the contradiction inherent in the verdict. All the defendants admitted membership in a party defined as organized for overthrow, yet only eight were found guilty of advocating overthrow! "The jury was insane. If any of us were guilty, all were," announced one.[11]

In 1937 the Third District Appellate Court noted the contradiction and reversed the decision, acquitting the defendants on all counts.[12] But the problems at issue remained unsettled: whether or not there was immediate danger of violence looking toward overthrow. No one mentioned either the Holmes "clear and present danger" doctrine or the later Holmes and Brandeis revision of it substituting "imminent danger" for "present danger," yet the U.S. Supreme Court on the Whitney case had inextricably linked them with the California Criminal Syndicalism Law.

Whether or not the Communist party advocated force and violence was at issue, too, raising the question: Do individual Communists advocate force and violence? Defense lawyers and witnesses, sundered in sectarian distrust, presented a solid front on this matter. Al Goldman bore in on the point with great urgency. But the appeals court, seeing the paradox in the verdict, rejected the party's claim that it did not "advocate." The court simply noted that the accused, found guilty of joining a party that (it was charged) "advocated" could hardly be acquitted of personally advocating it as they had been. The court accordingly wiped the slate clean.[13]

By this time, however, the California agriworkers union had disbanded, its labors nullified. The whole proceeding had the effect of putting very able strike leaders on ice for three years. It proved that when threatened with higher labor costs, businessmen acting in concert can mobilize an entire community in their behalf. The trial showed too how little rival radical sects can be counted on to cooperate. It showed how their spokesmen can alienate a middle-class jury with their compulsive use of jargon and frank articulation of political faith—exactly as they were to do in the Minneapolis trial in 1941. And for the first time, at Sacramento Trotskyists had mustered for combat their defense resources: the NPLD and the talents of Al Goldman.

The Minneapolis Smith Act Trial

By 1940 many of the state criminal syndicalism laws had been moderated or repealed. The Alien Registration Act, or Smith Act, which became operative in 1940 became in effect the federal criminal syndicalism law sought in the early 1920s. On June 29, 1940, it was signed into law. One year later the Federal Bureau of Investigation (FBI) raided

Socialist Workers party headquarters in Minneapolis and the story of
the subsequent trial and conviction of twenty-eight Trotskyist leaders
illuminates a less familiar facet of the Roosevelt years and reveals that
the president followed a pattern his predecessors established when beset by similar problems.

In the Smith Act were provisions requiring aliens over age fourteen
to register and be fingerprinted; criminals and subversives to be deported; and teaching and advocating the overthrow of the U.S. government by force and violence to be considered a criminal offense. One
more made it illegal to publish and distribute literature advising servicemen to disobey regulations or to advocate their disloyalty. The ven-
erable "clear and present danger" doctrine, accepted by the Supreme
Court in 1919 as a standard for determining the validity of a restriction
on freedom of expression when the Court backed unanimously Holmes's
decision, had been transmogrified by the Smith Act to "clear and probable" danger. The courts had to decide if a danger existed at a particular time. The American Civil Liberties Union (ACLU) opposed the
Smith Act and urged that such a determination is a "matter of fact"
for jury decision, and is not properly a "matter of law."[14]

While Farrell Dobbs was building the Central States Drivers' Council
(a network of Teamster locals covering eleven states), Europe plunged
into war and United States-Japanese hostilities deepened. President
Roosevelt wished to rely on Dan Tobin, general president of the International Brotherhood of Teamsters, AFL, as his labor lieutenant in the
current recession with its labor unrest. He needed Tobin's fealty, too,
during preparation for war, for, as Dobbs phrased it, Tobin was a labor
leader able to "dragoon workers into the ranks of the imperialist army
for World War II."[15] Tobin's rapprochement with the Democratic administration necessarily brought him into confrontation with Teamster
radicals, chiefly Trotskyists, in Minneapolis for the Trotskyists remained
staunchly antiwar. Dobbs insisted Trotskyists tried to avoid unnecessary
friction with Tobin, but conflict appeared inevitable as "reactionaries
and opportunists were becoming emboldened."[16] The Associated Industries, a new employers' group, paralleled the earlier Citizens' Alliance.
At a lower socioeconomic level, Dudley Pelley's Silver Shirts, a chauvin-
istic, antilabor, paramilitary organization of national scope but numeri-
cally small, became active in the Twin Cities. The two allegedly collaborated in vigilante actions against "reds" and strikers. To protect union

and party offices and the safety of their speakers, Local 544 formed the Union Defense Guard in 1938, and in 1940 just as quickly disbanded it as the Silver Shirt menace subsided. All the while, members of Local 544 stood loyally behind their Trotskyist leaders, reconfirming them in office time after time, even in the face of outside insistence that they be removed for radicalism, hence unfitness.[17]

Stepping up the intensity of the campaign for national unity and reflecting a general fear of radicals, local and national governments formulated a welter of measures to smother dissent. The Smith Act was one of these. Some state laws provided stiff sentences for "hindering national defense"; one allowed vigilantes to function almost immune from penalty. Congressman Jerry Voorhis of California introduced a bill requiring unions to file officers' names, addresses of branches and meeting halls, times of meetings, and names of contributors to their unions—legislation harmless in itself but subject to repressive application. The *Militant* reported that American Legionnaires urged firing of foreign-born workers, and that Attorney General Robert Jackson before moving to the Supreme Court had proposed placing undeportable aliens in concentration camps. The FBI enjoyed huge appropriations in 1941, and the Dies Committee received $150,000 early that year. (Representative Martin Dies of Texas chaired a freshly created House Committee on Un-American Activities charged with the duty of ferreting out both fascist and "red" subversives.) A wiretap bill was defeated by only two votes. The Federal Trade Commission bared its teeth and moved against certain unions for "conspiring in restraint of trade." The ACLU asserted that at no time in twenty years had it been faced with such an array of repressive measures.[18]

The explanation was that United States involvement in war was imminent; strikes and antiwar expression, useful in placid times, must be curtailed to facilitate defense preparations. As presented to the public, the campaign was waged to prevent radical aliens from disrupting the American way of life. When patriotism was invoked, average citizens agreed readily enough that crackdown was in order.

Tobin invoked patriotism in a move to wrest union control from the Trotskyist Teamster leaders. Long smoldering over his inability to control midwestern drivers, Tobin's ire was inflamed during the Teamster convention of September 1940 when Minneapolis Local 544 led

the successful opposition to his proposed constitutional amendment
that would have empowered him to enforce arbitration on every local.
The Minneapolis local fought Tobin's drive for a personal salary hike as
well, but Tobin got his raise. In the spring of 1941 after the defeat of
Tobin's candidates in the local's elections, he called a hearing before
Teamster officers in Chicago where union leaders answered charges of
radicalism. Vincent Ray Dunne ably fended off this assault. Tobin
attacked next in the Teamster press, vowing to rid the brotherhood of
Trotskyists.[19] At an executive board meeting in June, conceding that
Trotskyists had built the union to its present imposing membership,
Tobin insisted that they nevertheless be purged; the brotherhood must
rid itself of the blemish of radicalism. He demanded that the leaders of
544 resign and request him to send in to run the union a receiver with
full expulsion power. Of course, 544 leaders refused. No one expected
their next move. First they made ready a strike for the local, because
employers declined to renew the contracts that expired June 1 in retaliation for the local's refusal to cooperate with Tobin and make possible the ejection of radicals from its leadership. In accordance with a
recent Minnesota law, the local sent ten-day strike notices to the state
labor office. Two days later, the 4,000 members of the local voted to
separate from the Teamsters and affiliate with Denny Lewis's Motor
Transport and Allied Workers' Industrial Union, CIO. Soon they were
followed by a plethora of drivers' groups in the Midwest.[20]

Tobin then appealed to Roosevelt and reported the series of events
to the Department of Justice. Francis Biddle, acting attorney general,
anxious to receive a regular appointment, jumped into action. A sweeping raid in the early evening hours of June 27 on Socialist Workers party
headquarters in both the Twin Cities brought arrests of leaders and gar-
nered bushels of "seditious" literature such as the *Communist Manifesto*
and other titles easily available at local libraries. On July 15 a federal
grand jury convening in St. Paul, and according to the *Militant* constituted of men and women from rural counties, indicted twenty-nine
Trotskyists on charges of "seditious conspiracy."[21] There were two
counts. The first was based on an 1861 statute directed against the
Confederacy making it a federal crime to commit overt acts against the
state. In applying it to the Minneapolis case, the grand jury accused the
Union Defense Guard of concealing arms and ammunition with which
to overthrow the government by force and violence. The second count,

based on five provisions of the Smith Act, charged advocating overthrow by publishing and disseminating literature, by creating organizations, then joining them, to foster overthrow; and charges also inculcat-
ing disloyalty among servicemen.[22]

A few days earlier authorities had seized Karl Skoglund and held him
for deportation. Miles Dunne and Kelly Postal faced a separate indictment handed down by the Hennepin County grand jury on charges of
embezzling funds from Tobin's union. In all, sixty charges were filed.[23]
Trotsky's influence over the 544 leadership did not go unnoticed in the
indictment; one paragraph read:

> The said defendants and their co-conspirators would, and they did,
> accept as the ideal formula for the carrying out of their said ob-
> jectives the Russian Revolution of 1917, whereby the then exist-
> ing Government of Russia was overthrown by force and violence,
> and the principles, teachings, writings, counsel and advice of the
> leaders of that revolution, chiefly of V. I. Lenin and Leon Trotsky,
> would be, and they were, looked to, relied on, followed and held
> out to others as catechisms and textbooks directing the manner
> and means by which the aforesaid aim of the defendants could,
> and would be, accomplished; and accordingly, certain of the de-
> fendants would, and they did, go from the City of Minneapolis,
> State and District of Minnesota, and from other cities in the United
> States to Mexico City, Mexico, there to advise with and to receive
> the advice, counsel, guidance, and directions of the said Leon
> Trotsky.[24]

Labor groups reacted vigorously, the CIO regarding the indictments as
a pointed affront. Biddle hoped to prove the Union Defense Guard was
preparing for violent overthrow of the government. He did not succeed,
and in any event, they had disbanded the previous year. While writing
his memoirs in the 1960s Biddle claimed he believed the Smith Act and
the prosecutions under it were unconstitutional, and he had hoped to
have the Supreme Court confirm his opinion. Was he trying to refurbish
his reputation as a liberal? When the high court did not review the case,
he later said he regretted authorizing the prosecution. Of course, he did
receive the full attorney generalship.[25]

According to the *Militant,* Judge Matthew Joyce picked the jury from among personal friends of court officers who lived in the thirty-three counties of the Eighth Federal District. The judge alone could ask questions as prospective jurors were queried, so Goldman had to work through him; of course the judge could pick and choose from the questions submitted, and he tended to ignore most of Goldman's. The persons chosen included a working-class housewife, a farm laborer, two bankers, a publisher, and the remainder were businessmen. Judge Joyce refused to make public the list of veniremen from whom the jury was selected, but did disclose the voting preference of the jury as constituted: six Republicans, two Democrats, and four "independent voters."

On October 27, 1941, the first trial under the first federal peacetime sedition law since 1798 began. Victor Anderson, district attorney from St. Paul, opened for the prosecution with a two-hour speech (said the *Militant*). When Goldman's turn came, he told the jury they would soon be familiar with Socialist Workers party views and hopefully would grant the party its First Amendment right to propagate those views.[26] As at Sacramento, witnesses produced much ludicrous evidence. For example, Louis Adamic's book *Dynamite!,* far from being a manual for terrorists (as insinuated), was shown to be against violence. The *Communist Manifesto,* another trial exhibit, was thought valid evidence because the Socialist Workers party bookstore stocked it, because it had been basis for discussion at party meetings, and because an organizer explained its contents to one witness. However, the *Manifesto* was also found in local libraries and on University of Minnesota reading lists.

A witness brandished as a trial exhibit the ground plan of Minneapolis Socialist Workers party headquarters, solemnly declaring it was the plan he had helped FBI agents draw up before the trial. Equally solemnly, Judge Joyce upheld the "plan" as evidence. On the fifth day a witness read minutes of a local branch meeting where party anthems were sung, then gravely read into the record the lyrics of *Solidarity Forever, The Workers' Flag,* and the *Internationale.* On the sixth day, articles were read into the record, special attention directed to an anti-war statement and a diatribe against American courts.

In some ways the prosecution's efforts boomeranged. Several government witnesses praised Dobbs's organizing abilities as well as the work of Local 544. It was revealed that Tobin had brought in the FBI, and that the FBI had offered Skoglund citizenship papers if he would testify against the Dunnes. Skoglund had refused.

As at Sacramento, Goldman gave a socialist defense explaining points of doctrine, leaving it to M. J. Meyer, described by Novack as "a very able attorney" and Socialist Worker comrade, to use Constitutional arguments. Exaggerating, Felix Morrow commented, never before had revolutionaries "so deliberately, so systematically defended their revolutionary doctrines, using the courtroom as a forum from which to proclaim their ideas . . . ."[27] (Charles Ruthenberg had made the courtroom a propaganda arena in 1923.) But then, to give what Morrow called a "liberal defense" would have been to denigrate the party publicly. Such a defense would try to show how harmless was a little band of revolutionaries, and in effect would ask, Why bother to prosecute? because the mere thought that the SWP could overthrow the government was "fantastic." Morrow concluded, "We tried instead to make socialist sympathizers out of those jurors."[28] So, consistent with radical practice, the Socialist Workers party naïvely turned the courtroom into a forum to disseminate socialism but, as at Sacramento, with pitifully little effect except to alienate the jurors further.

On November 18, Goldman asked to have the case dismissed because the government had failed to prove the defendants conspired to overthrow the existing order. As for the party's antiwar stand, it was absurd to say that because the party opposed the war it abetted Hitler. The argument "lacks logic and common sense." The Socialist Workers party only tried to educate workers until it could win a majority. But the indictment had cited, too, the party's reverence for the Russian Revolution, so on the stand Cannon trumpeted that the comrades considered it "the greatest event in all history," then reminded the jury "it was not accomplished by force and violence on the part of the working class."

Meyer appealed to the "clear and present danger" test for free speech, referring to earlier decisions of Justices Holmes and Brandeis in the Whitney and Gitlow cases, respectively. Revolutionists have a right to freedom of speech as long as they do not threaten the existence of the state. Only "present conflagration" justified suppression of the rights of press and assembly. Moreover, the Socialist Workers party was not a conspiracy; it acted entirely in the open. Certainly belief in Marxism was no crime. No, he concluded, the prosecution has shown no conspiracy to overthrow the government.[29]

Al Russel, organizer for the Teamsters in Omaha and defendant, recollected a three-way conversation in the men's room. While he, Goldman, and federal prosecuting attorney Henry A. Schweinhaut stood at the urinal, Goldman asked the federal attorney, "How the hell can you put people like that up on the stand to testify that they hid guns in churches? You know that it's absolute nonsense," to which Schweinhaut replied, "I have a job to do; I'm unhappy about it, but I have to prosecute." Russel also recalled that as an eastern Jew he was kept in the background during the trial; "to make the best impression on the jury, they had to have good American types up front."[30]

Were the Trotskyists a serious threat to American institutions? Aware that a system of free speech is successful only when there is the narrowest basis for exceptions, and knowing the difficulty of calculating future effects of free expression with any certainty, Chief Justice Holmes went a step further in the Gitlow case (1925) than he did for Whitney (1927): "If in the long run the beliefs expressed in proletarian dictatorship are destined to be accepted by the dominant forces of the community, the only meaning of free speech is that they should be given their chance and have their way."[31] Justice Hugo Black argued in the later Communist cases that the founding fathers had clearly intended to permit untrammeled freedom of expression. Reviewing the case, Minneapolis ACLU attorneys saw no evidence of any clear and present danger, except, possibly, from the Union Defense Guard which had disbanded anyway. Consequently the ACLU protested that government officials had committed gross improprieties in securing the indictments.[32]

Judge Joyce overruled the acquittal motion, saying he denied the right of Constitutional guarantees to socialists who hoped to change the government. He could not conclude that any group "had the right to write and circulate material seditious and revolutionary in character, or material preaching force and violence against the government to set up an entirely new social order based on the principles of socialism." To defend their actions, Trotskyists simply could not "rush to the protection of the Constitution they would not amend but would absolutely destroy." Finally, the judge compared the Socialist Workers party and the National Socialists in Germany: "Hitler once ran around in a greasy old overcoat and was belittled for his efforts."

Schweinhaut, representing Biddle, repudiated the "clear and present danger" doctrine on the grounds that the Supreme Court had not ac-

cepted it, and insisted the government must prosecute because the Socialist Workers party seriously prepared for the likelihood of overthrow.
Anderson argued,

> Usually in connection with a conspiracy count or charge, it is in-
> cumbent on the prosecuting attorney to establish some overt act,
> some positive step or act done to bring about or in furtherance
> of the conspiracy; but it is the position of the Government in this
> case that the conspiracy itself is made unlawful, and that it will
> not be incumbent upon the government to do any more than to
> show the establishment of the conspiracy.

The prosecution concluded, "The government position is that even
though the defendants may never have done anything about overthrowing the government, the defendants can be punished for advocating its
overthrow."[33]

Despondent over his indictment, Grant Dunne committed suicide before proceedings, leaving twenty-eight to stand trial. Judge Joyce directed a verdict of acquittal for five defendants on the grounds that
they had no in-depth knowledge of party tenets. He ruled against acquittal for the rest. Finding all not guilty on one count, the jury found
eighteen guilty (but recommended leniency) of the five Smith Act offenses. They had urged insubordination in the armed forces; advocated
overthrowing the government by force and violence; printed material
and organized societies to advocate it; and belonged to the societies.
Goldman failed to impress, apparently, with his three-hour harangue on
the differences between "predicting" and "advocating" violence and on
the party preference for peaceful change but prediction that violence
will occur. By jury verdict, therefore, Trotskyists went on record as
encouraging overthrow of the government by force and violence. On
December 8, one day after the Japanese attack on Pearl Harbor, Judge
Joyce sentenced the defendants. The Eighth Circuit Court considered
an appeal. Relying on precedent from the Gitlow case, in October 1943
it conformed the convictions, and the Supreme Court denied *certiorari.*
With considerable party fanfare, on December 31, 1944, the eighteen
began serving their sentences for terms ranging from twelve to sixteen
months.[34]

The outcome pleased a variety of people. Minnesota's Governor
Harold Stassen applauded the action against Trotskyists. Some Teamster
affiliates trickled back to Tobin, who had succeeded in purging Trotskyists and in keeping presidential favor. Communists cheered the convictions. For example, Robert Minor, acting national secretary of the
Communist party during Browder's term in prison, called for a national
front of patriotic Americans against fifth columnists such as the "Trotskyites." Communist editor John Gates later insisted, despite contrary
evidence, that the Communist party disapproved of the prosecution,
but he admitted it did not defend the Trotskyists' civil liberties as it
should have done. In 1952 in *Dennis v. U.S.* the government tried
Communists under the Smith Act, and the Socialist Workers party consistently opposed this prosecution.[35] While the Communist party was
fighting conviction, Irving Abramson, eastern regional representative of
the CIO, believed his organization had good reason to deny support to
Communists. He harked back to the Minneapolis trial: "You were vin-
dictive. You hated the Trotskyites more than you loved civil liberties.
Yes, you were not even decent enough to be 'silent.' You saw the opportunity to get rid of hated political enemies . . . to help the hangman
do his work on the '18' even if your scaffold was the Smith Act."[36]
"The prosecution of the Trotskyites was not merely foolish, but scandalous," said Sidney Hook.[37] Reminiscing in 1963, Max Shachtman
thought of a remark by Rosa Luxembourg: "Freedom is always the
freedom of *andersdenkenden* [thinking other than the accepted view]."[38]

The Mini case had not been a party cause célèbre as had the Smith
Act case. In this one, the federal government arrested the most prominent Socialist Workers party members after the Shachtman split as well
as some lesser figures. The trial provided opportunity for reaffirmation
of party beliefs, and indeed, defendant Cannon's testimony published
as *Socialism on Trial* became a party classic and was later translated into
several languages. "It has remained a handbook of socialist propaganda
ever since," commented Novack. Goldman's final defense speech was
only slightly less revered. Again as at Sacramento the Nonpartisan
Labor Defense with the American Civil Liberties Union put together
defense and appeal committees enlisting the familiar roster of liberals,
but again, to no avail.

The convicted Trotskyists served their terms, and Al Russel grate-
fully recalled that James T. Farrell, still active in behalf of Trotskyists

and on the defense committee, wrote to them every week during their jail stay. The subsequent ACLU investigation disclosed that "the Government injected itself into an interunion controversy in order to promote the interests of the one side which supported the Administration's foreign and domestic policies." Novack in 1973 speaking of the atmosphere of the trial noted the "distortion and falsification of the prosecutors," and the justifiably very "political defense" of the Socialist Workers party "against what was essentially a political prosecution."[39]

* * *

The Sacramento and Minneapolis cases were essentially alike. In both, authorities raided radical headquarters, seized literature as evidence, and arrested leaders. Grand juries indicted the leaders on like charges, in one case under a state law, in the other under a federal law. The defendants in both cases faced the panoply of government prosecutory resources: police, FBI, and district attorneys, while chief executives praised the process. During the two separate trials Defense Attorney Al Goldman made the courtroom a forum to expound socialist theory and so alienated the jurors. In both cases, the government obtained convictions and the public cheered because radicals would be jailed and public safety restored.

The three most important factors both cases bring to light are first, the clear violation of the radicals' civil rights. Authorities arrested and jailed them for promoting views at variance with conventional ideology, therefore believed menacing, and for assembling with others who shared these views. The official response flew in the face of the professed commitment to "freedom." And with Rosa Luxembourg, we must insist that real freedom is the freedom to think otherwise.

But what if the "freedom to think otherwise" and to act on those thoughts portends violent overthrow of the existing order? Because of the natural instinct for self-preservation, a government in the philosophical scheme of things must try to maintain itself. The second factor rises from this consideration. Was there a "clear and present," or even "imminent" or "probable," danger to the existing order in allowing Trotskyists to continue unimpeded? In Sacramento no one raised the issue, and in Minneapolis, when a young defense lawyer did do so, an assistant U.S. attorney general mistakenly, but without challenge, dismissed it as a doctrine "not accepted." Although either ignored (Sacramento) or suppressed (Minneapolis), it lurked beneath the surface through both proceedings from first to last. Politicians and prominent citizens saw these radical organizers as a clear and probable, even a present, danger and could amass the facilities to convince the public that this was so.

The third, most significant, factor is the question of the labor movement. Did it pose a threat to the social order if not carefully checked? Marxist theory, touted as a philosophy of the underdog, assigns the laborer a prominent role in the redemption of society. Marxist parties, therefore, expected comrades to instruct workers in their redeeming role and to lead them to action to improve their present lot. When Communist organizers in California succeeded in this they upset the "stability" of the state, dependent as it was on cheap harvesting of crops. The labor question was of first importance in the Norman Mini case.

So was it in the Smith Act case. Trotskyists, successfully organizing and leading strikes in the industrial Midwest, refusing to take directions from a "labor lieutenant," menaced industry as it readied for the demands of war production.

To restore order (however exploitative) to the fields of California and to ensure the orderly progress of industrial retooling and war production without hazard of labor walkouts, authorities believed radical leaders had to be put away. "Sedition" was simply the facade. The tenet of Marxist philosophy central to both cases was the class struggle concept, which made conscientious radicals disruptors of the industrial system.

Epilogue

Any effort to write the postscript to the story of the Trotskyist movement to 1941 must try to fill the chinks in the main body of the narrative: topics omitted entirely or given only passing reference. The slighted topics fall in five categories: minorities, "literary Trotskyists," places in American life in the 1970s filled by Trotskyist leaders of the 1930s, the limits of Trotsky's personal authority, and the impact of Trotskyism (or lack of it) on American life.

Minorities in the Movement

Women, according to one sociologist a majority with primarily minority characteristics, in the Trotskyist sect not only were an actual minority but occupied a subordinate position that reflected their position in society at large. This was despite the inclusion of the Marxist classics in the party's body of doctrine: literature evaluating women's place, analyzing it in relation to the growth of economic systems, and prescribing equal status for them in the coming society.[1] Only in the youth group were women sometimes leaders. No figures paralleled the Communist party's Ella Reeve Bloor or Elizabeth Gurley Flynn. Seldom did members raise "the woman question" as an issue. Principally women were loyal wives, mistresses, and mothers of Trotskyist men. Often female relatives were not even party members. For instance, Arne Swabeck would not permit his wife to join. But Rose Karsner, Cannon's wife, played an active although an auxiliary part in national and local affairs. When asked if the party intentionally underplayed the role of women in order to attract blue-collar workers whose attitudes tended to be old world, hence conservative, respondents answered with a decisive "no." But all agreed that only "superior" women became known, and even these not nearly so well as their male counterparts. Some (male) respondents laughingly sloughed off the question about the role of women in the party as a joke, either making sexual allusions or disparaging remarks about women's deficiencies. As for the commonly held belief that Marxism sanctions a "community of women," Max Shachtman, married twice to movement women, conceded that a little "horsing around" took place about as it does in the established political parties, and "worse—as is everything else—in New York."

Some women did attain limited leadership rank or serve the party in a crucial capacity on a local basis. Antoinette Konikow held a revered and advisory position in the Boston branch; the three Agelof sisters had important courier and secretary roles in the functioning of the party nationally, even internationally; and Grace Carlson ran for local and national office on the party ticket in Minnesota. Anne Kracik, Hal Draper's wife, was district organizer in Los Angeles; Reva Crain, Al Glotzer's first wife, was district organizer in New York at one time, and his second wife, Maggie Bell, was district organizer in Akron. Myra Tanner Weiss, whose husband Al Russel persuaded authorities to incarcerate him at Danbury, Connecticut, rather than at Sandstone, Minnesota, because she lived in New York, was an organizer in that city; so too was Sylvia Bleecker, remembered as one of the outstanding women in the New York branch. To Max Geltman's quip that Trotskyists always liked to marry women who could type and make the living while they "made the revolution," Maggie Bell retorted that that was simply not so, adding that numerous women did support their husband's revolutionary activities, but the converse was just as true: "Many males worked and supported women who labored for the party."

Evelyn Reed, Maggie Bell, and Yetta Barsh all observed that when the male leaders were in jail during World War II, women held the titles and ran the party with all that responsibility entailed, including managing and editing the press and writing its articles. But Reed noted that although women had not been leaders in the 1930s, "Here you have to be fair and remember we don't transcend the conditions of life that we're in. There was no obstacle to their advancement" but neither was there special encouragement for it, as in the 1970s for example when the Trotskyist Socialist Worker party had women as 40 percent of the membership, with many female leaders.[2]

Women were in truth more active and influential than some male former members wished to acknowledge in 1972 and 1973. Yet the post of district organizer or a rare local candidacy for office appeared the ceiling to which a female Trotskyist could aspire. Not one from 1929 through 1941 appeared on either the national committee or the political committee. Despite Marxist theory which enjoins female equality, pressures from the social environment and the realities of day-to-day survival made women Trotskyists accept without resistance a subordinate place.

And despite classic Marxist writings, Trotskyists developed no special body of theory relating to pecular problems of women—the entrapment and politics of household labor, plus sex discrimination in the job market and in labor unions. Nor did the party try to recruit women or to organize them in trade unions in industries that relied chiefly on female labor, or in retailing where women made up much of the low-paid sales force. Trotskyists thus ignored a promising field for recruitment. It ignored too a particular kind of oppression on which Marx, Lenin, and Trotsky had commented, although briefly, and therefore, an opportunity to contribute uniquely to Marxist labor theory, the labor movement, and to radical politics in the 1930s.

With respect to a tally of blacks in membership and leadership a curious reversal with the position of women is evident. No women were national leaders, yet sizable numbers belonged. Although very, very few "colored comrades" entered the Trotskyist party, the largest influx taking place in the period following the one covered in this essay, two black men occupied top leadership positions through much of the decade. One, C. L. R. James of Trinidad, or "J. R. Johnson" as he was known in the party, served as policy-formulating specialist on the Negro question, was on both national committees and political committees, and was a major theoretician, racial problems and recruitment of blacks his chief concern. But his efforts to attract black members bore little fruit. He realized far more success in the 1950s and 1960s as writer and lecturer. The other, Ernest Rice McKinney, great grandson of a slave woman and a small town Virginia newspaper editor, was a full-time functionary. From 1920 a staff writer on the *Pittsburgh Courier* and the *Pittsburgh American,* he joined in 1929 the Musteite Conference for Progressive Labor Action. After Musteite-Trotskyist fusion took place in 1934, he came to New York to assume full-time duties as member of the political committee. McKinney's work focused less intensively on racial matters; he was a labor specialist and organizer, and in his field at that time was considerably more effective than was James in his.

Unlike the Trotskyists' sketchily defined policy on the woman question Trotskyists periodically made statements and formulated policy shifts on the Negro question from 1929 on, principally in response to Communist party policies. The Communist party had enjoyed greater successes in recruiting blacks and so bore scrutiny on that as on other accounts. Certainly nothing in the Trotskyist "answers" to the Negro question gave any substance to charges of white chauvinism sporadically made against them by Communists and Weisbordites alike.[3] A certain ambiguity nevertheless weakened their stand.

In the late 1920s the Communist party began formally to promote for the United States the slogans, "For a Negro Republic in the South," and "Self-Determination for Negroes in the Black Belt."[4] Drawn toward the Communist program yet aware that it was separatist and appeared to negate the desired unity of black and white proletarians, Trotsky vacillated for ten years, at length accepting the integrationist approach of C. L. R. James.

The first Communist League of America platform drafted in February 1929, rejected Communist slogans and urged black and white workers to unite. A resolution in 1935 on the Negro question similarly talked of cooperation between white and black, declaring that responsibility for fostering it fell on the shoulders of white workers who should realize their own emancipation depended on Negro emancipation, too, from the domination of capital. The Negro problem should be viewed as a combined development problem to which the world offered no parallel: "The situation of the American Negro is unique." The notion of the "National Negro Republic in the South—the state form of which they refuse to define—existing side by side with American imperialist rule" was as "fantastic and utopian as the idea of Socialism in One Country," the "self-determination" slogan itself "an inverted form of the petit bourgeois Garvey 'Back to Africa' movement." Because capitalist industry could not absorb the black worker freed from chattel bonds after the Civil War, he remained neither slave nor free, driven to a lower level of existence than before, his plight compounded in the South by legal discrimination and lynch law. "Self-determination" clouded the real issue of class struggle, and was inappropriately raised because the Negro problem was racial not national.[5] So ran the resolution, and in general it reflected a consistency in attitude: workers' solidarity must hold emphasis.

But Trotsky himself found the "self-determination" solution compelling, in 1933 pointing out that promoting it could set American Negroes against their nation's imperialism.[6] By 1939 as evidenced in an *Internal Bulletin* given over wholly to discussion of policy toward black Americans, the Trotskyist position had stabilized. As stated by James, the Socialist Workers members recognized the old Communist party program to be "economically reactionary" and "politically false" because desired by no Negroes "except CP [Communist party] stooges." The Socialist Workers party should foster a propaganda campaign steered by a "Negro committee" to "win the Negro for socialism" and by encouraging his reading of internationalist African periodicals and by letting him learn the realities of political activity through agitating for his full participation in unions, industries, schools, and universities, for his voting rights, and against oppressive rental exactions. Although led by party blacks, the Negro committee should push a few white comrades to acquaint themselves with Negro life and thought, to attend Negro meetings, and to "propagandize to Negroes on terms familiar to them."[7] James thus dismissed "self-determination" and defined a course of action.

Trotsky in 1939 was still intrigued by the idea of a Negro state in America and wary of scrapping a possibly promising program. The blacks themselves must decide the matter of "self-determination," he cautioned. Keep the party silent on the question, but ready to support "self-determination" if the 13,000,000 black Americans accept it. Trotsky reminded his party faithful that Marcus Garvey had certainly raised the level of imagination with his African Zionism.[8] In this way (and on Trotsky's insistence) leaving the tiniest reservation for approval

of black nationalism, the Socialist Workers party in 1939 agreed to subordinate the race question to class struggle as it had tacitly done with
the woman question. For the time being the party simply pursued that
policy toward all minority matters. Certainly the problem of anti-
Semitism did not surface with Trotskyists save in retrospect, nor was
the status of Asian-Americans raised at issue except in a broad condemnation of all racial discrimination. (The Trotskyist movement had no
counterpart to the early Socialist party's leader of Japanese birth, Sen
Katayama.)[9]

With the onset of World War II the leadership turned its attention to
bread-and-butter and other very practical problems facing blacks such
as blatant discrimination in the armed forces and defense industries,
attacks on Negro soldiers stationed in the South, President Roosevelt's
appointment of "Jim Crow" James F. Byrnes of South Carolina to the
U.S. Supreme Court, and A. Philip Randolph's march on Washington
movement.[10]

Literary Trotskyists

The term "literary Trotskyism" came first to the author's attention
by way of a turgid article in a Communist literary periodical. The piece
attacked V. F. Calverton of *Modern Monthly* as a literary Trotskyist
and "official corrupter of the left intelligentsia, serving up, through his
magazine, under the flag of Marxism, the most anti-Marxian, counter-
revolutionary rubbish"; and it set at poles Lenin's and Trotsky's views
on "proletarian culture" establishing Calverton solidly in Trotsky's
corner.[11]

If literary Trotskyism in fact existed, it did so in two manifestations.
Certain figures in arts and letters, Calverton, Max Eastman, William
Phillips and Philip Rahv of *Partisan Review*, Edmund Wilson, Mary
McCarthy, and Diego Rivera as examples, were appalled by the rigorous
exactions and stifling didacticisms of "proletcult" as enjoined by Communist officialdom in Lenin's name. As for Lenin's actual remarks on
proletarian culture, they were varied, diffuse, subject to interpretation,
and not within the scope of this essay. But Trotsky's allegedly contrary
approach had much greater appeal for these creative people because in
Literature and Revolution Trotsky projected proletarian culture only

for a future socialist society when the term "proletariat" would cease
to apply: the social order would be quite classless. One must designate
such art "socialist," not "proletarian," he explained. In that time, "the
average human type will rise to the heights of an Aristotle, a Goethe, or
a Marx. And above this ridge new peaks will rise." Until then, Trotsky
advised, let artists reflect the tumultuous and transient order in which
they live, for "art can and must be judged from the point of view of its
achievement in form . . . ." juxtaposed, of course, against the social
context from which it springs.[12]

Art has a history of its own:

> . . . each [generation], given a developing and not a decadent so-
> ciety, adds its treasure to the past accumulations of culture . . . .
> It appropriates existing culture and transforms it in its own way,
> making it more or less different from that of the older generation.[13]

And,

> Just as an individual passes biologically and psychologically through
> the history of the race . . . so . . . must the overwhelming majority
> of the new class which has only recently come out of prehistoric
> life, pass through the entire history of artistic culture. This class
> cannot begin the construction of a new culture without absorbing
> and assimilating the elements of the old cultures . . . . A new class
> cannot move forward without regard to the most important land-
> marks of the past.[14]

Nor did Trotsky dismiss the "historically utilitarian" role of art as "social servant":

> It finds the necessary rhythm of words for dark and vague
> moods, it brings thought and feeling closer or contrasts them
> with one another, it enriches the spiritual experience of the in-
> dividual and of the community, it refines feeling, makes it more
> flexible, more responsive, it enlarges the volume of thought in
> advance and not through the personal method of accumulated
> experience, it educates the individual, the social group, the class
> and the nation.[15]

But it does so only as distiller of a collective consciousness and adumbrator of contradictions in the social fabric, never as cheap giver of daily lessons in how-to-make-the-revolution.[16] The grand and cosmic ring of Trotsky's aesthetic philosophy and the free rein it left to the individual creator bore a built-in magnetism attracting irresistibly these essentially anarchistic spirits.

The second form literary Trotskyism took did not root itself in Trotsky's aesthetic. It comprised the personalities who may or may not have vaguely approved Trotsky's views, but who were drawn to him because he was a beleaguered exile shouting defiance to a despotic regime. The numbers lured into his orbit reached their highest level from 1936 to 1940, from the initial revelations about the Moscow trials to the Nazi-Soviet pact. The impetus tapered off when in June 1941 Hitler violated the pact and invaded Russia, and when half-a-year later the United States entered the war with Russia as ally.[17]

Trotsky of course attracted Eastman for similar reasons even before his exile. Dwight Macdonald exemplified this wing of literary Trotskyism in the late 1930s. Coming from an eastern upper-class background, he had had a traditional preparatory school and Yale education. After Yale, a stint in Macy's executive training program, then a writing assignment on *Fortune,* thoroughly disillusioned him with the management ethos. He read Marx, Lenin, and Trotsky, met people in radical circles, and when publicity about the first Moscow trial broke out, he became convinced that Trotsky was innocent and that the premise of the trial was absurd. With two Yale classmates, Phillips and Rahv, he revived the old Stalinist *Partisan Review* and opened its pages to anti-Stalinists. James T. Farrell, John Dos Passos, George Orwell, Mary McCarthy, André Gide, and Ignazio Silone among others wrote for *Partisan Review* under Phillips, Rahv, and Macdonald. Meantime Macdonald intensified his activities for radical causes, began contributing to *New International,* and drew yet closer to the Trotskyist party because, in James Gilbert's words, it "appealed to Macdonald's half-aristocratic, half-anarchistic critique of capitalism and his highly intellectualized radicalism." He liked the Socialist Workers party because "it was led by Trotsky whose career showed that intellectuals, too, could make history," because he liked theoretical politics, and because he believed small political groups were indeed relevant. He joined in the fall of 1939, then with gusto left the Cannonites to found the Workers party with Burnham and Shachtman in April 1940. As if to fulfill Trotsky's prediction that Macdonald would desert Marxism "into the camp of Burnham" a little later because "he is a little lazier," Macdonald did resign in April 1941.[18]

Important to remember, however, in reviewing the period when Trotsky's vicissitudes brought him a host of literary sympathizers is the truth that almost none enrolled in his party then or ever. James T. Farrell's short story, "The Renegade," about a young man's novitiate as Trotskyist in the 1930s and his difficulty in coping with the paradigmatic experience of narrow, constrained, and nervous party life and thought, best explained why this was so. Farrell's story, remarkably apt in capturing the spirit of life in a radical sect, also explained why the few creative souls who did enroll failed to remain after 1940 when the impulse to reform had been effectively stymied and the charismatic leader was gone.[19]

Trotskyist Leaders in American Life: The 1970s

Former leaders unanimously agreed that the camaraderie within the movement was as compelling as the cause for which they united. Another facet of party life came to light, too, one some ex-Trotskyists considered their greatest benefit from being part of the movement. Belonging was for them a great school for analytical thinking. Comrades began pondering in earnest about social questions, Widick recalled, and when they left the party to enter the mainstream they became leaders of one kind or another. Look at the old *Militant* staff, he ruminated a bit wistfully. On it sat "an impressive assemblage of talent—and it was a great paper, too."[20] Widick, in 1973 a professor of labor economics at Columbia University, came into the party in 1934 in Detroit. Agreeing that party life had been a marvelous school for thought ("but you'd better graduate!"), Harry Roskolenko remembered that he had entered in 1927, a merchant seaman stopping in Hamburg, Germany. After an eleven-year party career which he insisted he spent as a Jimmy Higgins, followed by a stint in the Federal Writers' Project and one on Voice of America, he turned to writing alternately with his memoirs "sexy, laugh" pulp books in his Greenwich Village apartment.

Shachtman brought Bert Cochran to Trotskyism from the Communist party in Communist League of America years and Cochran remained a Cannonite with Goldman and Russel, leaving the party in 1952. An accomplished pianist, his studies at the University of Wisconsin and a brief editorship of a short-lived socialist paper prepared him for his position as professor of economic history at the New School for Social Research. Hal Draper joined the socialist movement as a teenager in Brooklyn, New York. The French turn brought him to Trotskyism; he left the Socialist Workers party in 1940 with Shachtman. In his hilltop home overlooking San Francisco, the bay, and the Golden Gate Bridge, Draper, still a socialist, was in 1975 engaged in Marxist scholarship.

Felix Morrow and Herbert Solow with Sidney Hook, Lewis Corey, Anita Brenner, and others had been associated with the *Menorah Journal* and with Elliot Cohen on the *Encyclopedia of the Social Sciences.* Morrow, Solow, and George Novack (who came from the Socialist party) were early recruits in 1935 of the fusion Workers party. The Socialist Workers party expelled Morrow in the 1940s; he reportedly said then that the most foolish time of his life was that spent as a Trotskyist. In 1972 a commentator on the occult, he lived in semiretirement in New Hyde Park, New York. The author was unable to discover Solow's whereabouts. In the 1970s the steadfast Novack wore Shachtman's mantle as principal Socialist Workers party theoretician.

Albert Goldman joined the Musteite party after expulsion in 1934 from the Communist party and came to Trotskyism by that route. A Cannonite in 1940, he remained with the Socialist Workers party arguing its defense at Minneapolis, then went to Sandstone Prison as one of the convicted. After release, disbarred, he ran a taxicab business until his death a few years later. Meantime he had left the party with Morrow. When the government wished to revoke Danish-born Arne Swabeck's citizenship, officials allegedly promised to have Goldman reinstated at the bar if he would testify against Swabeck. Goldman refused.

Swabeck in 1976 lived near downtown Los Angeles. Because he believed the Republic of China had experienced a true socialist revolution in 1949 and because he agitated for a friendly "line" toward China within the Socialist Workers party, it expelled him in 1969. In the mid-1970s a member of the New American Movement (NAM), he was popular as a lecturer on the old left at their meetings.

Al Russel, in 1973 executive director of the Workers Defense League in New York, had been attracted to socialism as a youth attending Weisbordite rallies on the Lower East Side. Dispatched to Omaha in 1935 to aid Farrell Dobbs in building the Central States Drivers' Council, he was scooped up as a Trotskyist labor agitator, tried under the Smith Act, and sentenced with Dobbs, Goldman, Cannon, and the others.[21]

Through the early 1970s Cannon continued as the grand old man of the party, presiding as elder statesman from retirement in Los Angeles until he died on August 21, 1974.[22] Dobbs in the early 1970s lived on past laurels, delivering lectures and writing his recollections of the great Minneapolis days. Shachtman died on November 4, 1972. Except for his apostasy, he too would have merited the title of party patriarch. Two years earlier he had spent a semester at the University of Illinois, invited as Distinguished Visiting Radical. At the time of his demise, he was just beginning to write a history of the Communist International which he had been researching for eleven years. In 1972 an officer in the Socialist party, he had come to hold an abiding respect for Stalin and for what he viewed as an essential wisdom in the Communist party, an opinion he had not as yet adopted in 1962 and 1963 when interviewed for the Oral History Collection at Columbia University. Moreover, in 1972 he spurned the reasons which led him to follow Trotsky in 1928 as "all bunk." He remarked,

> The Communist party was fundamentally, essentially wisest, playing for time, maneuvering. It was ridiculous for us to call Stalin a reactionary, a fascist, a national socialist. He and the Communist party knew revolution would inevitably come—in a year, ten years, 100 years, but inevitably.

A few minutes later he reiterated the opinion:

> Stalin was no reactionary, he was for the permanent revolution, but he was just cooler, playing for time. By no means did he sell out to the Chinese bourgeoisie in any true sense. Hogwash. If he "sold out" to the Chinese bourgeoisie represented by Chiang Kai-shek, he was just maneuvering for time.[23]

This dramatic reevaluation of his prior analysis surprised former comrade

George Novack, who with others had no inkling that Shachtman's immersion in the papers of the third international would produce so startling a consequence. For Studs Terkel's oral history of the 1930s, Shachtman noted that only a few radicals of those years had kept their old commitments into the seventies. But, he added, "I feel more strongly about the ideals of socialism than I ever did. Still, many thousands of old radicals, like myself, vote for the goddam Democrats . . . ." Emanuel Geltman, Spartacus League leader in the 1930s, and editor of its *Young Spartacus,* was in 1975 senior editor for the *New York Time's* Quadrangle Press and with a number of former Shachtmanites a founder of the Democratic Socialist Organizing Committee. He looked forward to "doing something with the Shachtman papers" one day, certain he would be approached for this task.

Manny Geltman's brother Max in 1972 held views sufficiently conservative to merit him a position as staff writer for *National Review* under James Burnham's editorship. Max Geltman and Roskolenko had meantime also become Zionists. In the summer of 1972 these gentlemen and a few others gathered every Thursday to discuss current topics and old times.

Al Glotzer in 1972 was reporter for New York's municipal court and lived comfortably with his wife Maggie Bell. Glotzer had been among the first five expelled for Trotskyism from the Communist party in 1928, spent many of his party years as Chicago branch organizer, then left his indelible mark on party annals by officially recording the proceedings of the Dewey Commission of Inquiry in Mexico. Ernest Rice McKinney in 1975 lived in New York City, and at age eighty-nine was an assistant to Bayard Rustin, director of the A. Philip Randolph Institute. Despite his age, he retained the keenness of his senses, of his wit in particular, and with Max Geltman and Roskolenko retained the same old combativeness of party days in the 1930s. The other black leader, C. L. R. James, having left with Shachtman came back to the Socialist Workers party for two years, 1948 and 1949, only to be expelled. In 1973 James was teaching in Chicago.[24]

The Limits of Trotsky's Personal Authority

Inevitably the historian of Trotskyism in America must tackle the problem of Leon Trotsky's influence on his movement from exile. His instructions, his admonitions, and his analyses of current questions coming by letter, memorandum, and in the form of articles for the party organ run through the narrative as a continuous thread. To what degree were the comrades bound by them? Estimates have ranged all the way from insisting that he had "total authority" to belittling him as "a child in the hands of Cannon." There is some truth in both.

To his evaluation of international events, past and current, in the light of what he called "bolshevism-leninism," Trotsky commanded total assent. Pages of the early *Militant* were filled with his writings on such questions, from his "Draft Program of the Communist International: A Criticism of Fundamentals" in 1928 and 1929 to his "Foreign Policy of the Soviet Union" in the *Militant* of June 16, 1934. They formed the basis for the official "party line." Gradually Shachtman developed a greater and greater degree of skill in adapting Trotsky's verbose essays to a wider and less theoretically oriented reading audience, shortening them, but adhering faithfully to the author's intent. By the time American Trotskyists seriously considered fusion with the Musteites, about December 1933, they decided to change the format of the *Militant* to give it broader appeal. Shachtman now regularly employed his "popularizing" expertise to transform Trotsky's articles for the desired new readership. Trotsky continued to hold full authority, but Shachtman became (and remained until 1939) his principal American mouthpiece on international questions. Trotsky was an international figure of heroic, even legendary, proportions. Comrades proudly adopted his views as their own.

As for matters of overall strategy for the sections of the International Communist League and after 1934, the fourth international, again Trotsky's prescriptions served as commands. His lieutenant in the United States, Cannon, obeyed them loyally. On Trotsky's directions to enter the larger movement, Cannon and his henchmen negotiated for several months and then merged with a party of (chiefly non-Marxist) labor intellectuals, the Musteites. On his instructions, again Cannon prepared a merger, this time with the Socialist party, hoping to take advantage of its new menshevik "all-inclusive" policy. Just as obediently Trotskyists deliberately antagonized the Socialists to provoke their own expulsion, now hoping for a huge exodus of sympathetic radicals along with them.

To question Trotsky's analysis of world events, to disagree in the tiniest essential, was to court expulsion or be denied membership. Weisbord was an early example. Unable to come to terms on these and on matters of domestic tactics in the course of a protracted exchange of letters, he was denied admission to the Communist League of America. Several young members walked out of a meeting in 1937 and left Marxism altogether after being scolded by a leader for voicing disagreement with the "line" on the Russian question. A year and a half later began the dispute, over the same issue, that raged for nine months and culminated in permanent breach. The faction that adamantly stood by Trotsky's characterization of the Soviet Union remained the Trotskyist Socialist Workers party, the dissenters forced out to found their own sect.

In the same way, comrades who objected to Trotsky's dictation on party strategy found themselves slandered and ostracized. Their only recourse lay in finding supporters, building a faction of their own, and hoping to have their opinion prevail, all virtually impossible given Cannon's dominant role and the fact that in matters of this kind Cannon obeyed Trotsky. Oehler and Stamm, for instance, first opposed fusion with the Muste group, but yielded. Cannon's decision to follow Trotsky's orders and enter the Socialist party and his refusal to see entrism as a question to be debated at length forced them out. Muste, McKinney, and Abern similarly opposed entrism, but, unable to build a strong faction, relented. To be a Trotskyist meant to go along with party gyrations as ordered by Trotsky or to leave. Muste left when the Trotskyists fused with the Socialist party. Abern and McKinney left with Shachtman four years later.

On matters of party leadership and reform, Trotsky did not wield absolute authority. To do so would have been impossible, removed as he was by thousands of miles. Although he gave orders to Cannon on overall strategy and the "line" on foreign affairs, Cannon virtually instructed Trotsky on inner-party politicking. Trotsky placed great confidence in Cannon's judgment, far greater than his judgment merited, and Cannon used Trotsky's support to keep himself enthroned as monarch. When a clamor arose (as it did several times) to admit newer, younger faces to the cadre of leadership, Cannon derided the proposals and slandered those that made them as irresponsible or petty bourgeois. Cannon kept a corps of his own supporters at Trotsky's side in Mexico to whom he sent instructions regularly. Unable to be present, Trotsky heard details of every squabble second-hand, skewed by Cannon's "yes-men." Coached by Cannonites, Trotsky could be counted on to rebuke reformers and reaffirm faith in Cannon's leadership. Even Shachtman's considerable prestige could not prevail over Cannon's. In any event, Shachtman was not a political leader; "he was a facile writer and speaker, very gifted," in the words of Charles Curtis.[25]

In the quarrel that preceded the split of April 1940 Shachtman missed the chance to counteract Joseph Hansen's influence in Mexico. Afraid he was losing his brilliant journalist, Trotsky in December 1939 invited Shachtman down to Coyoacan to discuss the issues but Shachtman ignored the invitation, perhaps by then ceasing to care anyway. To be an American Trotskyist meant to accept without wavering Cannon's political leadership, labeled "bureaucratic conservatism" by the Shachtmanites, but perennially blessed by Trotsky himself.

Without Trotsky, the Trotskyists would not have held together in the 1930s. A tragic figure waiting all the rest of his life to relive the Russian Revolution, he felt himself cut off from great events and forced merely to interpret them. He "could not reconcile himself to the role of the outsider," Isaac Deutscher said.[26] Through directing his "parties," he lived vicariously in the great world of politics beyond his exile.

The Impact of Trotskyism

Meantime, the parade of international events and American politics went right on almost as though no group of Trotskyists existed. The internal struggles and resultant fragmentation that wracked the sect failed even to make a ripple on the sea of the Stalinist party which rolled right along on the ideological and financial foundation of a regime in power in an expansive and populous nation. Bert Cochran commented, "In the 1930s the Trotskyists were just a side show. The Communist party was the big show."[27] The Socialist party was dented by the Trotskyist invasion but was not ruined by it. Co-optation of some of its leaders and programs by the Roosevelt administration and the labor movement wounded it irrecoverably, but through these very means it made its mark on American life.

What mark, if any, did Trotskyists make on American life? For a
brief time because of their discipline and a few capable union leaders in
their ranks they made an impact in the labor movement, principally in
the organizing of midwestern truck drivers. But Shachtman even disputed this claim, saying, "The whole trade union effort came to zero.
The Minneapolis conflagration left nothing but ashes."[28] The Nonpartisan Labor Defense certainly did not affect the workings of the American
judicial system or the prejudices of the police. It may have in a few
individual cases gained acquittals and pardons or raised bail monies for
union organizers and radicals, but laws and popular attitudes, hostile
to both groups generally, remained the same.

Perhaps, as Widick believed in 1972, Trotskyism was a "first-rate
think-tank" that sent those who had been part of it out into the capitalist world as writers, editors, teachers, and lecturers, making its greatest
impact on American life this way.[29] As a party its influence was necessarily as limited as that of any narrow sect dealing in revealed truths
must be. To be sure, Trotskyists sometimes moved out beyond their
ideological borders on proselyting missions. They did not overlook the
interventionist quality in Marxism as did Daniel DeLeon and his Socialist Labor party. And they were a better, more humane group than the
Communists, according to Sidney Hook. But their appeal was minuscule: "That doctrine of theirs was deplorable," he concluded.[30] And
Shachtman sneered, "Then and now Trotskyists really have nothing to
say to the working class. 'Socialism in One Country'? What does that
mean to a working guy! He doesn't want socialism anywhere! 'Principled politics'? What's that to him!"[31] In the 1970s (as in the 1930s)
Trotskyism held greatest appeal for "city intellectuals"—principally
college students or dropouts. Shachtman was right. Trotskyists spoke
a language either unintelligible or distasteful to working people, the
class that party leaders most wanted to attract. All of its convolutions,
splits over minute points of doctrine, and internal struggles over power
seemed only tempests in a teapot. The American people neither heard
what they were saying, nor cared.

Notes

Chapter 1

1. The most readable and thorough account of socialism's early years in America is in Howard Quint, *The Forging of American Socialism* (Indianapolis, 1964). David Shannon provides an overview of the Socialist party through the Norman Thomas years in his *Socialist Party of America* (Chicago, 1955), as does Daniel Bell in *Marxian Socialism in the United States* (Princeton, N.J., 1967). For studies of periods in American socialism see Ira B. Kipnis, *The American Socialist Movement 1897-1912* (New York, 1952), and James Weinstein, *Decline of Socialism in America, 1912-1925* (New York, 1967). Good memoirs by participants are in Morris Hillquit, *Loose Leaves from a Busy Life* (New York, 1934) and Lillian Symes and Travers Clement, *Rebel America* (Boston, 1972). The Socialist Labor party is discussed in the Quint, Bell, and Symes and Clement volumes, passim. The IWW has had much more separate attention than has the Socialist Labor party. Older works are John Graham Brooks, *American Syndicalism* (New York, 1913) and the very pedestrian Fred Thompson, *The I.W.W.* (Chicago, 1955). A short later study is Patrick Renshaw, *The Wobblies* (New York, 1967). Melvyn Dubovsky best captures the flamboyance and the drama of American syndicalism in his *We Shall Be All* (Chicago, 1969); but the classic work on this movement remains Paul F. Brissenden's *The I.W.W.* (New York, 1919).

2. Shannon, *Socialist Party of America*, 99-104.

3. Theodore Draper, *The Roots of American Communism* (New

York, 1966), 77, 89-91; Trotsky, Biographical Dates Presented to the Commission, personal files of Bertram D. Wolfe.

4. Note Shannon's title for Chapter 2 of his *Socialist Party of America:* "Immigrants, Negroes, Intellectuals, Millionnaires, and Ministers," 43-61.

5. Draper, *Roots of American Communism,* 32, 137.

6. James P. Cannon, *The History of American Trotskyism* (New York, 1944), 5.

7. Draper, *Roots of American Communism,* 87.

8. Ibid., 89-91; James P. Cannon, *The First Ten Years of American Communism* (New York, 1962), 46, 49, 55.

9. Irving Howe and Lewis Coser, *The American Communist Party,* 2nd ed. (Boston, 1957); 153-154; Cannon, *First Ten Years of American Communism,* 189.

10. *Militant,* August 15, 1931; Draper, *Roots of American Communism,* 311-315; Cannon, *First Ten Years of American Communism,* 53-54.

11. This occurred again in the 1950s when Eugene Dennis was made titular head of the party. James Oneal and G. A. Werner, *American Communism* (New York, 1947), 239.

12. Claude McKay, *A Long Way from Home* (New York, 1937), 159; Benjamin Gitlow, *I Confess* (New York, 1939-1940), 161.

13. Max Shachtman, *Reminiscences,* 324, Columbia University Oral History Collection (hereafter cited as COHC).

14. Shachtman, *Reminiscences,* 25; 332-333, COHC; "Twenty-Five Years of American Trotskyism," *New International* (January-February 1954), 19; cf. birthday tribute to eighty-one-year-old Cannon in *Militant,* April 23, 1971.

15. See *Militant,* January 15, 1929; Cannon, *History of American Trotskyism,* 29-30; Draper noted, "The most damaging thing that Lovestone could think of saying of Foster was that he had been and would always be a 'trade union syndicalist,'" and the most contemptuous thing that Foster could think of saying of Lovestone was that he would never get over being a 'City College intellectual.' " *American Communism and Soviet Russia* (New York, 1960), 252-253.

16. Interview with Yetta Barsh, August 15, 1972; Betty Yorburg with Max Shachtman for Socialist Movement Project, 2: 3, 6, COHC.

17. Introduction by Howard Maclay to Max Shachtman, "Radicalism in the Thirties," in Rita James Simon, ed., *As We Saw the Thirties* (Chicago, 1967), 8-9; Max Eastman, *Love and Revolution* (New York, 1964), 516.

18. Cannon, *First Ten Years of American Communism,* 181; Trotsky,

"His Last Article," *Fourth International,* 1 (October, 1940), 128-131;
Eastman, *Love and Revolution,* 510-515. Eastman told of a five-
member discussion circle called together as a nucleus of an American
Trotskyist party in which he and his wife, Eliena Krylenko, participated;
Lore was one of the five. Sidney Hook, "As to Max Eastman's Mentality," *Modern Quarterly,* 5 (November 1928-February 1929), 88-91, a
very pointed rebuttal article.

    19. Cannon, patriarch of American Trotskyism, said in his memoir,
"By 1928, when the big fight started, all the organized revolutionists—
that is to say, all those who professed allegiance to socialism and were
willing to do something about it—were organized in the Communist
Party, and nowhere else . . . . The original Trotskyists in the United
States, the initiating nucleus of the revolutionary party of the future
victory, came from the Communist Party because the Communist
Party—and the Communist Party alone—contained the human material
prepared by the past for the work of reconstruction." *First Ten Years
of American Communism,* 31-32; interview with Charles Curtis, June
3, 1970.

    20. Lenin said, "Practice is higher than (theoretical) knowledge for
it has not only the dignity of universality, but also of immediate actuality." Quote by Mao Tse Tung in "On Practice," *Selected Works* (Peking,
1967), 1: 297; but he also stressed the necessity of theory for action,
in "What Is to Be Done?" Henry M. Christman, ed., *Essential Works of
Lenin* (New York, 1966), 65, 69-70; and see E. R. Carr, *Studies in Revolution* (New York, 1964), 149; R. N. Carew Hunt, *The Theory and Practice of Communism* (Baltimore, 1964), 58-59, 181; and Schlomo Avineri,
The Social and Political Thought of Karl Marx (Cambridge, 1968), 134-
149 on unity of theory and *praxis* in Marx. Norman Cantor itemized
the ingredients of protest movements and found the two personalities,
the trade union (or other) activist and the party intellectual, integral to
all that have endured, in *The Age of Protest* (New York, 1969), 332-334.
Radicals believed so fully in the need of theory for action that they
thought every sacrifice justified to keep the revolutionary press intact.

    21. See chart, "Contemporary Marxian Political Parties at a Glance,"
Appendix 1 in William Isaacs, "Contemporary Marxian Political Movements in the U.S." (Ph.D. dissertation, New York University, 1940);
also, Harry Ring, "History of the Socialist Workers Party," lecture,
Socialist Workers party Tape Collection, New York.

    22. Max Shachtman, "Footnote for Historians," *New International,*
4 (December, 1938), 377; Max Eastman quoted in *Sacramento Bee,*
January 23, 1935.

    23. Peter Gay, *The Rise of Modern Paganism,* in *The Enlightenment:*

An Interpretation, 2 vols. (New York, 1966), 1: 4-5.

24. Interview with Ann Snipper, June 1, 1970; Gay, *Rise of Modern Paganism,* 6.

25. Howe, "A Memoir of the Thirties," in *Steady Work* (New York, 1966), 364. Howe concluded, "There is nothing I desire more than a revival of American radicalism."

Chapter 2

1. Cannon quoted in Theodore Draper, *The Roots of American Communism* (New York, 1957), 265.

2. Draper, ibid., 165, 169; James Weinstein, *The Decline of Socialism in America, 1912-1925* (New York, 1969), 201-202.

3. On the founding of the Communist International, see Franz Borkenau, *World Communism* (Ann Arbor, 1962), 161-170; Leonard Schapiro, *The Communist Party of the Soviet Union* (London, 1963), 196-197; Ross Dowson, "The Rise and Fall of the *Third International,*" Ernest Mandel, ed., *Fifty Years of World Revolution, 1817-1967* (New York, 1968), 99-100. In 1975 Mandel was the leading Trotskyist theoretician of international stature.

4. Weinstein, *Decline of Socialism in America,* 210-215. Draper noted that with the passage of time the foreign-born categories decreased in the American party, but there was very, very little numerical increase in numbers of women and black members. The radical movement, labor, socialist, and communist, was a white, male world. *Roots of American Communism,* 186-193.

5. Charles Ruthenberg, first real Communist party leader, and Max Bedacht were chief spokesmen for the liquidators, according to Draper; goose caucus spokesmen (who claimed they cackled to save the party as in the legend geese had cackled, saving Rome) included Israel Amter, Robert Minor, and Alfred Wagenknecht. Wolfe merged his "rurals" with the liquidators at the eleventh hour. Draper, *Roots of American Communism,* 360-361; Cannon, *First Ten Years of American Communism* (New York, 1962), 56-57; interviews with Bertram D. Wolfe, November 8, 1975; with Arne Swabeck, August 13, 1976.

6. Draper, *American Communism and Soviet Russia* (New York, 1960), 106-107.

7. Cannon added, "American CP [Communist party] politics, beginning with Pepper, was a devious and vicious business." *First Ten Years,* 55, 77, 79, 193; Pepper's less-than-revolutionary past in Hungary was chronicled in *Militant,* March 1, 1929.

8. Draper, *Roots of American Communism,* 274-276; Schapiro, *Communist Party of Soviet Union,* 196-197.

9. Cannon, *First Ten Years,* 119-120; *History of American Trotsky-ism,* 23. And see Draper, *American Communism and Soviet Russia,* 30-51.

10. Talks between the Conference for Progressive Political Action (CPPA) and the Workers (Communist) party were severed with much acrimony. La Follette called the communists "mortal enemies of . . . democratic ideals"; Foster characterized La Follette's following as "future American fascists." Draper, *Roots of American Communism,* 113-118.

11. Cannon, *First Ten Years,* 128-129, 134-136; Draper, *American Communism and Soviet Russia,* 131, 239.

12. Cannon, *First Ten Years,* 134.

13. Louis Budenz noted that the Soviet representative's "original job in America had been to make certain that Stalin rather than his rivals, Trotsky and Bukharin, would control the party here." *Men Without Faces* (New York, 1948), 68; Benjamin Gitlow, *I Confess* (New York, 1929-1940), 416-417.

14. E. H. Carr found a "fundamental theme of east and west" underlying the conflict and concluded, "It is possible to read the whole story of the defeat of Trotsky and the 'old Bolsheviks,' who had spent their formative years in Europe and whose revolutionary outlook was predominantly western, by Stalin and a group whose background and training were mainly Russian and non-European, as a reemergence in Russian history of the eastern factor temporarily eclipsed by its western counterpart." *Studies in Revolution* (New York, 1964), 103. In journalist Eugene Lyons's more picturesque language, "Trotsky—the intellectual, steeped in European ideas, was grappling with Stalin, the provincial-minded Asiatic for whom the west was a hateful mystery . . . . When Stalin won out, Asia triumphed over Europe, Ivan the Terrible conquered Karl Marx." *The Red Decade* (Indianapolis and New York, 1941), 159.

15. Before Eastman left for Moscow, Cannon persuaded him to join the Workers party so he could carry a card with him in Russia. But Eastman never introduced himself as a party member or used the card, as it turned out. This was the closest Eastman came to enrolling in a radical party. Max Eastman, *Love and Revolution* (New York, 1964), 272, 410-411; *Reflections on the Failure of Socialism* (New York, 1962), 13-14; Leon Trotsky, *My Life* (New York, 1960), 479-480.

16. Eastman, *Love and Revolution,* 420-421; 446.

17. Revolutionists viewed Eastman with either friendly or hostile suspicion. Lenin's wife in 1925 called him a "petty bourgeois anarchist" who has woven "a network of lies"; we must presume that she too was

acting in the interest of harmony or under severe pressure. Trotsky
called *Since Lenin Died* "trivial." Three years later, Trotsky made Eastman "a friend of the revolution." At the Dewey Commission hearings
in 1937 Trotsky claimed Eastman was his friend, but "more or less of a
free lance," and not a disciplined member. "It is his right, but it is my
right as a disciplined member of the organization to disavow him when
it is necessary." Eastman, *Love and Revolution,* 513-514; Dewey Commission, *The Case of Leon Trotsky* (New York, 1969), 429; W. Rork
[Trotsky] to Joseph Hansen, February 29, 1940, Socialist Workers party
Papers, Wisconsin State Historical Society (hereafter cited as SWPP).

18. Cannon, *First Ten Years,* 181; Shachtman, *Reminiscences,* 174,
Columbia Oral History Collection (hereafter cited as COHC).

19. *Militant,* January 15, 1929; Draper, *American Communism and
Soviet Russia,* 359-362.

20. ". . . Weisbord—a brash young egocentric fresh out of college
. . . a powerful mass orator and a human dynamo if there ever was
one . . . ." said IWW alumnus Cannon, not fully agreeing with Foster's
policy. Apparently he at the time was still attached to the IWW "dual"
or "red" union idea, in contrast to "boring from within" existing unions
which Foster, in the AFL, espoused. He believed it would be "better to
'lose' the strike than to end it with a disgraceful settlement." Cannon,
First Ten Years, 140-144. Weisbord later was expelled from the Communist party, flirted briefly with the Trotskyists, then formed a splinter
group that at last disintegrated.

21. According to the Trotskyist press, it formed to "struggle against
. . . the socialist fakers and A.F. of L. lieutenants of capitalism who repeatedly betray the workers' interests, against the machinery of the government which works hand in hand with the bosses . . . ." *Militant,*
April 1, 1929.

22. Lovestone, Bertram D. Wolfe, and Benjamin Gitlow had been
part of the Ruthenberg alignment. Their trade union-oriented rivals re-
sented them and denigrated them as "composed mainly of a special
type of intellectual developed by N.Y.C. College, and graduated from it
or similar institutions into the leadership of our party without appreci-
able experience in the class struggle." The faction comprised "students,
teachers, artists, philanthropic society and commercial investigators, insurance agents, etc. . . ." *Militant,* January 15, February 15, 1929.

23. "Lovestone's 'exceptionalism' for the United States is only an
American translation of Stalin's exceptionalism for Russia." *Militant,*
May 7, 1932. Trotsky called this analysis the law of uneven development: "For America there is one scale of uneveness [sic]; for Europe
there is another." *Militant,* November 15, 1928.

24. In his memoirs Cannon berated Lovestone as "unscrupulous in his ceaseless machinations and intrigues . . . . Lovestone was downright crooked . . . [a] crookedness [that] was purposeful and utilitarian." "He was like an anarchistic cancer cell running wild in the party organism." Cannon ascribed to Foster the remark that were not Lovestone a Jew, "he would be the most likely candidate for leadership of a fascist movement." Arne Swabeck called him "ruthless." Cannon, *First Ten Years,* 155-156. Trotskyists viewed "exceptionalism" as only two small steps away from national socialism.

25. William Isaacs, "Contemporary Marxian Political Movements in the U.S." (Ph.D. dissertation, New York University, 1940), 61. Later to the charge that he was "counter-revolutionary" Communists added that Trotsky had conspired against socialism, his path opposing Lenin and bolshevism, and later collaborated with Japanese military-fascism and the Hitler regime to overthrow the Soviet government. See Alexander Bittelman, *Trotsky the Traitor* (New York, 1937), 8-12; Trotsky schemed to deceive the people with his copious use of Marxist-Leninist phrases, added Moissaye J. Olgin in *Trotskyism: Counter-Revolution in Disguise* (New York, 1935), 152. Both Stalin and Trotsky knew the necessity of building all the socialism possible in Russia while promoting to the fullest extent possible world revolution; no other route was considered until the political contest, which defeated Trotsky, was joined. See R. N. Carew Hunt's excellent chapter entitled "The Doctrines of 'Socialism in One Country' and of 'Permanent Revolution' " in *Theory and Practice of Communism* (Baltimore, 1963), 216-223.

26. Abern described events surrounding Trotsky's ouster in *Militant,* January 1, and March 15, 1929; see Cannon, *First Ten Years,* 195; and Trotsky, *My Life,* 538-557.

27. Cannon, *First Ten Years,* 200.

28. Gitlow, *I Confess,* 491.

29. Cannon, *First Ten Years,* 181.

30. Irving Howe and Lewis Coser, *American Communist Party* (Boston, 1957), 153-154; Cannon insisted that Lore was never fully a Communist, and it was therefore simple for him to "slip backwards" into bourgeois democracy. *First Ten Years,* 181, 189.

31. Shachtman, "Twenty-Five Years of American Trotskyism," *New International* (January-February 1954), 14-15; Draper, *American Communism and Soviet Russia,* 364.

32. *Militant,* November 18, December 1, 1928.

33. Interview with Shachtman, August 17, 1972.

34. Gitlow, *The Whole of Their Lives* (Boston and Los Angeles, 1965), 158.

35. Draper appeared to believe that principle alone brought Cannon to support Trotsky. See also his account of conversion in *American Communism and Soviet Russia,* 364-367. Trotsky's "Draft Program" appears in first *Militants,* November 18 and December 1 and 15, 1928. See too Jack Alan Robbins, *The Birth of American Trotskyism, 1927-1929* (n.p., 1973), 21-44.

36. Shachtman, *Reminiscences,* 151-152, COHC.

37. Draper, *American Communism and Soviet Russia,* 367; Cannon, *History of American Trotskyism,* 49-51, 212.

38. Cannon, ibid., 52-54; Max Eastman, *Love and Revolution,* 515; Shachtman, *Reminiscences,* 154-155, COHC.

39. Cannon, *History of American Trotskyism,* 54-64; Shachtman in *Socialist Appeal,* October 22, 1938.

40. Shachtman, *Reminiscences,* 163, COHC.

41. Cannon, *History of American Trotskyism,* 54.

42. Fosterites moved for instantaneous irrevocable expulsion, the Lovestoneites, for suspension or expulsion, with right of appeal to the next plenum. Shachtman, *Reminiscences,* 166, COHC.

43. Vincent Ray Dunne in *Militant,* November 8 and December 15, 1928; Abern in *Militant,* December 1, 1928; Victor Serge, *Memoires d'un revolutionnaire* (Paris, 1951), 275-276; interview with Charles Curtis, June 3, 1970; Shachtman, *Reminiscences,* 169-170, COHC.

44. Cannon's speech in *Militant,* January 1, 1929.

45. "Others will demand our reinstatement," the first *Militant* proclaimed. See issues of November 15, December 15, 1928, and January 15, 1929; Eastman, *Love and Revolution,* 515; Shachtman, *Reminiscences,* 172-175, COHC.

46. *Militant,* November 15, December 1, 1928.

47. Joseph Hansen, "Introduction," *Militant,* vols. 1-7, *Radical Periodicals in the United States,* 1st series (New York, 1968).

48. Konikow in *Socialist Appeal,* October 22, November 5, 1938. An article about Konikow by Diane Feeley, a Los Angeles Trotskyist, entitled "Antoinette Konikow, Marxist and Feminist," is in *International Socialist Review* (January, 1972), 42-46.

49. Konikow in *Socialist Appeal,* October 22, November 5, 1938.

50. Interview with George Weissman, August 4, 1973.

51. Ibid.

52. Gitlow, *Whole of Their Lives,* 233-235; James Oneal and George Werner, *American Communism* (New York, 1947), 216; Patricia Eames, "Attitude of the American Civil Liberties Union Toward the CPUSA, 1920-1940" (M.A. thesis, Columbia University, 1951), 27-50 passim; *Militant,* February 1, 15, 1929.

53. *Militant,* December 10, 1928; January 15, 1929; April 1, June 14, 1941; Harry Roskolenko, *When I Was Last on Cherry Street* (New York, 1965), 135; Shachtman, *Reminiscences,* 176-179, 181-188, COHC.

54. Shachtman, *Reminiscences,* 192-195, COHC; *Militant,* January 1, 15, 1929. Different accounts of the robbery gave conflicting dates for it. One gave December 23; another December 27; yet another, January 14.

55. *Militant,* January 15, 1929.

56. Trotsky in *Militant,* February 1, 1929; Cannon, *History of American Trotskyism,* 80-81.

57. Lovestone was replaced by Jack Stachel, who (Shachtman noted) "had a very sinister reputation in the party," and was a man who made Lovestone look like a "scrupulous, responsible political leader." Shachtman, *Reminiscences,* 196, 431, COHC. See also *Militant,* March 15, July 1, August 1 and 15, 1929.

Chapter 3

1. Max Shachtman, *Reminiscences,* 167, Columbia Oral History Collection (hereafter cited as COHC).

2. James P. Cannon, *The First Ten Years of American Communism* (New York, 1962), 162-164.

3. Theodore Draper, *American Communism and Soviet Russia* (New York, 1960), 181-182.

4. Shachtman, *Reminiscences,* 112-113, COHC.

5. William C. Seyler, "The Rise and Decline of the Socialist Party in the U.S." (Ph.D. dissertation, Duke University, 1952), 553; editorial, *Modern Quarterly,* 4 (November 1928-February 1929), 28-29.

6. Shachtman in *Militant,* December 1, 1928.

7. Irving Howe and Lewis Coser, *The American Communist Party* (Boston, 1957), 282; Seyler, "Rise and Decline of the Socialist Party," 553; William Pratt, "The Reading Socialist Experience" (Ph.D. dissertation, Emory University, 1969), 151; Martin Diamond, "Socialism and the Decline of the American Socialist Party" (Ph.D. dissertation, University of Chicago, 1954), 139, 158; Mauritz Hallgren, *Seeds of Revolt* (New York, 1933), 333; Richard B. Morris, ed., *Encyclopedia of American History,* rev. ed. (New York, 1965), 336, 340.

8. Frank Warren, *The Red Decade Revisited* (Bloomington, Ind., 1966), 101; for the history of the doctrine of "social fascism," including its application to the New Deal, see Theodore Draper, "The Ghost of Social Fascism," *Commentary* 47 (February 1969), 29-72.

9. Trotsky at times came perilously close to calling the Roosevelt programs "fascist." Norman Thomas in 1934 called them "state capitalism," and denied that they were liberal. The difference between Trotskyists, Socialists, and Communists lay in the fact that in 1935 after the Seventh Comintern Congress, Communists reversed the third period policy and sought to ally with the Democratic party in a "popular front" against war and fascism. Socialists and Trotskyists continued their criticism and sought no such alliance. Trotsky, "Trade Unions in the Epoch of Capitalist Decay," *Fourth International* 2 (February 1941), 40-43; Diamond, "Socialism and the Decline of the American Socialist Party," 145-146.

10. Republished in paperback. Ann Arbor, 1965, 111-113. See Shachtman, "Struggle for the New Course," *New International* 4 (October 1938), 5.

11. Irving Howe, "Leon Trotsky: The Costs of History," *Steady Work* (New York, 1966), 146.

12. Shachtman, "Twenty Five Years of American Trotskyism," *New International* (January-February 1954), 18-19, 21.

13. Trotsky, "Lessons of October," George Breitman and Bev Scott, eds., *Writings of Leon Trotsky, 1935-1936* (New York, 1970), 121.

14. Ibid.

15. Lenin, quoted in William Isaacs, "Contemporary Marxian Political Movements in the U.S." (Ph.D. dissertation, New York University, 1940), 359-360. Lenin was true to Marx, who regarded socialism in one country as a self-destroying hypothesis. Schlomo Avineri, *The Social and Political Thought of Karl Marx* (Cambridge, England, 1968), 167.

16. Trotsky in *Militant,* November 15, 1928.

17. *Militant,* August 29, 1931; Vincent Ray Dunne in *Socialist Appeal,* October 22, 1938; Trotsky and F. Robertson, "An Interview with Leon Trotsky," in Breitman and Scott, eds., *Writings of Trotsky, 1935-1936,* 72; David M. Schneider, *The Workers (Communist) Party and American Trade Unions* (Baltimore, 1928), 105-110.

18. Trotsky, "Trade Unions in the Epoch of Capitalist Decay," *Fourth International* 2 (February 1941), 40-43.

19. Hugo Oehler in *Militant,* July 29, 1933; Lydia Bennett, "Discussion of the Chicago United Front Proposal," *Internal Bulletin* 4 (August 1943); James P. Cannon, *Notebook of an Agitator* (New York, 1958), 107-109.

20. Cannon in *Militant,* August 15, 1929.

21. *Militant,* July 1, August 15, 1929.

22. Shachtman, "Foreword," in Trotsky, *Problems of the Chinese Revolution* (Ann Arbor, 1967), v-xvii; Donald McCoy, *Angry Voices*

(Lawrence, Kan., 1958), 73-74.

23. "Resolution on the Internal Situation," *Internal Bulletin* 7 (January 1938); "Conference Thesis Draft on the League and the New Party" (n.d. but 1934), Socialist Workers Party Papers; and see Trotsky's statement on terrorism in Dewey Commission, *The Case of Leon Trotsky* (New York, 1969), 488-494, and Lenin on terrorism in "What Is to Be Done?" Henry M. Christman, ed., *Essential Works of Lenin* (New York, 1966), 110-111.

24. James Burnham, "Fascism's Dress Clothes," *New International* 4 (July 1938), 207-209; Trotsky, *Death Agony of Capitalism and the Tasks of the Fourth International* (New York, 1970), passim; and "Whither France?" (New York, 1936), 15-16; "His Last Article," *Fourth International* 1 (October 1940), 128-131; Cannon, *Notebook of an Agitator*, 355.

25. Mark Braden in *Internal Bulletin* 5 (September 1942).

26. Shachtman, *Reminiscences*, 34, COHC.

27. Dewey Commission, *Case of Leon Trotsky*, 476.

28. Trotsky, "The Way Out," in Breitman and Scott, eds., *Writings of Leon Trotsky, 1934-1935* (New York, 1971), 82; "Stalin Has Signed the Death Certificate of the Third International," ibid., 299-300; Trotsky et al., "Open Letter for the Fourth International," Breitman and Scott, eds., *Writings of Trotsky, 1935-1936*, 16-17; Trotsky, *Death Agony of Capitalism and Tasks of Fourth International*, 33. Some scholars acknowledged the Comintern's role in the rise of Hitler. According to Milorad M. Drachkovitch and Branko Lazitch, Moscow directives were "given the German Communist Party, which was obliged to consider the 'social fascism' of the German Socialists the main enemy, [serving as] a boon to Hitler and his quest for power . . . ." "The Communist International" in Drachkovitch and Lazitch, eds., *The Revolutionary Internationals, 1864-1943* (Stanford, 1966), 186. Stefan T. Possony said "the Communists could have saved German democracy simply by breaking the voting alliance with the Nazis in the Reichstag . . . . even a temporary change in Communist voting behavior could have prevented the immediate collapse of the German Republic," in "The Comintern as an Instrument of Soviet Strategy," ibid., 215. Marx saw political democracy as the path to socialism; Comintern strategy was ill-advised.

29. Shachtman, "Struggle for the New Course," in Trotsky, *The New Course* (Ann Arbor, 1965), 246; *My Life*, 476-478.

30. Trotsky, "In Closed Court," Breitman and Scott, eds., *Writings of Trotsky, 1935-1936*, 137.

31. These are the themes found in Trotsky, *Death Agony of Capitalism and the Tasks of the Fourth International*, passim; see too "Discus-

sion with Crux [Trotsky] on the Transitional Program," *Internal Bulletin*, I, 6 (July 1938); Trotsky, "On the Revolutionary Intellectuals: An Open Letter to V. F. Calverton," *Modern Quarterly* 7 (March 1933), 85.

32. William F. Warde, "The Right of Revolution," *Fourth International* 2 (August 1941), 209-212.

33. Isaac Deutscher, *The Prophet Outcast* (London, 1963), 202-208.

34. Trotsky, my translation, in Pierre Broué, ed., *Le mouvement communiste en France, 1919-1939* (Paris, 1967), 432.

35. Cannon, *History of American Trotskyism*, 92.

36. Ibid., 92-93.

37. Cannon, *History of American Trotskyism*, 94. The *Militants* of the early years perpetually pleaded for funds. *Militant,* September 15, 1929; July 26, October 1, November 1, 1930; the issue of December 19, 1931, advertised a benefit Christmas party in New York, proceeds for the *Militant* fund.

38. *Militant,* June 1, 1929.

39. To the question whether or not the group should have participated in electoral politics, Shachtman replied it should not have done so; participation had been "a completely wasted effort," and worst of all, "an exposure of weakness." Interview with Shachtman, August 17, 1972. See *Militant,* May 1-15, June 1, 1929 for Hedlund's campaign.

40. *Militant,* June 1, 1929; Cannon, *History of American Trotskyism,* 83-85. Delegates and alternates came from Chicago, Cleveland, Detroit, Kansas City, Minneapolis (the largest delegation), New York, Philadelphia, Springfield (Illinois), St. Louis, St. Paul, Toronto, and Youngstown. Greetings arrived from Trotskyists in other cities unable to send representatives.

41. Cannon, *History of American Trotskyism,* 86.

42. *Militant,* September 15, 1929; January 1, February 1, 15, March 1, September 12, 1931.

43. *Militant,* July 25, September 12, 1931.

44. *Internal Bulletin* 1 and 2 (July 1932).

45. Trotsky in *Militant,* July 1, 1929.

46. *Internal Bulletin* 1 (July 1932); Cannon quoted in Abern, Glotzer, and Shachtman, "The Situation in the American Opposition," June 4, 1932, SWPP.

47. Interviews with Max Geltman, November 24, 1972; with Emanuel Geltman, November 25, 1972; and with Hal Draper, November 7, 1975.

48. Lillian Symes and Travers Clement, *Rebel America* (Boston, 1972), 346; Cannon, *First Ten Years of American Communism* (New York, 1962), 141.

49. *Internal Bulletin* 4 [Nov. ?] 1932, SWPP.

50. Ibid.

51. *Militant,* September 15, 1933.

52. Isaacs, "Contemporary Marxian Political Movements," 683-684; *Militant,* January 15, May 15, 1931.

Chapter 4

1. James P. Cannon, *The History of American Trotskyism* (New York, 1944), 108.

2. Arne Swabeck in *Militant,* March 29, 1930; Farrell Dobbs, lecture, "The Minneapolis Strikes and the Tasks of the Revolutionary Party," Socialist Workers Party Tape Collection, New York.

3. *Militant,* June 1, August 15, 1929, and August 29, 1931; Trotsky and F. Robertson, "An Interview with Leon Trotsky," George Breitman and Bev Scott, eds., *Writings of Leon Trotsky, 1935-1936* (New York, 1970), 69-73; Trotsky, "Trade Unions in the Epoch of Capitalist Decay," *Fourth International* 2 (February 1941), 40-43.

4. Vincent Ray Dunne in *Socialist Appeal,* October 22, 1938.

5. Arne Swabeck in *Militant,* December 7, 1929.

6. A. Swabeck and B. Crane in *Socialist Appeal,* December 1936; Cannon in *Labor Action,* February 20, 1937; Irving Bernstein, *Turbulent Years* (Boston, 1970), 778.

7. *Militant,* May 1, 1929; Earl Browder, *The Communists and the People's Front* (New York, 1938), 66; Bernstein, *Turbulent Years,* 777, 781-782.

8. Joseph B. Matthews, *Odyssey of a Fellow-Traveler* (New York, 1938), 125; Louis F. Budenz, *The Techniques of Communism* (Chicago, 1954), 290-298.

9. Interview, Betty Yorburg with Max Shachtman for Socialist Movement Project, 2: 18, Columbia Oral History Collection; author with B. J. Widick, August 3, with Bert Cochran, August 16, with Ernest Rice McKinney, November 25, all in 1972.

10. *Militant,* January 15, April 1, August 1, 15, 1929.

11. *Militant,* April 15, July 1, August 1, 15, September 15, 1929; and see Louis Waldman, *Labor Lawyer* (New York, 1944), 65; Waldman defended Fred Beal, Communist party member indicted as agitator in the Gastonia violence.

12. The National Miners Union enrolled 4,000-5,000 miners in 1928 and was in fact a Trade Union Unity League affiliate. When by 1931 John L. Lewis's United Mine Workers was accused under Kentucky's

criminal syndicalism law and so quit the effort (evidence of IWW activity was uncovered by Harlan County law officers, and members were charged with murder of a mine guard), the NMU heightened its action. It too was driven out of Harlan County by the end of 1931 by terrorism, mail tampering, raids, and arrests for criminal syndicalism. It thereupon moved its action center to the Pennsylvania coal fields. Swabeck in *Militant,* February 1, 1929; also, *Militant,* March 1, 1930; Irving Bernstein, *The Lean Years* (Cambridge, Mass., 1960), 134, 343, 379-388; Cannon, *History of American Trotskyism,* 105.

13. Bernstein, *Turbulent Years,* 217-218.

14. In 1932 the League had expelled Field. Trotsky mildly objected and ordered reinstatement, respecting his ability in theoretical economics: "His study on economic crisis I recommend for publication . . . . I insist—you let the Left Opposition have the benefit of his talents." Field duly approached the national committee on March 11, 1933. Obediently and promptly the membership by unanimous vote reinstated Field. Trotsky in NC, August 18, October 10, November 13, 1932, *Internal Bulletin* 4 [November ?] 1932, Socialist Workers Party Papers (hereafter referred to as SWPP); *New Internal Bulletin,* January 1936, SWPP. Kaldis under Works Progress Administration auspices later became a lecturer on Greek art. Interview with Emanuel Geltman, November 25, 1972; Cannon, *History of American Trotskyism,* 126-127; Harry Roskolenko, *When I Was Last on Cherry Street* (New York, 1965), 143-144.

15. "Statement on the Expulsion of Field and Kaldis," February 19, 1934; Swabeck to League Branches, May 15, 1934, in SWPP; Cannon, *History of American Trotskyism,* 133-134.

16. B. J. Field et al., "The Lessons of the New York Hotel Strike," n.d., SWPP.

17. The Communist party's *Daily Worker* of March 1, 1934 reported the strike settlement as a betrayal of the food workers by Cannon, Field, and Gitlow. Shachtman, "Footnote for Historians," *New International* 4 (December 1938), 377-378; "From CLA to WP: A Political Autobiography," *New International Bulletin,* October 1935, SWPP; Cannon, *History of American Trotskyism,* 134.

18. Daniel Bell, *Marxian Socialism in the U.S.* (Princeton, 1967), 111-112; William Isaacs, "Contemporary Marxian Political Movements in the U.S. (Ph.D. dissertation, New York University, 1940), 696-697.

19. *What Is the Non-Partisan Labor Defense?* (New York, n.d.), Tamiment Institute Library.

20. *Militant,* February 1, 1929; Dobbs, lecture, "Minneapolis Strikes," SWP Tape Collection; Civil Rights Defense Committee, *Who Are the 18*

Prisoners in the Minneapolis Labor Case? (New York, n.d.), Tamiment Institute Library; Bernstein, *Turbulent Years,* 231-233; Arthur M. Schlesinger, *The Coming of the New Deal* (Boston, 1959), 386; for the entire story told from the perspective of a Minneapolis worker turned urban historian, see Charles Rumford Walker, *American City* (New York, 1937), passim.

21. As quoted in Thomas E. Blantz, "Father Haas and the Minneapolis Truckers' Strike of 1934," *Minnesota History* (Spring 1970), 7.

22. Dobbs, "The Minneapolis Strikes," Socialist Workers party Tapes; Cannon, *History of American Trotskyism,* 135.

23. *Militant,* February 4, 1934; Cannon, *History of American Trotskyism,* 135.

24. Vincent Ray Dunne in *Militant,* January 4, 1930; interview with B. J. Widick, August 3, 1972.

25. The League demands for relieving unemployment appeared repeatedly in *Militant.* See June 28, 1930; Sam Gordon in ibid., April 1, 1931 and Hugo Oehler in ibid., December 12, 1931.

26. Gordon in *Militant,* April 1, 1931; Swabeck in *Militant,* February 1, 1931 and July 30, 1932.

27. See *Militant* from February through June 1930, Tom Stamm in ibid., June 15, 1931, Oehler in ibid., April 15, 1931. Chicago convention proceedings described in ibid., May 20, 1931.

28. Leonard Howard de Caux, *Labor Radical* (Boston, 1970), 162-163.

29. Hook to author, October 5, 1972.

30. *Daily Worker,* March 29, 1934; July 7, 9, 11, 13, 16, 23, 25, 1934; August 3, 9, 1934; *Militant,* October 17, 31, 1931; February 13, November 26, 1932; February and March 1933; Sidney Lens, *Radicalism in America* (New York, 1969), 307; A. J. Muste, "Sketches for an Autobiography," in Nat Hentoff, ed., *Essays of A. J. Muste* (New York, 1967), 156; telephone interview with Sidney Hook, November 19, 1973.

31. *Militant,* January 30 and August 27, 1932; August 11, 1934.

32. A splinter from the "self-helpers" in Los Angeles formed the "Hermits," which met in cells of twenty at private homes and subscribed to mystical formulas handed down from the top, bureaucratically. *Militant,* August 11, 1934; Oehler in ibid., January 28, 1933.

33. Mauritz Hallgren, leftist commentator who was by no means a Trotskyist, describing the movement called the scheme a "pipe dream of a man ignorant of the workings of modern economic society." *Seeds of Revolt* (New York, 1933), 194-195, 200.

34. Art Preis wrote *America's Permanent Depression* (New York, 1938) and *Labor's Giant Step* (New York, 1972). For Muste's prior

connection with self-help, see Louis Breier in *New Militant,* December 15, 1934.

35. *Militant,* February 24, July 15, 1933; in 1939 Muste wrote, "personally I was moving rapidly along the road which made me become an inwardly-convinced Marxist-Lenist—though critical of the official Communist Party's course . . . ." in "True International," Hentoff, ed., *Essays of Muste* (New York, 1967), 208; interview, Yorburg with Muste for Socialist Movement Project, 5: 6-7, COHC.

36. Muste, "Sketches for an Autobiography" in Hentoff, ed., *Essays of Muste,* 61-63, 82.

37. Muste, "Sketches," in Hentoff, ed., *Essays of Muste,* 82-129; Bernard Johnpoll believed Woll's hostility to Brookwood stemmed from "Brookwood's threat to his own view of a labor utopia: docile, conservative unions, based on crafts and limited to the most highly skilled artisans using tactics totally devoid of militancy." *Pacifist's Progress* (Chicago, 1970), 74. Leonard de Caux was impressed. "Labor idealists liked Brookwood. To the romantic it had aspects of a quasi-utopian colony. To the more practical, if optimistic, it was a step toward advancing labor from the rear end to the vanguard of progress. To me, at my age and in my state of mind, it was altogether enchanting . . . . Spiritually, Brookwood was a labor movement in microcosm without bureaucrats or racketeers—with emphasis on youth, aspiration, ideals." *Labor Radical,* 94-96.

38. *Militant,* May 27, June 3, 1933.

39. Muste, "The World Task of Pacifism," Hentoff, *Essays of Muste,* 223-224; Muste,"The Problem of Violence," *Modern Monthly* 10 (March 1937), 7-9; in the Fellowship of Reconciliation, whose organ *The World Tomorrow* was edited by Norman Thomas, Muste's assistants were for a time James Farmer and Bayard Rustin. The Congress of Racial Equality was launched by FOR; Ernest Rice McKinney came into the Trotskyist movement as a follower of Muste and in 1975 was Rustin's assistant.

40. Shachtman in *Militant,* January 1, 1931; Cannon in ibid., April 1, 1931.

41. *Militant,* July 1, August 1, 1929.

42. Hentoff, "Introduction," *Essays of Muste,* v-xi.

43. Telephone interviews with Sidney Hook, November 19, 1973; with James Burnham, November 20, 1973.

44. A. J. Muste, "An American Revolutionary Party," *Modern Monthly* 7 (January 1934), 713-719; "Open Letter to American Intellectuals," ibid. (March 1934), 87-92; American Workers party *Toward an American Revolutionary Labor Movement* (New York, 1934), 3-19.

45. Louis Budenz, "For an American Revolutionary Approach," *Modern Monthly* 9 (March 1935), 14-18; Sidney Hook, "On Workers' Democracy," ibid., 8 (October 1934), 529-544.

46. Muste, *Automobile Industry and Organized Labor* (n.p.), 37-39; Louis Budenz, *This Is My Story* (New York and London, 1947), 96-97; Budenz, "Strikes Under the New Deal," Alfred M. Bingham and Selden Rodman, eds., *Challenge to the New Deal* (New York, 1934), 100-102; Muste, "Trade Unions and the Revolution," Hentoff, ed., *Essays of Muste,* 189; Louis Adamic, *Dynamite!* (New York, 1934), 450-453; Bernstein, *Turbulent Years* (Boston, 1970), 223-227; Philip Taft, *Organized Labor in American History* (New York, 1964), 489; Associated Press release to *Augusta Chronicle,* May 25, 1934.

47. Taft, *Organized Labor in American History,* 489.

48. Budenz, "Strikes Under the New Deal," Bingham and Rodman, eds., *Challenge to the New Deal,* 103.

49. Muste, *Automobile Industry and Organized Labor,* 37-39.

50. Muste, "Sketches," Hentoff, ed., *Essays of Muste,* 158-160.

51. Comment by B. J. Widick in interview with author, August 3, 1973.

52. *Militant,* June 16, 1934; Bernstein, *Turbulent Years,* 235; Taft, *Organized Labor in American History,* 445-446; Cannon, *Notebook of an Agitator,* 75-81; see Dobbs's volume devoted entirely to events of the strike: *Teamster Rebellion* (New York, 1972).

53. Cannon in *Militant,* June 16, 1934; Schlesinger, *Coming of the New Deal,* 387.

54. AP release to *Augusta Chronicle,* May 22, 1934; Bernstein, *Turbulent Years,* 236-237.

55. *Militant,* May 26, 1934; *Daily Worker,* May 21, 1934; and see ch. 10, "Civil War in July," in Walker, *American City,* 155-183.

56. Quoted by Schlesinger in *Coming of the New Deal,* 388.

57. Dobbs, "Minneapolis Strikes," Socialist Worker party Tapes; AP to *Augusta Chronicle,* May 24, 1934; *Militant,* June 16, 1934.

58. Authorities "shot fifty pickets down and killed two of them in cold blood . . . whitewashed the murderers and defamed the victims . . . raided our headquarters with full military force and equipment . . . imprisoned our leaders . . . confined our union doctor in their stockade . . . ." Cannon reported in *Notebook of an Agitator,* 82; Dobbs, "Minneapolis Strikes," Socialist Worker party Tapes; Blantz, "Father Haas and the Minneapolis Strike," *Minnesota History* (Spring 1970), 5-6; *Militants* through July and August 1934.

59. *Augusta Chronicle,* May 22, 1934.

60. Bernstein claimed employers plotted riot for July 20: they drove

a truck of police, firing, into a picket line, wounding sixty-seven and killing two, most shot in the back. *Turbulent Years,* 243-246; Walker in *American City* agreed to that extent (see 165-169). But Bernstein added that Trotskyists knew a trap had been set as the governor's adjutant-general had warned them. Nevertheless they sent unsuspecting pickets out and obtained slain martyrs for whom a big funeral with Veterans of Foreign Wars marchers took place. The conflict came to be known as the "battle of bloody Friday." Briefly, too, during this second strike Governor Olson imposed martial law on Minneapolis.

61. For instance, the *Daily Worker* proclaimed: "Trotskyite Leaders Try to Split the Ranks of Men on Strike," and Clarence Hathaway said in an editorial that while Olson prepared martial law, Trotskyist leaders knifed the strike in the back. See issues of July 19, 25, 1934.

62. *Militants* of June 1934, and August 18, 1934; Blantz, "Father Haas and the Minneapolis Strike," *Minnesota History* (Spring 1970), 15.

63. "The I.B.T.C.W.H.," *Fortune* 23 (May 1941), 47; Paul Jacobs, *The State of the Unions* (New York, 1963), 11-14; interviews with Alfred Russel, July 14, 1973; and George Novack, July 29, 1973.

64. Ralph C. James and Estelle James, *Hoffa and the Teamsters* (Princeton, 1965), 89-99.

65. James R. Hoffa, *The Trials of Jimmy Hoffa* (Chicago, 1970), 91.

66. Ibid., 91-92.

67. Shachtman, *Reminiscences,* 221, COHC.

Chapter 5

1. G. Gourov in *Internal Bulletin* 12 (April 19, 1933), Socialist Workers Party Papers (hereafter referred as SWPP), Wisconsin State Historical Society; *Militant,* October 14, 1933.

2. Trotsky, my translation, in Pierre Broué, ed., *Le mouvement communiste en France, 1919-1939* (Paris, 1967), 428; Gourov in *Internal Bulletin* 15, n.d., SWPP.

3. Trotsky in George Breitman and Bev Scott, eds., *Writings of Leon Trotsky, 1934-1935* (New York, 1971), 10; Isaac Deutscher, *The Prophet Outcast* (London, 1963), 264; *Bulletin* of the International Communist League (June, 1934), SWPP; *Militants* February through September 1933; Max Shachtman, *Reminiscences,* 231, Columbia Oral History Collection (hereafter referred to as COHC).

4. *Militant,* September 30, 1933.

5. *Militant,* October 7, 1933.

6. *Militant,* November 18, December 16, 30, 1933. Al Goldman

suggested an ad hoc federation of communist groups to meet and discuss "questions of principles and tactics" for forming the party.

7. Alfred M. Bingham and Selden Rodman, "Postscript," in Bingham and Rodman, eds., *Challenge to the New Deal* (New York, 1934), 281; Mauritz Hallgren, *Seeds of Revolt* (New York, 1933), 348-351.

8. John Dewey, "Imperative Need: A New Radical Party," Bingham and Rodman, eds., *Challenge to the New Deal,* 271.

9. Eastman, "Am I a Technocrat?" Bingham and Rodman, eds., *Challenge to the New Deal,* 149.

10. Hardman, "Is a New Party Possible?" Bingham and Rodman, eds., *Challenge to the New Deal,* 273.

11. Muste, "Middle Class or Working Class," Bingham and Rodman, eds., *Challenge to the New Deal,* 242.

12. Calverton, *Modern Monthly* 7 and 8 (January-June 1934; July-December 1934), passim.

13. American Workers Party, *Toward an American Revolutionary Labor Movement* (New York, 1934), 37-45; Herbert Solow, "After Madison Square Garden," *Modern Monthly* 7 (April 1934), 182; *New Militant,* July 20, 1935.

14. *Militant,* June 11, 1932.

15. John Spargo and Morris Hillquit quoted in Bernard Johnpoll, *Pacifist's Progress* (New York, 1970), 17-20; *Militant,* September 15, 1929, and August 8, 1931.

16. *Militant,* August 1, September 15, October 15, 1929; January 25, 1930; March 1, July 25, 1931.

17. *Militant,* July 25, 1931.

18. American Workers party, *Toward an American Revolutionary Labor Movement,* 30-31, 37-48; V. F. Calverton (pseudonym for George Goetz) and seventeen CPLA-American Workers party leaders signed "An Open Letter to American Intellectuals," *Modern Monthly* 7 (February 1934), 87-92, appealing to "professional workers . . . doctors, architects, engineers, scientists, teachers, lawyers, artists, writers—to help build the A.W.P. Your condition is becoming steadily and rapidly worse. There is no chance under the present order for its betterment." But there was hope. The American Workers party understood the revolutionary nature of change that alone could save society and would establish a "free workers' democracy guaranteeing peace, security, and the opportunity of individual betterment for all." The appeal rested on an assumption that these professionals were in reality a white-collar proletariat, long guilty of misplaced loyalty to the big bourgeoisie. It purported to instruct them where their interests in fact lay, with the blue collar proletariat and in a revolutionary party. Calverton and his col-

leagues overlooked the truth that very, very few of these professionals would be consulting the left-wing *Modern Monthly* at all, and so would escape their message.

19. Hardman quoted in Walter Goodman, *The Committee* (New York, 1968), 66.

20. Louis Budenz, "For an American Revolutionary Approach," *Modern Monthly* 9 (March 1935), 14-18; and "Winning America," ibid. (April 1935), 142-146.

21. Muste, "Sketches for an Autobiography" in Nat Hentoff, ed., *Essays of A. J. Muste* (New York, 1967), 122-123.

22. Sidney Hook, "On Workers' Democracy," *Modern Monthly* 8 (October 1934), 544.

23. *Militant,* December 16, 1933.

24. Shachtman, *Reminiscences,* 241-242, COHC.

25. *Militant,* January 27, 1934.

26. Shachtman in *Militant,* February 24; Cannon in ibid., March 10, both 1934.

27. Cannon in *Militant,* March 10, 1934; Felix Morrow in ibid., May 26, June 2, 1934.

28. "Conference Thesis Draft on the League and the New Party for Third League National Conference" (mineographed), n.d. but 1934, SWPP.

29. Communist League of America to International Secretariat and L. D. Trotsky, March 9, 1934, SWPP.

30. Shachtman, *Reminiscences,* 243-244, COHC.

31. Hook to author, October 5, 1972.

32. Cannon distrusted Hardman as much as Hardman did the League, calling him a "half-and-half man," a "moral weakling," the "flunkey editor of *Advance* [Amalgamated Clothing Workers' organ], intellectual sharpshooter who did all kinds of dirty work for that ignorant boor and trickster . . . Sidney Hillman." Also recollecting meetings to negotiate fusion, Cannon remembered Hardman's remark, "I always read the *Militant,* I like to see what Trotsky has to say," which forced the caustic Cannon to bite his lip and restrain himself from responding, I always read the *Advance* because I like to see what Hillman has to say. Still, Hardman had adamantly taken Trotsky's side against Stalin, calling his persecution "a deed of disgrace" and "criminality," because his "only 'crime' was insubordination to . . . leadership of the Russian Communist Party at present in power," and was not "against the Revolution, the working class, or the labor state." Cannon, *History of American Trotskyism* (New York, 1944), 174-175; Muste to Provisional Organizing Committee-American Workers party, "Summary of Negoriations," Aug-

ust 30, 1934, SWPP; *Militant,* September 22, 1934; J. B. Salutsky-
Hardman quoted in Peter S. Filene, *Americans and the Soviet Experiment, 1917-1933* (Cambridge, Mass., 1967), 178.

33. Trotsky, *Whither France?* (New York, 1946), 83; André Philip, *Les socialistes* (n.p., 1967), 79-80; Maurice Thorez, *Fils du peuple* (Paris, 1960), 88.

34. Trotsky, "The Way Out," Breitman and Scott, eds., *Writings of Trotsky, 1934-1935,* 81-88.

35. Shachtman, *Reminiscences,* 233, COHC.

36. Shachtman's enthusiasm for the French turn may have taken form in retrospect; a comrade reported that at the time he regarded it as a retreat and was "impatient, panicky." The comrade, Max Geltman (Max Glee in the party) opposed entry picturesquely: "Enter the SFIO as a surgeon penetrates a rotting corpse in order to remove healthy living organisms from it . . . . Not enter as maggots which is part of a carrion," but enter "scientifically by building a strong faction inside it, keeping organizational independence, then pull all our people . . . out of it and build up the Ligue." *Internal Bulletin* 17 (October 1934), SWPP; Trotsky to Polish Comrade V, February 28, 1935, Breitman and Scott, eds., *Writings of Trotsky, 1934-1935,* 204-205; Shachtman, *Reminiscences,* 238, COHC.

37. Trotsky, *Death Agony of Capitalism and Tasks of the Fourth International* (New York, 1970), 44; Linier in *Internal Bulletin* 16 (September 1934), SWPP.

38. Linier in *Internal Bulletin* 16 (September 1934); J. Thulier in ibid.; Glee in *Internal Bulletin* 17 (October 1934); for Oehler's role at the plenum see ibid.; all in SWPP.

39. Trotsky to National Committee-Workers party, August 11, 1935, Breitman and Scott, eds., *Writings of Trotsky, 1934-1935,* 22; Trotsky to National Committee, August 12, 1935 in ibid., 24; Crux [Trotsky] to International Secretariat, June 10, 1935, *International News* 2 (October 1935), SWPP; Trotsky in Broué, ed., *Le mouvement communiste en France,* 404-405.

40. Editorials exclaimed "For the New Party—For the Fusion of the League and the AWP!" and, "For the New Revolutionary Party!" *Militant,* September 15, November 17, 1934.

41. Communist League of America leaders urged a speedy course: ". . . we must hurry and fuse before the dot is put on every 'i' and every hair is split in two." *Militant,* September 29, 1934; "[we] should speed up and press for action," declared the CLA "Statement," *Internal Bulletin* 16 (September 1934), SWPP; Cannon, *History of American Trotskyism,* 180-181.

42. Bittelman in *Daily Worker* quoted by Cannon, *History of American Trotskyism,* 182.

43. It "will speedily attract the scattered revolutionary militants as a magnet attracts steel particles"; thousands will join, beamed Cannon in *Militant,* September 15, 1934.

44. *Militant,* October 6, 1934.

45. Cannon incorrectly claimed more dues-paying members at time of fusion. It was indeed more tightly knit, but about one-sixth the size of the American Workers party in paid memberships. Interviews with Hook, November 19, 1973; with Burnham, November 20, 1973; Cannon, *History of American Trotskyism,* 180-181.

46. The program covered the topics so important to radicals. In order of mention they were: deficiencies of other parties, crisis of capitalism, imperialism and fascism, role of United States in the world emergency, the New Deal, what to do and who must do it, road to power, condition of democracy, need for revolutionary party, workers' state to come, goals of socialist society, critical defense of Russia, united fronts, the new fourth international, "tasks" of new party, trade union policy, policy toward agricultural workers, Negroes, colonized peoples, professional and technical workers, the unemployed, youth, and a stand on war. *Militant,* October 27, 1934; interviews with Ernest Rice McKinney, November 26, 1972 and December 29, 1975. Hook to author, October 5, 1972.

47. Cannon, *History of American Trotskyism,* 180-181; Shachtman, *Reminiscences,* 428, COHC.

48. Cannon, *History of American Trotskyism,* 182-188; *Militant,* November 3, 1934; *New Militant,* December 8, 1934; telephone interviews with Hook, November 19, 1973; with Burnham, November 20, 1973.

49. George Weissman, in 1973 an editor of the Socialist Workers party press, remembered Shachtman's brilliance and wit as speaker, dimmed only once in Weissman's experience. When Weissman was a student at Harvard in 1939, Shachtman came on invitation to speak. Unaware that campus Trotskyists held Harvard's pretensions in contempt, Shachtman was apparently so overwhelmed with awe that his delivery went sour. Interview with Weissman, August 4, 1973; with Shachtman, August 17, 1972, with Swabeck, August 13, 1976; Cannon, *History of American Trotskyism,* 204-205.

50. *New Militants,* December 15, 19, 1934 and January through April 1935.

51. *New Militant,* February 2, 1935; Cannon, *History of American Trotskyism,* 136.

52. Workers party's *Organizational Bulletin,* May, 1935, SWPP.

53. Hook to author, October 5, 1972.

54. Still needing the psychological security of an ideological home, Budenz followed the same pattern inside the Communist party. He claimed his parents' prayers, Monsignor Fulton J. Sheen, and intercession of the Virgin Mary brought him back to the Christian fold. He remained in the party for four weeks after all arrangements were complete for his return to Catholicism. Budenz then went on to become an anti-Communist witness for the House Un-American Activities Committee. Budenz, *This is My Story* (New York, 1947), 99-100; Muste, "Sketches for an Autobiography," Hentoff, ed., *Essays of Muste,* 116, 170, 173, and in *New Militant,* May 25, 1935; Shachtman, *Reminiscences,* 245-247, COHC.

55. Workers party's *Organizational Bulletin,* May 1935, SWPP.

56. The Revolutionary Policy Committee was a tiny fraction intending to capture the Socialist party for hard-line Marxism. In 1932 Jay Lovestone "sent" Irving Brown into the Socialist party to put it together. Interviews with Hal Draper, November 7, 1975; with Bertram D. Wolfe, November 8, 1975.

57. *New Militant,* April 6, 1935; telephone interview with Hook, November 19, 1973.

58. Martin Abern, Al Glotzer, Max Shachtman, "The Situation in the American Opposition: Prospect and Retrospect," June 4, 1932, SWPP; *New Militant,* December 22, 1934.

59. Shachtman, *Reminiscences,* 247-248, 255, COHC.

60. "To NC, Branches, Members of the WPUS," May 15, 1935; "Statement of PC on Expulsion of Joseph Zack," June 4, 1935; Muste, "How the Cannon-Shachtman Group 'Builds' the Party," July-August 1935; Basky, Oehler, Stamm, "On Zack," July 8, 1935, all in SWPP.

61. Cannon, *History of American Trotskyism,* 211.

62. *New Militant,* December 22, 1934; also ibid., March and May, and October 5, 1935. Muste published his views separately from his Trotskyist comrades in *Automobile Industry and Organized Labor* (n.p.), 40-43, 54-56, in Tamiment Institute Library.

63. *New Militant* charged that the local businessman from whom Local 173 rented the building "had taken out riot insurance the previous Friday." April 6, 1935 and see ibid., February 2, November 30, 1935.

64. Ibid., March 20, April 6, 1935.

65. Workers party's *Organizational Bulletin,* April 1935; "Report on Activity of New York District, WPUS," n.d. but May 1935, SWPP.

66. *New Militant,* October 13, all November 1935 issues; Paul Jacobs, *State of the Unions* (New York, 1963), 11-14.

67. *New Militant,* November 23, 1935, January 4, February 15, 1936; Farrell Dobbs, "Minneapolis Strikes and Role of the Revolutionary Party," Socialist Workers party's Tape Collection.

68. *What Is the Non-Partisan Labor Defense?* (New York, n.d.), Tamiment; interview with George Novack, July 29, 1973.

69. Nonpartisan Labor Defense attorney Francis Heisler of Chicago argued the Fargo case; Al Goldman and Raymond Henderson handled separate phases of the Sacramento case. *New Militant,* December 15, 1934; February 16, May 18, 25, June 1, 15, September 7, October 12, November 2, 30, December 21, 28, 1935; February 1, March 36, 1936.

70. *New Militant,* January through October 1935. James Burnham wrote under the pen name "John West."

71. Muste in *New Militant,* May 11, 1935, November 2, 1935; "West" in ibid., October 1935 issues; Leighton Rigby in ibid., November and December 1935; Trotsky in *Militant,* August 15, 1931; April 9, 16, May 7, 1932; in *New Militant,* November 2, 1935.

72. Articles by Swabeck, Ruth Wilson, "John West," Muste, Dan Eastman (Max Eastman's son and until 1937 a Trotskyist) in *New Militant,* December 1934 through May 1935.

73. "Statement on Third Plenum, WPUS," October 5, 1935, SWPP; "Convention Resolutions," *New Militant,* March 14, 1936.

74. Cannon, *History of American Trotskyism,* 209-211; "Resolutions. Minutes." June 1935, SWPP.

75. "Resolution by Oehler on International Plenum," n.d. but 1935, SWPP; *New Militant,* July 6, 1935.

76. Muste in *New Militant,* November 9, 1935.

77. Cannon, *History of American Trotskyism,* 189, 192; interviews with Novack, July 29, 1973; with Weissman, August 4, 1973; with Bert Cochran, August 16, 1972; with Emanuel Geltman, November 25, 1972; with Arne Swabeck, August 13, 1976.

78. Shachtman, *Reminiscences,* 251, COHC.

Chapter 6

1. The Workers party had made some unspectacular progress . . . . "[but with the Communist and Socialist parties] still constituted an absolutely insignificant portion, not of the population in general alone but of the labor movement in striking contrast to Europe . . . ." Max Shachtman, *Reminiscences,* 250, Columbia Oral History Collection (hereafter referred to as COHC).

2. Hook to author, October 5, 1972.

3. Trotsky, noting expulsion of youth leaders in his diary on July 10, 1935, remarked that it was "the price of the forthcoming merger of the Social Democrats with the Stalinists." He referred to the impending united front of the SFIO with the French Communist party, which would not tolerate Trotskyists in their midst. Trotsky, *Diary in Exile, 1935* (New York, 1963), 155; Trotsky to Comrade Rous, July 30, 1935, George Breitman and Bev Scott, eds., *Writings of Leon Trotsky, 1935-1936* (New York, 1970), 46; Trotsky in Pierre Broué, ed., *Le mouvement communiste en France, 1919-1939* (Paris, 1967), 405-406; Pivert to Expelled Comrades, July 30, 1935, in *New Militant,* September 7, 1935.

4. Pierre Naville was the other French Trotskyist leader. Naville followed *Truth* out of the SFIO. Trotsky in Broué, ed., *Le mouvement communiste en France,* 404-406; Trotsky to French Bolshevik-Leninists, August 11, 1935, Breitman and Scott, eds., *Writings of Trotsky, 1935-1936,* 49; Trotsky, *Whither France?* (New York, 1936), 4; *New Militant,* April 13, 1935.

5. Trotsky to National Committee, Workers party, August 11, 12, 1935, Breitman and Scott, eds., *Writings of Trotsky, 1935-1936,* 23-24; to Comrades, December 30, 1935, ibid., 31; to Cannon and Shachtman, January 24, 1936, ibid., 32.

6. "Symposium on Important Problems of the SP," *American Socialist Monthly* 5 (June 1936), 27; Haim Kantorovich, "Notes on the United Front Problem," ibid. (May 1936), 9-11; Bernard Johnpoll, *Pacifist's Progress* (Chicago, 1970), 77, 80; William E. Seyler, "Rise and Decline of the Socialist Party in the U.S." (Ph.D. dissertation, Duke University, 1952), 494-496.

7. Twenty-year-old Hal Draper joined the Revolutionary Policy Committee (RPC) immediately, the only YPSL comrade to do so. After printing about five issues of *Revolutionary Socialist,* the RPC changed its name to "Revolutionary Publishing Association." Draper recalled that "the whole thing was smeared right away as a Lovestone front." Interviews with Draper, November 7, 1975; with Bertram D. Wolfe, November 8, 1975. Trotskyists viewed these developments in the Socialist party with utmost cynicism. Shachtman in *Militant,* February 5, March 1, 1931; also, ibid., May 28, June 4, 1932.

8. The stenographic report of the debate on the declaration of principles is in *American Socialist Monthly* 3 (July 1934), 7-58, Waldman's comment on p. 9, and see *Labor Lawyer* (New York, 1945), 261-270; see also J. B. Matthews, *Odyssey of a Fellow Traveler* (New York, 1938, 43; William C. Pratt, "The Reading Socialist Experience" (Ph.D. dissertation, Emory University, 1969), 248-250; Johnpoll, *Pacifist's*

Progress, 77; Felix Morrow, "New Socialism in America," *Modern Monthly* 8 (August 1934), 402. The literature on the dramatic events and aftermath of the Detroit convention is enormous. Herbert Zam, "Is the SP Going Revolutionary?" *Modern Monthly* 9 (March 1935), 44-47; V. F. Calverton, "Socialism Leans Left," ibid., 8 (January 1935), 645-649. Johnpoll said the Militant-Old Guard split was initially more a struggle between generations than ideologies. Pratt, speaking of Reading, Pennsylvania, concurred that ideology was less important than other factors; in Reading rivalry for control of the local movement motivated split.

9. Trotskyists nonetheless complained that the platform carried no condemnation of League of Nations' sanctions or of sanctions by one capitalist power against another. Nor did it criticize pacifism. It did reject armed insurrection as "romantic impossibilism." Editorials, *Socialist Appeal,* April, May, and July, 1936; Waldman, *Labor Lawyer,* 273-274; Bruno Fischer in *Modern Monthly* 10 (June 1936), 5 and Aaron Levenstein in ibid. (July 1936), 9; Haim Kantorovich in *American Socialist Monthly* 5 (July 1936), 11; Robert Delson in ibid. (June 1936), 5-6, and Murray Gross in ibid., 9. Also, *New Militant,* January 4, 11, 1936.

10. Oehler in *Militant,* May 7, 1932; Calverton in *Modern Monthly* 8 (July 1934), 326; Felix Morrow in ibid. (August 1934), 401; and in *New Militant,* August 10, 1935.

11. "A pool of Methodist preachers shows that 34% voted Socialist," claimed *New Militant,* November 16, 1935. See Tom Stamm in *Militant,* January 6, 1934; Muste, "Statement on Attitude of WP to SP and CP," July 1935, Socialist Workers Party Papers (hereafter referred to as SWPP).

12. "Conference Thesis Draft on League and New Party," n.d. but 1934, SWPP.

13. Ibid.

14. Thomas and Senior quoted by William C. Seyler in "The Rise and Decline of the Socialist Party in the U.S." (Ph.D. dissertation, Duke University, 1952); Johnpoll, *Pacifist's Progress,* 156-157; *Militant,* November 3, 1934; *Socialist Call,* November 17, 1936.

15. Arne Swabeck commenting on the Norman Thomas-Earl Browder debate of November 27, 1935, observed that although both were wrong, "Thomas was more right—that is, more left." He presented "the important arguments on every fundamental point, militantly critical and arguing from the left against the reactionary position of Browder." The Socialist party "has taken one step leftward." *New Militant,* December 31, 1935. The figure on Workers party membership in 1935 is an

approximate one supplied by Sidney Hook in telephone interview, November 19, 1973.

16. Minutes, June 1935; Minutes, October 1935, SWPP; *New Militant,* October 19, December 14, 1935.

17. Cannon insisted, "If we had allowed the opportunity in the SP to cool, we would have missed our chance. We had to strike while the iron was hot." *History of American Trotskyism* (New York, 1944), 213, 222-223.

18. Cannon quoted in leaflet, *Shall the International Proletariat Give Material Aid to the Spanish Loyalist Government?* July 19, 1937, SWPP.

19. *New Militant,* March 14, 1936; "John West" (Burnham) in ibid., April 18, 25, 1936; "West" and Shachtman in ibid., May 30, 1936.

20. Zam, Gus Tyler, Murry Baron, Andrew Biemiller, and Paul Porter met with Workers party negotiators. Cannon, *History of American Trotskyism,* 224-226.

21. Emanuel Geltman recalled that Shachtman's views were actually at the extreme right end of the remaining Socialist party, not differing substantially from Porter's or Laidler's, yet Socialists feared he would turn them into rabid revolutionaries. His habitual use of Marxist jargon disturbed them. Interview with Geltman, November 25, 1972; see *Socialist Appeal,* April and May 1936, and Robert Carson in ibid., July 1936; William C. Pratt, "The Reading Socialist Experience" (Ph.D. dissertation, Emory University, 1969), 312.

22. Citing his role in the American Workers party and League merger, Hook added, "I also acted as a marriage broker between them and Norman Thomas to my regret." He favored the two mergers because he wanted the Communist party to have some substantial opposition. Hook to author, September 13, 1972, and telephone interview with Hook, November 19, 1973; Harry Fleischman, *Norman Thomas* (New York, 1969), 170.

23. Cannon, *History of American Trotskyism,* 232; *New Militant,* June 6, 1936; Shachtman, *Reminiscences,* 265-266, 270, COHC.

24. *Militant,* June 21, 1930; *Internal Bulletin* 17 (October 1934), Communist League of America. On organic unity and factional identity, see Oehler, "Reply to Crux Letter," February 18, 1935, both SWPP.

25. On Stamm's background I find little information. Emanuel Geltman remembered him simply as a "nothing," who played ping-pong and invented the term "table tennis." Shachtman referred to him as "second in command of the Oehlerites," recalling a picturesque verbal exchange with him. Prescribing mutual confidence within the new Workers party, Shachtman admonished, "This is a baby . . . you have to nurse

the baby," to which Stamm assented, adding that he was concerned that
the baby be nursed at the left breast of revolutionary Marxism, not at
the right breast of opportunism, conciliationism, and centrism. Shachtman retorted that he, too, favored nursing baby at the proper breast,
but above all at a breast and not at an organ designed for other functions. *Reminiscences,* 249-250, COHC; interview with Emanuel Geltman, November 25, 1972.

26. Oehler, "Proposed Amendment to Draft Thesis of NEC [national
executive committee] on New Party," n.d. but 1934; "Minutes," June
1935; Muste, "How the Cannon-Shachtman Group 'Builds' the Party,"
August 1935; "West" in Workers party's *Internal Bulletin* 2 (January
1936), and ibid. 3 (February 1936), all SWPP.

27. Muste, "How the Cannon-Shachtman Group 'Builds' the Party"
and "Footnote on Organizational Methods," August 1935; "Minutes,"
June 1935, SWPP.

28. The *News* noted four positions on the French turn. At the far
right stood Cannonite liquidators; moving one notch left, a buffer
group, "the tail of the Cannon caucus"; next over, Muste, against the
turn as a tactic; and farthest left, Basky, Oehler, and Stamm, standing
for an independent Marxist party. Louis Basky, the eldest of the three,
was a middle-aged Communist party veteran. Basky, Oehler, and Stamm,
in *International News* 2, 1 (October 1935), SWPP.

29. Muste to Workers party branches, October 29, 1935, SWPP;
New Militant, November 2, October 19, 1935.

30. *International News* 2, 1 (October 1935); Muste to Workers party
branches, October 29, 1935; SWPP.

31. Cannon, *History of American Trotskyism,* 197; *New Militant,*
November 2, 1935.

32. Trotsky to Vereecken, November 19, 1935, Breitman and Scott,
eds., *Writings of Trotsky, 1935-1936,* 29.

33. Fragmentation went right on. Karl Mienov left Oehler's Revolutionary Workers League (RWL) in disagreement over the Spanish Civil
War and created the Marxist Workers League. Continuing, another
Oehlerite, George Marlen (party name contracting Marx and Lenin)
formed the Leninist League after he quarreled with the Revolutionary
Workers League and Trotsky on the nature of the Stalinist state. Several
subsequent efforts to merge the splinter sects failed utterly. Revolutionary Workers League leaflet, March 15, 1936; Revolutionary Workers
League, "Open Letter to Those Who Are Opposed to Joining the SP,"
1936, SWPP; Shachtman, *Reminiscences,* 259, COHC, and "Footnote
for Historians," *New International* 4 (December 1938), 378-379;
William Isaacs, "Contemporary Marxian Political Movements in the

U.S." (Ph.D. dissertation, New York University, 1940), 688-691; Oehler, "Crisis of Capitalism and Revolutionary Marxism," *Modern Socialism* 1 (Winter 1941-1942); interview with Max Geltman, November 24, 1972.

34. Benjamin Gitlow, *I Confess* (New York, 1939-1940), 574; Dwight Macdonald, *Memoirs of a Revolutionist* (Cleveland, 1957), 17; Norman L. Levy, "Radicalization of Dwight Macdonald" (M.A. Thesis, University of Wisconsin, 1966), 48; Shachtman, "Radicalism in the Thirties: the Trotskyist View," Rita James Simon, ed., *As We Saw the Thirties* (Urbana, Ill., 1967), 32.

35. Harry Roskolenko, *When I Was Last on Cherry Street* (New York, 1965), 180.

36. *New International Bulletin* (October 1935), (January 1936); Larry Cohen in *Internal Bulletin* 2 (January 1936); three circulars by "Marxist Action Group"; Bessie Shapiro to Workers party, all dated February 1936, in SWPP.

37. Muste in *New Militant,* August 10, 1935; Muste, McKinney, Johnson et al., in Workers party's *Internal Bulletin* 2 (January 1936); SWPP; and Muste, "Sketches for an Autobiography," Nat Hentoff, ed., *Essays of A. J. Muste* (New York, 1967), 164.

38. The Allentown group kept close contact with Arnold Johnson who did join the Communist party. "There was always a taint of Stalinist ideology in the position of the Allentown comrades," recalled Cannon in *History of American Trotskyism,* 229. Max Geltman in 1972 suspected Muste was himself a Stalinist infiltrator of the Trotskyists. "The young Trots felt they had been invaded by the barbarians—by Goyim—planted by Stalinists," the very assassination of Trotsky having been plotted through this maneuver. Interview with Geltman, November 24, 1972; Muste interviewed by Betty Yorburg for Socialist Movement Project, 5: 9-11, COHC.

39. New York branch *Bulletin* 5 (January 28, 1936), SWPP; Trotsky to Cannon and Shachtman, January 24, 1936, Breitman and Scott, eds., *Writings, 1935-1936,* 32.

40. Muste in *New Militant,* May 25, 1935; "True International," in Hentoff, ed., *Essays of Muste,* 207-214.

41. Max Geltman related an anecdote intended to give the lie to Muste's profession of pacifism. One day Geltman visited Muste in his office and asked him how he, as head of a pacifist group [the Fellowship of Reconciliation], could at the same time be head of an organization dedicated to overthrow of the political and economic system by force and violence. Muste allegedly winked and replied, "In the revolution as in life there are more ways than one to skin a cat." Geltman,

obviously repelled by Muste's memory ("I distrusted him entirely. He
gave me a feeling of butterflies in my guts"), reported that Muste moved
with palsied tremor and was "the most addicted chain smoker" Geltman had ever seen. More importantly, Geltman, in 1972 a Zionist, believed Muste was part of the international Communist conspiracy during the period chronicled here. A fellow Zionist in 1972, Harry Roskolenko, was convinced of Muste's basic Christian commitment, but
appeared similarly repelled by the man's memory. Muste was "an
exercise in theological vanity," in Roskolenko's language. Yet Roskolenko remarked that the year of Trotskyist-Musteite fusion was the best
period of the movement, but added sardonically that Muste's presence
made it fully an *American* movement replete with preacher. Contra-
dicting Geltman, Ernest Rice McKinney insisted Muste never condoned
revolutionary violence and to Muste, whom he described as "a pacifist—
absolutely," he attributed the saying, "If you can't love Hitler you
can't love anybody." Certainly Trotsky appeared to regard Muste
highly, according to Isaac Deutscher. Nat Hentoff, *Peace Agitator*
(New York, 1963), 95-96; interviews with Geltman, November 24,
1972; with Roskolenko, August 15, 1972; with McKinney, November
26, 1972 and December 29, 1975.

 42. Muste interviewed for Yorburg, Socialist Movement Project, 5:
6-7, COHC.

 43. Muste interviewed for Yorburg, 5: 15-17, COHC; Rudolph
Vecoli, "Introduction" to Muste, "My Experience in Labor and Radical Struggles," Simon, ed., *As We Saw the Thirties,* 124-125. According to Bernard Johnpoll, Norman Thomas said in 1963 Muste had
warned him of Cannon's and Shachtman's intentions. Johnpoll to author, August 1975.

 44. Muste, "World Task of Pacifism," Hentoff, ed., *Essays of Muste,*
220; interview with B. J. Widick, August 3, 1972. For Muste's career
as head of Labor Temple at Second Avenue and East Fourteenth Street,
see JoAnn Ooiman Robinson, "The Pharos of the East Side, 1937-1940:
Labor Temple under Direction of A. J. Muste," *Journal of Presbyterian
History* 42 (Spring 1970), 18-37.

 45. Hook to author, October 5, 1972.

 46. Interview with Shachtman, August 17, 1972.

 47. Cannon, *History of American Trotskyism,* 177.

 48. Burnham, "Socialists and the Coming War," *American Socialist
Monthly* 5 (August 1936), 26-27.

Chapter 7

1. Max Shachtman, *Reminiscences,* 262, 267-268, Columbia Oral History Collection (hereafter referred to as COHC); George Novack, address to Socialist Workers party banquet, November 21, 1970 in *Militant,* December 18, 1970.

2. According to Shachtman in *Behind the Moscow Trial* (New York, 1936), 128.

3. *Socialist Appeal,* December 16, 1936; interview with Hal Draper, November 7, 1975; Frank Trager to Norman Thomas, January 18, 1937, Norman Thomas Papers, New York Public Library.

4. Interview with Draper, November 7, 1975; *Socialist Appeal,* February 1937. Other leading Altmanites were Dan Hoan, also in Wisconsin, and in New York, Aaron Levenstein, Murry and Sam Baron, Hal Siegel, and Murray Gross. The Altmanites' Wisconsin arm had strong AFL ties and did not wish to support a party stand for the CIO against the AFL although Altman was a CIO organizer and Gross was in the pro-CIO International Ladies' Garment Workers Union (ILGWU).

5. Shachtman because of later violent disagreements with Clarity-ites caustically commented in 1962, "I assume that the reason they took that name was because they had the least clarity of all about the problems of the party." Zam and Tyler espoused bolshevism with greater zeal than did other leading Clarity figures, some of whom were Frank Trager, labor secretary for the Socialist party, Maynard Krueger of Chicago, and young lawyer Robert Delson of New York. Shachtman, *Reminiscences,* 268, COHC; *Socialist Appeal,* February and March 1937; Tyler, "How Shall We Conduct Our Election Campaign?" *American Socialist Monthly* 5 (October 1936), 14-16; telephone interviews with Emanuel Geltman, November 29, and Gus Tyler, December 4, 1973. Tyler was reached at his ILGWU office at 1710 Broadway, where in 1973 he was assistant to the president.

6. "Advance in Chicago," *American Socialist Monthly* 6 (May 1937), 9-12; "Party Affairs: A Paper for SP Members," 2, I (February 1937), Socialist Workers Party Papers (hereafter referred to as SWPP), Wisconsin State Historical Society.

7. Al Goldman in *Socialist Appeal,* September 1936; Tyler, "How Shall We Conduct Our Election Campaign?" *American Socialist Monthly* 5 (October 1936), 14-16; Harry Laidler, "Some Issues of the Campaign," ibid., 5.

8. John L. Lewis in symposium, "Why Labor Should Support the SP," *American Socialist Monthly* 5 (July 1936), 2.

9. Thomas in ibid., 3-6; Bruno Fischer, book review of Thomas,

After the New Deal, What? in *Modern Monthly* 7 (May 1937), 14.

10. Cannon, *Notebook of an Agitator* (New York, 1958), 102-103; William C. Pratt, "The Reading Socialist Experience" (Ph.D. dissertation, Emory University, 1969), 360-364.

11. Martin Diamond, "Socialism and the Decline of the American Socialist Party" (Ph.D. dissertation, University of Chicago, 1954), 144; Pratt, "Reading Socialist Experience," 364; *Socialist Appeal*, December 1936. Voting figures from Richard B. Morris, ed., *Encyclopedia of American History* (rev. ed., New York, 1965), 355.

12. Editorial, *American Socialist Monthly* 5 (December 1936), 6-7; Robert Delson and Louis Mann, "Some Problems of Party Organization," ibid. (February 1937), 59-62; *Socialist Appeal*, December 16, 1936; John Scott Wilson, "Norman Thomas" (Ph.D. dissertation, University of North Carolina, 1966), 331.

13. Thomas to Altman, December 5, 1936; to Senior, January 19, 1937, Norman Thomas Papers, New York Public Library. And see Earl Browder, *Trotskyism Against World Peace* (New York, 1936), 9-10 and Alexander Bittelman, *Trotsky the Traitor* (New York, 1937), 1-30 passim.

14. *Socialist Appeal*, March, 1937.

15. Richard Babb Whitten in *Socialist Appeal*, February 1937.

16. Notably absent at the institute was James P. Cannon, in Tijunga, California at the time. Appeal Institute, "Minutes," February 20-22, 1937, SWPP; *Socialist Appeal*, March 1937; Shachtman, *Reminiscences*, 272-273, COHC.

17. *Socialist Appeal*, March 1937.

18. Ibid.

19. Appeal Institute, "Minutes," February 20-22, 1937, SWPP.

20. Histories and analyses of this conflict abound. Trotsky's writings, chiefly letters, are collected in Naomi Allen and George Breitman, eds., *The Spanish Revolution, 1931-1939* (New York, 1973). A good Trotskyist interpretation written contemporaneously is in Felix Morrow, *Revolution and Counter-Revolution in Spain* (New York, 1938). A superb account by an Englishman who fought with the POUM militia is George Orwell's *Homage to Catalonia* (New York, 1952). The above writers disagreed in their comparison of Franco with Hitler and Mussolini. Orwell saw in Franco a throw-back to feudalism, not a fascist; the big bourgeoisie won him with generous financing coming from an array of international industrialists. The Loyalists, according to Orwell, feared social revolution and resultant expropriation far more than a feudal-fascist coup. Trotskyists, the POUM, the FAI, and the CNT embodied these fears. Felix Morrow declared the "land question is a capitalist

question," that "Spanish fascism is no more feudal than is Italian."
Frank Warren described some American reactions in *Red Decade Revisited* (Bloomington, Indiana, 1971), 133-140. Recent histories that
lend support to Morrow's and Orwell's earlier appraisals are Allen
Guttman's *Wound in the Heart* (New York, 1962) and Robert Rosenstone's *Crusade of the Left* (New York, 1969). Good descriptions of
Spanish anarchist groups active in the civil war are in James Joll, *The
Anarchists* (New York, 1963). In favoring the POUM and CNT, Appeal
closely followed Trotsky's admonitions from Norway. He approved
POUM cofounder and leader Andrés Nín, described by Victor Serge as
"an erudite socialist and a first rate intellectual" and Joaquin Maurín,
until they moved POUM into the popular front government. Then
Trotsky poured invective: "passive dilettantes," whose policy was "not
only false but criminal," "reactionary in its entire essence," "menshevism." Both Nín and Maurín were kidnapped and presumed killed as
Trotskyists by Spanish Communists in 1937. Trotsky to Dutch Trotskyists, July 19, 1935 in Breitman and Scott, eds., *Writings, 1935-1936*,
42; Crux [Trotsky] in *Internal Bulletins* 3 and 5, 1938, and in *New International* 5 (April 1939), 125-126; issues of *Spanish Revolution*
[short-term paper published by POUM in English]; Victor Serge, *Memoires d'un revolutionnaire* (Paris, 1951), 367-368; V. F. Calverton, "Will
England Give Spain to Franco?" *Modern Monthly* 10 (August 1937),
6-8; John Newton Thurber, "People's Front Tried and Found Wanting,"
American Socialist Monthly 5 (October 1936), 19-23; *Socialist Call,*
August 14, 1937.

21. *Socialist Appeal,* March 1937; Shachtman, *Reminiscences,* 281,
COHC.

22. Shachtman, *Reminiscences,* 277, COHC.

23. *Socialist Appeal,* March 1937; Trager to Norman Thomas, January 18 and March 14, 1937, Norman Thomas Papers.

24. Harry W. Laidler, "The Socialist Convention: Opportunity and
Challenge," *American Socialist Monthly* 6 (February 1937), 9-12.

25. Seidler, *Norman Thomas,* 174; Wilson, "Norman Thomas," 313;
Socialist Call, March 27, 1937.

26. Laidler, "Socialist Convention: Opportunity and Challenge,"
American Socialist Monthly 6 (February 1937), 12.

27. Quoted in *Socialist Appeal,* March 1937.

28. Wilson, "Norman Thomas," 332-333; Goldman and Shachtman
in *Socialist Appeal,* August 28, 1937.

29. Ibid.

30. Shachtman, *Reminiscences,* 280, COHC.

31. Travers Clement, interviewed by Betty Yorburg, Socialist Move-

ment Project, 7: 34, COHC. James Maurer quoted Cannon to Local
Berks County to the effect that Trotskyists fully intended to cohere
even within the Socialist party, in memo dated June 27, 1936, Norman
Thomas Papers.

32. Trotsky, Biographical Dates Presented to Defense Committee,
Bertram D. Wolfe personal files; Trotsky, "Exile in Norway, 1935-1936,"
International Socialist Review 31 (September 1970), 9; *Socialist Appeal,*
January 1937; Joseph Hansen, "Foreword" to Trotsky, *Stalin's Frame-
Up System and the Moscow Trials* (New York, 1950), ix-x.

33. The Committee to Obtain Right of Asylum for Trotsky issued
this statement: "The American Committee for the Defense of Trotsky
protests against this outrageous violation of democratic rights by the
Norwegian Government and demands that the full rights of asylum be
restored to Trotsky. The most elementary notions of justice dictates
that this world famous revolutionist should be given the fullest and
freest opportunity to state his case." *Socialist Appeal,* December 16,
1936; *Socialist Call,* February 13, 1937. Typed address December 18,
1936 in Wolfe personal files; interview with George Novack, July 29,
1973; Eastman, *Heroes I Have Known* (New York, 1942), 317-318.

34. Interview with Novack, July 29, 1973; Shachtman, *Reminiscences,* 378-384, COHC.

35. Dwight Macdonald, *Memoirs of a Revolutionist* (Cleveland,
1957), 10-11; Sidney Hook to author, October 5, 1972; James T. Farrell,
Reflections at Fifty and Other Essays (New York, 1954), 101; Trotsky,
"Let Us Know the Facts," Breitman and Scott eds., *Writings, 1935-
1936,* 129.

36. Other members of the full commission were Wendelin Thomas,
Edward A. Ross, John Chamberlain, Carlo Tresca, and Francisco
Zamora. Novack, "Introduction," in Dewey Commission of Inquiry,
The Case of Leon Trotsky (New York, 1968), x; for endorsement of
commission by the Socialist party see *Socialist Appeal,* December 16,
1936.

37. Shachtman, *Reminiscences,* 291-292, COHC.

38. Cannon, *History of American Trotskyism,* 241; Shachtman,
Reminiscences, 291, COHC.

39. *Partisan Review,* literary monthly published by the John Reed
Clubs, publicly broke with Stalinism as a result of the Moscow trial
controversy, thereafter taking "a quasi-Trotskyist position in politics."
Skeptical liberals Alfred Bingham and Selden Rodman of the monthly
Common Sense moved from giving equal weight to both sides in April
1937 to deciding with the commission that Trotsky was not guilty by
December 1937. A chapter explaining the disenchantment of Commu-

nist party intellectuals is in Daniel Aaron's *Writers on the Left* (New York, 1965), 325-334; on *Partisan Review,* see James Gilbert, *Writers and Partisans* (New York, 1968), 157-159; Trotsky, *I Stake My Life,* pamphlet (Ceylon, 1950).

40. Mauritz A. Hallgren, *Why I Resigned from the Trotsky Defense Committee* (New York, 1937), 13; Eugene Lyons, *The Red Decade* (New York, 1941), 250-255; Hook in *Socialist Appeal,* February 26, 1938; and Hook, "Corliss Lamont: 'Friend of the G.P.U.,' " *Modern Monthly* 10 (March 1938), 5-8.

41. Herbert W. Schneider—Dewey's student, colleague, and collator of Dewey's papers—claimed John Dewey took interest in the Moscow trials "because he realized that Trotsky was being misrepresented by the Stalinists. He was pushed into this by Sidney Hook but he was quite willing to be pushed into it . . . He wasn't a Trotskyite the way Sidney Hook was . . . he took Socialism very seriously because he thought the Socialists had the same general aim he had, at least the American Socialists. But he wasn't willing to formulate it as Marxian." "Recollections of John Dewey," *Claremont Quarterly* 2 (Winter 1964), 31-32. The pragmatists' rejection of inevitability of class struggle as against the Marxists' absolute faith in it as determinant in shaping social relations is discussed (from the Trotskyist perspective) by Novack in "Liberal Morality: the Controversy between John Dewey and Leon Trotsky," *International Socialist Review* (Fall 1964), 118-124; and from the perspective of a left-liberal in Farrell, "Dewey in Mexico," *Reflections at Fifty,* 114-117. Yet for all their hostility to experimentalism, Eastman was right: Bolsheviks (Trotsky included) were exemplary in their flexibility to meet the exigency of the moment. Eastman, *Stalin's Russia and the Crisis in Socialism* (New York, 1940), 229-230.

42. Warren, *Red Decade Revisited,* 164-166; Matthew Josephson, *Infidel in the Temple* (New York, 1967), 456-457; Alfred Kazin, *Starting Out in the Thirties* (Boston, 1962), 97-98; John Chamberlain, Jerome Davis, Theodore Dreiser, Clifton Fadiman, Henry Hazlitt, John Haynes Holmes, Leo Huberman, Henry Goddard Leach, Robert Morss Lovett, Ludwig Lore, A. J. Muste, and Burton Rascoe, "Is Trotsky Guilty? A Symposium," *Modern Monthly* 10 (March 1937), 5-8.

43. Shachtman, *Behind the Moscow Trial,* passim; *Socialist Appeal,* September 25, 1937.

44. Hook quoted in *Socialist Appeal,* April 9, 1938.

45. See Thomas Ray Poole, " 'Counter-Trial': Leon Trotsky on the Soviet Purge Trials" (Ph.D. dissertation, University of Massachusetts at Amherst, 1974).

46. Shachtman, *Reminiscences,* 297, COHC.

47. Howard Zinn, *LaGuardia in Congress* (New York, 1958), 268-269; Wilson, "Norman Thomas," 336.

48. Shachtman, "Against LaGuardia Socialism," *Socialist Review* 6 (September 1937), 21-22.

49. Gus Tyler, "Socialist Discipline and Action!" *Socialist Review* 6 (September 1937), 23-25; Goldman in *Socialist Appeal,* August 28, 1937.

50. Report, National Action Committee Plenum, July 24-25, 1937, SWPP.

51. *Socialist Appeal,* August 14, 28, September 21, 1937; Tyler, "Socialist Discipline and Action!" *Socialist Review* 6 (September 1937), 23-25; *Socialist Call,* August 21, 1937.

52. Shachtman, *Reminiscences,* 298, COHC; Hal Draper insisted in retrospect that the letter from Trotsky ordering Trotskyists to provoke expulsion was placed by Abern in an incorrectly addressed envelope and fell into the hands of Altman. Already piqued by the Trotskyists and envious of their superior theoretical and rhetorical abilities, Altman seized the chance to accelerate the anti-Trotskyist drive and to expel them. Interview with Draper, November 7, 1975.

53. Because Clarity had placed much stress on discipline, it was compelled to support expulsion of those who plainly had broken discipline. This was despite the ideological affinity of the two factions. Frank Warren, *An Alternative Vision* (Bloomington, Ind., 1974), 114.

54. Travers Clement, interviewed by Yorburg, Socialist Movement Project, 7: 34 COHC.

55. *Socialist Appeal,* August 28, September 4, 11, 1937; the *Socialist Call* of September 11, 1937 reported that Ernest Erber at the meeting rose and declared he could no longer accept National Executive Committee authority, thus "consummating" expulsion.

56. Shachtman, *Reminiscences,* 298, COHC.

57. In his inimitable style of invective Shachtman announced, "The American Socialist Party had succumbed to a malignant malady known as centrism . . . . The mass expulsion of the left wing, carried out in as brutally bureaucratic a manner as ever under that Stalinist regime . . . ripped the revolutionary heart out of the Socialist Party . . . [which] today is reduced to the icon of Norman Thomas." "Head Without a Body," *New International* 4 (June 1938), 175-177; Cannon, *History of Trotskyism,* 251.

58. Harry Roskolenko, *When I Was Last on Cherry Street* (New York, 1965), 168.

59. To David Shannon, "Their invasion was like a slight cerebral stroke for one already dying of malnutrition." *Socialist Party of America* (Chicago, 1965), 254. See too Daniel Bell, *Marxian Socialism in the*

U.S. (Princeton, 1967), 177.

60. Muste interviewed by Yorburg, Socialist Movement Project, 5: 25-26, COHC; figures on party membership are from Sidney Lens, *Radicalism in America* (New York, 1969), 325. "The flirtation with Communism brought destruction to the organized Socialist movement in the United States," concluded James Oneal and George Werner in *American Communism* (New York, 1947), 293; Donald Drew Egbert and Stow Persons said, "The Trotskyist faction wrecked the Socialist Party organization before it was expelled in 1937," in *Socialism and American Life* (2 vols.; Princeton, 1952), 1: 154. "The general result of the admission of the Trotskyites was bedlam," said Murray Seidler in *Norman Thomas, Respectable Rebel,* 175-176. Pratt recorded the complaint of Local Berks County that the Trotskyists tried to wreck the local, "causing many members to give up lifelong membership in disgust." "Reading Socialist Experience," 404fn.

61. Interview with Bert Cochran, August 16, 1972.

62. Interviews with Emanuel Geltman, November 15; with Al Glotzer, November 24; with Shachtman, August 17; all in 1972.

63. Isaac Deutscher, *The Prophet Outcast* (London, 1963), 424-425.

64. Shachtman, *Reminiscences,* 264, COHC, and interview with Shachtman, August 17, 1972.

65. Shachtman, *Reminiscences,* 304, COHC.

66. Cannon in *Socialist Appeal,* October 22, 1938; Cannon to majority groups, January 24, 1940 in John Wright, ed., *Struggle for a Proletarian Party* (New York, 1943), 154.

67. Benjamin Gitlow, *I Confess* (New York, 1939-1940), 584.

68. Harry Ring, "History of the SWP, 1933-1939," Socialist Workers party's Tape Collection, New York.

69. Trotsky to Sherman Stanley, October 22, 1939 in Joseph Hansen and William F. Warde, eds., *In Defense of Marxism* (New York, 1970), 35.

70. Interview, J. R. Johnson (C. L. R. James) with Trotsky, April 1939 in Pierre Broué, ed., *Le mouvement communiste en France, 1919-1939* (Paris, 1967), 638.

Chapter 8

1. James Burnham, "Socialists and the Coming War," *American Socialist Monthly* 5 (August 1936), 25; "From Formula to Reality: Notes on the Nature of the Soviet State," *Internal Bulletin* 5 (December 1937).

2. In Trotsky's *The Revolution Betrayed,* written in 1936 (New York, 1970) appear the exposition of his views on the nature of the Soviet state under Stalin: his analysis of Soviet economic growth; the myth of Stalinist "socialism"; Stakhanovism and labor; the currency; religion; the family, women, and youth; foreign policy and the military; the constitution of 1936; his analogies with the French post-revolutionary period labeled by him "Soviet Bonapartism" and the "Thermidorean reaction"; and the Soviet break with Marxism through "socialism in one country." Isaac Deutscher called it "one of the seminal books of the century" in *The Prophet Outcast* (London, 1963), 296. See Trotsky, "Not a Workers' and Not a Bourgeois State?" in George Breitman and Evelyn Reed, eds., *Writings of Leon Trotsky, 1937-1938* (New York, 1970), 90-94.

3. Harry Roskolenko, *When I Was Last on Cherry Street* (New York, 1965), 176-180; Max Shachtman, "Footnote for Historians," *New International* 4 (December 1938), 378; interview with Max Geltman, November 24, 1972.

4. Shachtman held that the Russian question, seemingly at first "a brief and auxiliary discussion," became the decisive one for the Trotskyist movement, suggesting that the disputes over it ruptured the Socialist Workers party irremediably. Interview with Shachtman, August 17, 1972. He was not alone. Albert Glotzer agreed in his retrospective interview with author, November 24, 1972. Cannon understood that the structure of the party was very much at issue too, and Max Geltman saw that profound antipathies were part of the equation. James P. Cannon, *History of American Trotskyism* (New York, 1944), 254; interview with Max Geltman, November 24, 1972.

5. *Socialist Appeal,* December 25, 1937; January 8, 15, 1938; editorial, *New International* 4 (January 1938), 5; *Declaration of Principles and Constitution of the Socialist Workers Party* (New York, n.d. but 1938), 1-18.

6. Resolutions adopted at Chicago convention printed in *Internal Bulletin* 6 (January 1938). See also *Declaration of Principles and Constitution of Socialist Workers Party,* 25.

7. *Socialist Appeal,* March 12, April 2, 1938; *Internal Bulletin* 2 (May 19, 1938), Socialist Workers Party Papers (hereafter referred to as SWPP); Trotsky, *The Death Agony of Capitalism and the Tasks of the Fourth International* (New York, 1970), 36-40.

8. Of the Munich pact, a Trotskyist commented, "In this pact the Galahads are lined up with the dragons." *Socialist Appeal,* October 3, 1938; of the Ludlow Amendment, an editorial charged "another of many pacifist illusions by which the masses are distracted from the only

means whereby imperialist war can be fought, namely, the continuous prosecution of the class struggle." *Socialist Appeal,* February 5, 1938; Browder quoted by Burnham in *How to Fight War: Isolation, Collective Security, Relentless Class Struggle?* (New York, 1938), 6, SWPP.

9. Trotsky in *Internal Bulletin* 3 (1938), SWPP; Burnham in *Socialist Appeal,* September 25, 1937.

10. Each unit could have been represented by only one or less than one individual. The impressive-sounding scope belies the pitiful reality. Sections represented at the conference were reported as: the United States, Mexico, Cuba, Puerto Rico, Brazil, Colombia, Argentina, Uruguay, Peru, Chile, Indo-China, China, Union of South Africa, Australia, Great Britain, France, Belgium, Holland, Spain, Germany, Norway, Austria, Czechoslovakia, Denmark, Canada, Poland, Switzerland, and Russia, with notice that small groups were just forming in Lithuania, Rumania, Yugoslavia, Bulgaria, Italy, New Zealand, Sweden, Ireland, Palestine, "etc.," *Socialist Appeal,* October 22, 1938; editorial, *New International* 4 (September 1938), 278; Shachtman, "Fourth International Is Launched," ibid. (November 1938), 325-327; Leon Trotsky, " 'For the Fourth International'? No! The Fourth International!" *Internal Bulletin* 3 (1938), SWPP; interview with Arne Swabeck, August 13, 1976.

11. *Socialist Appeal,* July 23, September 3, 1938; Shachtman, *Reminiscences,* 363-364, Columbia Oral History Collection (hereafter referred to as COHC).

12. Trotsky, "A Great Achievement," *New International* 4 (October 1938), 12.

13. Deutscher, *The Prophet Outcast,* 68, 272, 419; E. Victor Wolfenstein, *The Revolutionary Personality* (Princeton, 1971), 275; William Isaacs, "Contemporary Marxian Political Movements in the U.S." (Ph.D. dissertation, New York University, 1940), 538-539.

14. An anecdote exemplifying this trend described a New Year's Eve meeting (1938) in Cannon's apartment, only selected members of both political and national committees present, these constituting Cannon's alleged clique. At the meeting, to which clique members had been summoned from as far away as Minneapolis and Flint, comprehensive plans were devised for a specific labor campaign. Finally the group schemed to present the plans to the entire political committee in such a light as to secure approval. Responsibility officially lay with the political committee itself, or with the national committee, to formulate such policies, not with factional cliques. Shachtman and Burnham (who later deplored these practices) were there and reported the incident apologetically. Political committee minority, "War and Bureaucratic Conservatism,"

John G. Wright, ed., *Struggle for a Proletarian Party,* 286; this was the "auto crisis." Cannon defended that method of decision-making in his rebuttal essay, "The Struggle for a Proletarian Party" in ibid., 77-79; and George Clarke related the same incident also from the Cannonite viewpoint in a mimeographed memorandum, "The Truth about the Auto Crisis," March 4, 1940, SWPP.

15. "I want a genuinely collective leadership that operates, discusses, and decides collectively," not a monolithic leader cult. The leadership showed "arrogance and contempt for the membership," Shachtman believed, *Internal Bulletin* II, 3 (November 14, 1939); Hiram Eifenbein, "Seeds of Bureaucracy," *Internal Bulletin* II, 9 (January 1940), both SWPP.

16. Abern, Glotzer, Shachtman, "The Situation in the American Opposition: Prospect and Retrospect," June 4, 1932; "Resolution of the NC-CLA," *Internal Bulletin* 14 (June 29, 1933), SWPP.

17. Political committee minority, "War and Bureaucratic Conservatism," Wright, ed., *Struggle for a Proletarian Party,* 268.

18. In November 1938 Shachtman warned that Stalin would seek and reach agreement with Hitler due to collapse of popular fronts everywhere. He would preserve socialism in one country first by agreements with the democracies, and when that should fail, with fascist imperialisms, but "Hitler's price will be high." Shachtman, "Stalin Agonistes," *New International* 4 (November 1938), 325; and in *Internal Bulletin* II, 3 (November 14, 1939), SWPP.

19. Burnham in *Internal Bulletin* II, 2 (November 6, 1939), SWPP.

20. Trotsky to Cannon, September 12, 1939, in Joseph Hansen and William F. Warde, eds., *In Defense of Marxism* (New York, 1970), 1-2; Cannon to national committee, September 8, 1939, Wright, ed., *Struggle for a Proletarian Party,* 85-88.

21. Members who had seldom or never spoken up now joined the discussion. See, e.g., Ben Hall, "Stalin's War in Poland," *Internal Bulletin* II, 4 (December 1939); Roger Cross, "Why Not Analyze the Russian Economy?" ibid. 6 (December 1939); Sylvia Remarre, "On Comrade Cannon's Formula of Revolutionary Defeatism," ibid. 11 (February 1940); Samuel Meyers, "Is the USSR a Workers' State? Need for Reexamination," ibid. 12 (February 1940), all SWPP. Stalwart party leaders found their writing responsibilities doubled as they chronicled party discussions, answered points raised by theoretical adversaries, challenged or defended cherished doctrine. For instances, see Cannon to locals and branches, *Internal Bulletin* 1 (October 10, 1939); political committee minority, "What Is at Issue in the Dispute on the Russian Question?" ibid. 8 (January 1940); John B. Wheelwright, "Not Soviet

Patriotism, but Bolshevik Renaissance," ibid. 12 (February 1940); George Clarke and Sam Gordon, "The Real Issue: Revelation or Marxist Analysis?" ibid.; Murry Weiss, "Marxist Criteria and the Character of the War," ibid.; Joseph Carter, "The Soviet Union Is a Big Trade Union, or, How the Cannonite Argument Becomes a Boomerang" (mimeographed memorandum); March 8, 1940, all SWPP.

22. Shachtman, *Reminiscences,* 308, COHC, and in *Internal Bulletin* II, 3 (November 14, 1939), SWPP; interview with Weissman, August 4, 1973.

23. Trotsky to Hansen and Warde, eds., *In Defense of Marxism,* 24-33.

24. Cannon to Socialist Workers party on Russian Question, *Internal Bulletin* II, 1 (October 10, 1939), SWPP; Trotsky, "Referendum and Democratic Centralism," October 21, 1939 in Hansen and Warde, eds., *In Defense of Marxism,* 33.

25. Cannon to Vincent Ray Dunne, October 25, 1939, Wright, ed., *Struggle for a Proletarian Party,* 92-95; to Joseph Hansen, October 26, 1939, ibid., 96-97; political committee minority, "War and Bureaucratic Conservatism," ibid., 272.

26. Dwight Macdonald, *Memoirs of a Revolutionist* (New York, 1963), 17.

27. Cannon to Trotsky, November 8, 1939, Wright, ed., *Struggle for a Proletarian Party,* 103-105; to C. Charles, December 1, 1939, ibid., 107-113; political committee minority, "War and Bureaucratic Conservatism," ibid., 272.

28. Trotsky to national committee majority, December 26, 27, 1939; January 3, 4, 1940, Hansen and Warde, eds., *In Defense of Marxism,* 65-69, 161-163; Cannon to Trotsky, December 21, 1939, Wright, ed., *Struggle for a Proletarian Party,* 122; "War and Bureaucratic Conservatism," ibid., 257-293. Rizzi's book, *Le bureaucratisation du monde,* published in 1939 in Paris, claimed that the USSR, Nazi Germany, and the New Deal were all part of the same revolution. James Gilbert, *Designing the Industrial State* (Chicago, 1972), 279.

29. Shachtman, *Reminiscences,* 309, 311, COHC.

30. Max Eastman doubted Trotsky's mental stability in his last months, because he viewed as unbalanced Trotsky's tenacity in maintaining that it was only possible for workers to expropriate private capitalists and as these had been expropriated in the USSR, it must of course be a workers' state. Trotsky's desperate suspicions of Stalinist infiltration of the Socialist Workers party lend credence to Eastman's doubts. Eastman, *Heroes I Have Known* (New York, 1942), 244.

31. Quotation from letter, Trotsky to Cannon, May 27, 1939, Wright, ed., *Struggle for a Proletarian Party,* 90fn.; "War and Bureau-

cratic Conservatism," ibid., 285.

32. Trotsky, "A Petty Bougeois Opposition in SWP," Hansen and Warde, eds., *In Defense of Marxism*, 43-62.

33. Trotsky, "From a Scratch—to the Danger of Gangrene," Hansen and Warde, eds., *In Defense of Marxism*, 103-150 passim.

34. Ibid.; and Shachtman in *Internal Bulletin* II, 7 (January 1940), SWPP.

35. Workers party's *Organizational Bulletin*, January 1936, SWPP; Shachtman, *Reminiscences*, 45-47, COHC.

36. Cannon to Trotsky, January 18, 1940, Wright, ed., *Struggle for a Proletarian Party*, 139.

37. A selection from the early 1940 Cannon correspondence appears in Wright, ed., *Struggle for a Proletarian Party*, 122-208. The letters present a chronology of party activities (from the Cannonite perspective) before the April convention. He addressed branch and local leaders individually; his "majority" (the "Cannon clique" in Shachtman's words), the entire membership, and Trotsky, the latter usually with a detailed therefore highly informative presentation of developments in the dispute.

38. The Twin Cities reported fifteen meetings devoted solely to the crisis, plus the "daily discussions in party headquarters and union halls." Grace Carlson, V. R. Dunne, and Carlos Hudson, "Minnesota Answers the Minority," n.d. but February or March 1940, SWPP.

39. Carter, "Socialist Democracy or Bolshevik Mythology?" March 12, 1940, SWPP. On offer of seats on *New International,* see Goldman to locals and branches, February 12, 1940; Abern to Trotsky, January 24, 1940; Trotsky to Abern, January 29, 1940; Goldman to Trotsky, February 5, 1940; Trotsky to Goldman, February 10, 1940, all SWPP.

40. Cannonites assigned colorful labels: "bohemian free lancers," "literary panic-mongers," "calamity howlers," among many, many others. Echoing Trotsky, they proclaimed in "Letter to Party Membership," March 5, 1940, "The slogan of split is the slogan of class betrayal." Wright, ed., *Struggle for a Proletarian Party*, 192.

41. Abern to Trotsky, February 6, 1940, SWPP.

42. Shachtman in *Internal Bulletin* II, 7 (January 1940); Burnham in *Internal Bulletin* II, 9 (January 1940), both in SWPP.

43. Macdonald, *Memoirs of a Revolutionist*, 18.

44. Hansen, "From 'Science' to Slander," February 22, 1940, SWPP; "Trotsky's Last Battle Against the Revisionists," *Fourth International* 1 (November 1940), 171; Trotsky, "Back to the Party!" February 21, 1940; Trotsky to Goldman, August 9, 1940, in Hansen and Warde, eds., *In Defense of Marxism*, 184-185; Macdonald *Memoirs of a Revo-*

tionist, 18.

45. Burnham, "Science and Style," Hansen and Warde, eds., *In Defense of Marxism,* 187-206.

46. Trotsky to Comrades, February 23, 1940, Hansen and Warde, eds., *In Defense of Marxism,* 156-157; Trotsky, "Petty-Bourgeois Moralists and the Proletarian Party," April 23, 1940, ibid., 166-169 and passim; Hansen, "Trotsky's Last Battle," *Fourth International* 1 (November 1940), 165-172.

47. Trotsky to Goldman, February 19, 1940, Hansen and Warde, eds., *In Defense of Marxism,* 152; Cannon to minority conference, February 24, 1940, in Wright, ed., *Struggle for a Proletarian Party,* 183; Cannon to Isadore Bern, February 24, 1940, SWPP.

48. Letter to Membership, March 5, 1940, Wright, ed., *Struggle for a Proletarian Party,"* 187; "An Answer to the Splitters," March 5, 1940, SWPP; Trotsky to Farrell Dobbs, March 4, 1940, Hansen and Warde, eds., *In Defense of Marxism,* 161.

49. Shachtman differentiated between two kinds of split. One occurred when both sides agreed in advance to split peacefully, amicably. The other, a "cold split," also called for advance agreement to part, similarly in a peaceful, amicable way, but it involved too a fair, proportionate division of party property. Shachtman, *Reminiscences,* 317-318, COHC, and interview with Shachtman, August 17, 1972.

50. Dated April 1, 1940 in Wright, ed., *Struggle for a Proletarian Party,* 1-82.

51. The four resolutions are in Wright, ed., *Struggle for a Proletarian Party,* 227-240. Cannon's report of the convention is in ibid., 242-247.

52. Telephone interview with Burnham, August 15, 1972; interview with Shachtman, August 17, 1972; with Novack, July 29, 1973.

53. Shachtman, *Reminiscences,* 319, COHC.

54. "The Suspension of the Burnham-Shachtman-Abern Group," Wright, ed., *Struggle for a Proletarian Party,* 241; and ibid., 251-254; *Militant,* October 18, 1941.

55. James quoted by Marc Loris in "On Some Critics of Trotsky," *Fourth International* 3 (August 1942), 231.

56. Shachtman, *Reminiscences,* 316, COHC.

57. Remembering that people of the calibre of YPSL theoretician Hal Draper, literary critic Irving Howe, and trade union expert, professor of labor economics at Wayne State and Columbia Universities B. J. Widick left the party at that time, Harry Ring lamented, "They took some of our best." Ring, "History of the SWP since 1940," Social Workers party Tape Collection, New York; Hansen, "Trotsky's Last Battle Against the Revisionists," *Fourth International* 1 (November

1940), 164; Macdonald, *Memoirs of a Revolutionist,* 17; Jim Robertson and Larry Ireland in *Marxist Bulletin* 2 (n.d. but September 1965).

58. *Labor Action* carried on its masthead, "An Organ of Revolutionary Marxism," and proclaimed the Workers party to be a section of the fourth international. "Expulsion of the Shachtman-Abern Group," Wright, ed., *Struggle for a Proletarian Party,* 253; and ibid., 248-250.

59. Shachtman, interviewed by Yorburg, *Socialist Movement Project,* 2: 31, COHC. In 1973, a number of veterans of the old Shachtmanite grouping now associated together in producing the magazine *Dissent,* including Emanuel Geltman, Stanley Plastrik, Irving Howe, and Michael Harrington (who entered the Shachtmanite party in 1948), created the Democratic Socialist Organizing Committee to work for socialist aims within the Democratic party.

60.

1928	to Alma Ata, Kazakhstan
1929	to Prinkipo on the Sea of Marmora
November 1932	to Denmark (to lecture)
December 1932	back to Prinkipo
July 1933	leave Prinkipo; to France
July-October 1933	St. Palais
November 1933-April 1934	Barbizon
April-July 1934	wandering in France incognito, pursued
July 1934-June 1935	Domesne, near Grenoble
June-December 1935	Honefoss, Norway
January 1936-August 1940	Mexico City and Coyoacan, Mexico

The above table compiled in part from L. D. Trotsky, Biographical Dates Presented to the Commission [of Inquiry], in Bertram D. Wolfe files.

61. Trotsky said, "The fascists steal my papers in Norway, the G.P.U. steals them in Paris, and this unity of action engenders a solidarity of interest." Gouged from both right and left, he felt squeezed by pincers. But the reaction of the right was unpredictable. So widely had the rumors of his "capitalist connections" circulated that on one occasion "Signor Trotsky" received fascist honors due "a great military commander" in Naples. Shachtman, *Reminiscences,* 366, COHC; Trotsky, "In Closed Court," George Breitman and Bev Scott, eds., *Writings of Leon Trotsky, 1935-1936* (New York, 1970), 139-140.

62. Trotsky's assassin allegedly later admitted the GPU had had Leon Sedov murdered. *Socialist Appeal,* December 18, 1937; February 26, September 10, 1938; Hansen, "With Trotsky in Coyoacan," *International Socialist Review* 31 (May 1970), 34, 38; "With Trotsky to the End,"

Fourth International 1 (October 1940), 121.

63. August 16, 1940, printed in *Fourth International* 1 (October 1940), 127.

64. Hansen, "Attempted Assassination of Leon Trotsky," *Fourth International* 1 (August 1940), 85-89; interview with George Novack and Evelyn Reed, July 29, 1973.

65. Shachtman, *Reminiscences,* 475, COHC; Walter Rourke, "The Murder of Robert Sheldon Harte," *Fourth International* 3 (May 1942), 139-142; interview with Novack and Reed, July 29, 1973; Hansen, "With Trotsky to the End," *Fourth International* 1 (October 1940), 91. The plaque was inscribed thus:

In Memory
of
Robert Sheldon Harte
1915-1940
Murdered by Stalin

66. Louis F. Budenz, *Men Without Faces* (New York, 1948), 123-128; Benjamin Gitlow, *The Whole of Their Lives* (Boston, 1965), 344-345; interviews with Emanuel Geltman, November 25, 1972; with Novack, July 29, 1973; U.S. House of Representatives, 92d Cong., 1 sess., *Communists in the Trotskyite Mold* (Washington, D.C., 1971), 4.

67. Budenz, *Men Without Faces,* 128; Hansen, "With Trotsky to the End," *Fourth International* 1 (October 1940), 117-120.

68. Shachtman, *Reminiscences,* 482, COHC.

69. Hansen, "With Trotsky to the End," *Fourth International* 1 (October 1940), 117; Natalya Trotsky, "How It Happened," ibid., 2 (May 1941), 100-103.

70. Walter Rourke, "Trial of the Assassin of Trotsky," *Fourth International* 3 (August 1942), 233-236; Hansen, "With Trotsky to the End," ibid., 1 (October 1940), 120-123; Shachtman, *Reminiscences,* 483-484, COHC.

71. The correspondence concerning the Dies Committee invitation and retraction is in George Breitman and Evelyn Reed, eds., *Writings of Leon Trotsky, 1939-1940* (New York, 1969), 51-53; on the suit pressed by the Communist party of Mexico against Trotsky for his accusation that it tried in May to assassinate him, and that the directors of the party organ received financial aid from Stalin, see ibid., 91-107. Hearing of the progress of his biography by Trotsky, Stalin "flew into a rage and cursed the CPUSA and the GPU," according to Gitlow (who did not give his source) in *Whole of Their Lives,* 345-353; and see Mary McCarthy,

On the Contrary (New York, 1961), 20, 103. Shachtman spoke of
Trotsky's theoretical genius, and when I asked him if Trotsky was perhaps a bit flamboyant, Shachtman replied, "No, *magnetic.*" Interview
with Shachtman, August 17, 1972.

72. Interview with Arne Swabeck, Los Angeles, August 13, 1976;
and see *The News Line* (publication of the Workers Revolutionary
League), July 15, 1976.

Chapter 9

1. *Militant,* August 15, 1931.

2. Progress of the Morgenstern–Goodman case is detailed in *Militant,* July 4, 11, 18, November 28, 1931; February 13, 20, May 21,
1932; June 17, 1933.

3. See *New York Times,* January 20, 1935; Carey McWilliams,
Factories in the Field (Boston, 1939), 214; Herbert Solow, *Union-
Smashing in Sacramento* (New York, 1935), 10.

4. Clark A. Chambers, *California Farm Organizations* (Berkeley,
1952), 42-45; Donald D. Ranstead, "District 13" (M.A. thesis, University of California, Berkeley, 1963), 70.

5. Woodrow C. Whitten, *Criminal Syndicalism and the Law in California* (Philadelphia, 1969), 40-50; Eldridge F. Dowell, *A History of
Criminal Syndicalism Legislation in the U.S.* (Baltimore, 1939), 56, 143.

6. *Sacramento Bee,* July 20, 25, August 28, 29, 1934; *Daily Worker,*
August 18, 23, September 5, 1934; *New Militant,* December 29, 1934;
Marion R. Hardy, "Politico-Economic Implications of the Pat Chambers
Criminal Syndicalism Trial" (M.A. thesis, Sacramento State College,
1964), 37-40; Michael Quin (Communist party alias for Paul W. Ryan),
The Criminal Syndicalism Case against Labor (San Francisco, 1935), 2,
17; Travers Clement, "Red Baiting Holiday in Sacramento," *Nation* 140
(March 13, 1935), 307.

7. *Sacramento Bee,* February 15, 1935; Hardy, "Politico-Economic
Implications of the Pat Chambers Trial," 90-91.

8. *Daily Worker,* February 8, 9, 11, 16, 1936.

9. Oswald G. Villard, "Come Laugh at California," *Nation* 140
(May 15, 1935), 563; *Sacramento Bee,* January 16, February 9, April
11, 1935; *Daily Worker,* January 24, 1935; *New Militant,* January 15,
1935.

10. *Sacramento Bee,* March 6, 26, 27, 28, 1935; interview with Rabbi
Norman O. Goldburg, April 3, 1973.

11. *New York Times,* April 2, 1935; *Daily Worker,* April 2, 12, 1935.

12. Ranstead, "District 13," 65-66.

13. Hardy, "Politico-Economic Implications of Pat Chambers Trial," 123.

14. *Socialist Appeal,* July 4, 1940; American Civil Liberties Union, *The Smith Act and the Supreme Court* (New York, 1952), 4-5.

15. Farrell Dobbs, "Minneapolis Strikes and Role of the Revolutionary Party," Socialist Workers party's Tapes, New York. Roger Baldwin, national director of ACLU, was quoted in *Militant,* November 22, 1941 as saying everyone knew Tobin was Roosevelt's man.

16. Dobbs, "Minneapolis Strikes," Socialist Workers party's Tapes; *Socialist Appeal,* June 1, 1940; *Militant,* November 22, 1941.

17. Albert Goldman, *In Defense of Socialism* (New York, 1942), 57-58; Earl Latham, *Communist Controversy in Washington* (Cambridge, Mass., 1966), 415; *Socialist Appeal,* January 13, December 14, 1940; Novack, *Witch Hunt in Minnesota* (New York, n.d.), 15-16.

18. *Socialist Appeal,* June 8, 15, July 6, 27, 1940; Farrell Dobbs in ibid., December 28, 1940; *Militant,* July 12, 1941; ACLU, *Liberty's National Emergency* (New York, 1941), 16-17.

19. Editors, "FBI-Gestapo Attack on the Socialist Workers Party," *Fourth International,* 2 (July 1941), 164-165; Novack, *Witch Hunt in Minnesota,* 6; Goldman, *In Defense of Socialism,* iii-vi.

20. Ralph James and Estelle James, "The Purge of the Trotskyists from the Teamsters," *Western Political Science Quarterly* 19 (March 1966), 6-8; Civil Rights Defense Committee, *Who Are the Eighteen Prisoners in the Minneapolis Labor Case?* (New York, n.d.), 5-6.

21. In *Militant,* July 5, 1941.

22. Text of indictment is in *Fourth International* 2 (August 1941), 212-214; and see Daniel Eastman, "Minneapolis 'Sedition' Trial," *New Republic* 105 (October 20, 1941), 503-504.

23. Novack, *Witch Hunt in Minnesota,* 9-10.

24. James P. Cannon, *Socialism on Trial,* 4th ed., (New York, 1965), 2.

25. Francis Biddle, *In Brief Authority* (Garden City, N.Y., 1962), 151-152.

26. *Militant,* November 1, 8, 1941.

27. *Militant,* November 22, 1941; Felix Morrow, "The Minneapolis Sedition Trial," *Fourth International* 3 (January 1942), 4, 7.

28. Ibid.

29. *Militant,* November 22, 1941.

30. Interview with Al Russel, July 20, 1973. Schweinhaut had some-

thing of a reputation as a liberal. In 1939 when the Justice Department created a special civil liberties unit, Schweinhaut was named to head it.

31. Holmes quoted by Irving Brant in *The Bill of Rights* (Indianapolis, 1965), 401.

32. Thomas I. Emerson, *Toward a General Theory of the First Amendment* (New York, 1966), 204; Philip L. Sirotkin, "Evolution of the Clear and Present Danger Doctrine" (M.A. thesis, University of Chicago, 1947), 63-64; ACLU, *Sedition!* (New York, 1941), 3-4.

33. *Militant,* November 22, 1941.

34. *Militant,* December 13, 1941; March 21, 1942; Goldman, *In Defense of Socialism,* iv-v.

35. *Militant,* November 22, 1941; Walter Goodman, *The Committee* (New York, 1968), 99fn.; Paul Jacobs, *The State of the Unions* (New York, 1963), 89; John Gates, *The Story of an American Communist* (New York, 1958), 127; Cannon, *Socialism on Trial,* 4.

36. Abramson quoted by Art Preis in *Labor's Giant Step* (New York, 1964), 400.

37. Hook quoted in Milton R. Konvitz, *Fundamental Liberties of a Free People* (New York, 1957), 403fn.

38. Shachtman, *Reminiscences,* 501, Columbia Oral History Collection.

39. An ACLU spokesperson quoted by Felix Morrow in "Introduction" to Goldman, *In Defense of Socialism,* iii; interviews with Al Russel, July 20, 1973; with George Novack, July 29, 1973.

Epilogue

1. Helen Mayer Hacker, "Women as a Minority Group," *Social Forces* 3 (October 1951), 60-69. Standard Marxist classics on the position of women in both present capitalist and future socialist societies include certain crucial observations made by Karl Marx and Friedrich M. Engels in *The Communist Manifesto;* the writings of V. I. Lenin on the subject collected by his wife, N. K. Krupskaya, in *On the Emancipation of Women* (Moscow, 1934); Engels' historico-anthropological treatment of it in his *Origin of the Family, Private Property, and the State* (Chicago, 1902); and August Bebel's *Woman Under Socialism* (New York, 1971; reprint of 1904 publication).

2. Interviews with Max Geltman, Yetta Barsh, Ernest Rice McKinney, Maggie Bell, Max Shachtman, Harry Roskolenko, George Novack, and Evelyn Reed.

3. "Statement of the Communist League of Struggle" [Weisbord

group], *Internal Bulletin* 4 (November ?, 1932), Socialist Workers party Papers (hereafter referred to as SWPP), Wisconsin State Historical Society; *Militant,* August 29, 1931.

4. From colonization schemes to "internal statism" and black Zionism, Theodore Draper discussed the history of black nationalism, especially in America and in relation to Communist party policy in "The Fantasy of Black Nationalism," *Commentary* 48 (September 1969), 27-54. Fearful of sounding prescriptive, Communists stressed "the right" to Negro self-determination without going so far as to promote action toward its realization.

5. Cannon, Swabeck, Abern et al., *Militant,* February 15, 1929; "Resolution of the Negro Problem," n.d. but 1935, SWPP. Draper showed that the problem was vastly more complicated than one of ethnicity; the fact of *color* made it unique and uniquely difficult. *Commentary* 48 (September 1969), 53.

6. "The Negro Question in America," *Internal Bulletin* 12 (April 19, 1933), SWPP.

7. J. R. Johnson in *Internal Bulletin* II, 9 (June 1939), SWPP.

8. "Self-Determination for American Negroes," *Internal Bulletin* II, 9 (June 1939), SWPP; editorial, *New International* 5 (August 1939), 227-229.

9. In 1972 former Trotskyists accused the movement of anti-Semitism traceable to Marx's and Trotsky's own, and a story from the Trotsky apocrypha bears repeating here. During the Russian Revolution when some Jews with their rabbi called on Trotsky to protest Bolshevik anti-Semitism, Trotsky said, "Go home to your Jews, and tell them I am no Jew, and I care nothing for the Jews and their fate." To this the Rabbi retorted, "The Trotskys make the revolution and the Bronsteins pay for it." Harry Roskolenko, *When I Was Last on Cherry Street* (New York, 1965), 183, and interview with Max Geltman, November 24, 1972. Trotsky's real name was Lev Davidovitch Bronstein; his parents were apostate Jews.

10. *Militant,* March 29, May 31, June 21, July 1, October 18, 1941; Albert Parker, *The March on Washington, One Year After* (New York, 1942). Parker excoriated Randolph for "selling out" demands for full equality made by blacks who subscribed to the March on Washington movement, and settling for mere promises in Executive Order #8802 and a gutless Fair Employment Practices Commission.

11. A. Stork, "Mr. Calverton and His Friends: Some Notes on Literary Trotskyism in America," *International Literature* 3 (July 1934), 97-124.

12. Trotsky, *Literature and Revolution* (Ann Arbor, 1960), 256, 179.

13. Ibid., 194.

14. Ibid., 226.

15. Ibid., 168.

16. See Trotsky, "Art and Politics," *Partisan Review* 5 (September 1938), 3-10.

17. See the doctoral dissertation by Allen Wald, "James T. Farrell: The Revolutionary Years" (University of California, Berkeley, 1974).

18. Norman Levy, "The Radicalization of Dwight Macdonald" (M.A. thesis, University of Wisconsin, 1966), 491; James Gilbert, *Writers and Partisans* (New York, 1968), 171; Dwight Macdonald, *Memoirs of a Revolutionist* (Cleveland, 1957), 6-15; Trotsky to Albert Goldman, August 9, 1940, in Joseph Hansen and William F. Warde, eds., *In Defense of Marxism* (New York, 1970), 184.

19. Farrell, "The Renegade," in *An American Dream Girl* (New York, 1950), 299-302.

20. Interview with B. J. Widick, August 3, 1972.

21. Jere Mangione, *The Dream and the Deal* (Boston, 1972), 175-176, 181; interviews with Roskolenko, August 15, 1972; with Novack, July 29, 1973; with Russel, July 20, 1973; with Hal Draper, November 7, 1975; with Swabeck, August 13, 1976.

22. Obituary in *Los Angeles Times,* August 23, 1974. At his death he held the title "national chairman emeritus." On August 23, 1974 a "political tribute" to him launched a fund drive to "Educate, Agitate, Organize" for the Socialist Workers party. Speeches delivered in his honor by close associates and party leaders (almost all representing a generation that did not experience the tumult of the 1930s) were printed in *Militant: James P. Cannon Special Issue,* September 6, 1974.

23. Interview with Shachtman, August 17, 1972; and see Shachtman's obituary, *New York Times,* November 6, 1972.

24. Terkel, *Hard Times* (New York, 1970), 347. Interviews with Widick, August 3; Max Geltman, November 24; Emanuel Geltman, November 25; Albert Glotzer, November 24, all in 1972; with Alfred Russel, July 20, 1973; with Hal Draper, November 7, 1975. Also, telephone conversation with James Burnham (in Kent, Conn.), July 23, 1973 during which after thinking it over Burnham declined a personal interview, a reaction predicted by Farrell and Widick. Burnham insisted, "I am not a public person," a contention with which many would find serious disagreement. It is only fair to note, however, that Burnham answered cordially the questions posed to him during three telephone interviews: August 15, 1972; July 23, 1973; November 20, 1973.

25. Interview with Charles Curtis, June 2, 1970.

26. Deutscher, "Trotsky at His Nadir," in *Ironies of History* (London, 1966), 176.

27. Interview with Cochran, August 16, 1972.

28. Interview with Shachtman, August 17, 1972.

29. Interview with Widick, August 3, 1972.

30. Telephone interview with Sidney Hook (in New York), November 19, 1973.

31. Interview with Shachtman, August 17, 1972.

Selected Bibliography

Unpublished Sources

Special Collections

Columbia Oral History Collection, Columbia University: A. J. Muste, *Reminiscences;* Max Shachtman, *Reminiscences;* Betty Yorburg, compiler, *Socialist Movement Project: Travers Clement, A. J. Muste, and Max Shachtman*
New York Public Library: Norman Thomas Papers
Palo Alto, California: personal files of Bertram D. Wolfe
Socialist Workers Party Tape Collection, New York: lectures by Farrell Dobbs and Harry Ring
Tamiment Institute Library, New York University, Radical Pamphlets
Wisconsin State Historical Society, Socialist Workers Party Papers

Interviews

Yetta Barsh, New York, August 15, 1972; Maggie Bell, New York, November 24, 1972; James Burnham (telephone), August 15, 1972; July 23 and November 20, 1973; Bert Cochran, New York, August 16, 1972; Charles Curtis, Los Angeles, June 2, 1970; Hal Draper, Albany, Cal., November 7, 1975, August 7, 1976; James T. Farrell, New York, July 25, 1973; Emanuel Geltman, New York, November

25, 1972; Max Geltman, New York, November 24, 1972; Albert
Glotzer, New York, November 24, 1972; Norman O. Goldburg,
Augusta, Ga., April 3, 1973; Dorothy Healey, Los Angeles, August
9, 1976; Sidney Hook (telephone), November 19, 1973; Ernest Rice
McKinney, New York, November 26, 1972 and Atlanta, Ga., Decem-
ber 29, 1975; George Novack, New York, July 29, 1973; Evelyn
Reed, New York, July 29, 1973; Harry Roskolenko, New York,
August 15, 1972; Alfred Russel, New York, July 20, 1973; Max
Shachtman, Floral Park, N.Y., August 17, 1972; Ann Snipper, Los
Angeles, June 1, 1970; Arne Swabeck, Los Angeles, August 13, 1976;
Gus Tyler (telephone), December 4, 1973; George Weissman, New
York, August 4, 1973; B. J. Widick, New York, August 3, 1972;
Bertram D. Wolfe, Palo Alto, Cal., November 8, 1975.

Theses and Dissertations

Diamond, Martin. "Socialism and the Decline of the American Socialist
    Party." Ph.D. dissertation, University of Chicago, 1954.
Eames, Patricia. "The Attitude of the American Civil Liberties Union
    Toward the Communist Party, U.S.A., 1920-1940." M.A. thesis,
    Columbia University, 1951.
Hardy, Marion R. "The Politico-Economic Implications of the Pat
    Chambers Criminal Syndicalism Trial." M.A. thesis, Sacramento
    State College, 1964.
Isaacs, William. "Contemporary Marxian Political Movements in the U.S.,
    1917-1939." Ph.D. dissertation, New York University, 1940.
Levy, Norman Louis. "The Radicalization of Dwight Macdonald."
    M.A. thesis, University of Wisconsin, 1966.
Poole, Thomas Ray. " 'Counter-Trial': Leon Trotsky on the Soviet
    Purge Trials," Ph.D. dissertation, University of Massachusetts at
    Amherst, 1974.
Pratt, William C. "The Reading Socialist Experience: A Study of Work-
    ing Class Politics." Ph.D. dissertation, Emory University, 1969.
Ranstead, Donald Davitt. "District 13: A History of the Activities of
    the California Communist Party, 1929-1940." M.A. thesis, Univer-
    sity of California at Berkeley, 1963.
Seyler, William C. "The Rise and Decline of the Socialist Party in the
    U.S." Ph.D. dissertation, Duke University, 1952.
Sirotkin, Philip Leonard. "Evolution of the Clear and Present Danger
    Doctrine." M.A. thesis, University of Chicago, 1947.
Wald, Allen. "James T. Farrell: The Revolutionary Socialist Years."
    Ph.D. dissertation, University of California at Berkeley, 1974.

Wilson, John Scott. "Norman Thomas: Critic of the New America." Ph.D. dissertation, University of North Carolina at Chapel Hill, 1966.

Newspapers

Augusta (Georgia) *Chronicle; Daily Worker; Internal Bulletin* (Communist League of America, Workers party, and Socialist Workers party): *International News* (Oehler-Stamm faction); *Labor Action* (Socialist party, West Coast Trotskyist faction); *Los Angeles Times; Militant* (Communist League of America and Socialist Workers party); *New International Bulletin; New Militant; New York Times; Organizational Bulletin* (Workers party); *Party Affairs: A Paper for SP* [Socialist party] *Members; Sacramento Bee; Socialist Appeal; Socialist Call; Spanish Revolution.*

Periodical Articles

Blantz, Thomas E. "Father Haas and the Minneapolis Truckers' Strike of 1934." *Minnesota History* (Spring 1970): 5-15.

Budenz, Louis F. "For an American Revolutionary Approach." *Modern Monthly* 9 (March 1935): 142-146.

Burnham, James. "Fascism's Dress Clothes." *New International* 4 (July 1938):207-209.

———. "Socialists and the Coming War." *American Socialist Monthly* 5 (August 1936): 26-27.

Calverton, V. F. "An Open Letter to American Intellectuals." *Modern Monthly* 7 (March 1934): 87-92.

———. "Socialism Leans Left." *Modern Monthly* 8 (January 1935): 645-649.

———. "Stalin on Trial." *Modern Monthly* 10 (October 1936): 3-4.

———. "Will England Give Spain to Franco?" *Modern Monthly* 10 (August 1937): 6-8.

Clement, Travers. "Red Baiter's Holiday in Sacramento: The Criminal Syndicalism Trial." *Nation* 140 (March 13, 1935): 306-308.

Delson, Robert. "A New Flag for the Socialist Party." *American Socialist Monthly* 5 (April 1936): 5-6.

———, and Louis Mann. "Some Problems of Party Organization." *American Socialist Monthly* 5 (February 1937): 59-62.

Draper, Theodore. "The Fantasy of Black Nationalism." *Commentary* 48 (September 1969): 27-54.

————. "The Ghost of Social Fascism." *Commentary* 47 (February 1969): 29-42; (May 1969): 8.

Eastman, Daniel. "The Minneapolis 'Sedition' Trial." *New Republic* 105 (October 20, 1942): 503-504.

Eastman, Max. "The End of Socialism in Russia." *Harper's* 174 (January 1937): 306-308.

————. "An Open Letter to the Nation: A Letter the Nation Did Not Publish." *Modern Monthly* 10 (April 1937): 4-7.

Editorial, "Advance in Chicago." *American Socialist Monthly* 6 (May 1937): 9-12.

Editorial, "The FBI—Gestapo Attack on the Socialist Workers Party." *Fourth International* 2 (July 1941): 163-166.

Editorial, "The Fourth International Meets." *New International* 4 (September 1938): 278.

"F.M." [Felix Morrow?]. "The Role of Burnham and the Apology of Shachtman." *Fourth International* 3 (May 1942): 158-159.

Fischer, Bruno. "The Old Guard Dies." *Modern Monthly* 10 (June 1936): 5.

Gross, Murray. "Trade Union Policy for the Socialist Party." *American Socialist Monthly* 5 (June 1936): 9.

Hacker, Helen Mayer. "Women as a Minority Group." *Social Forces* 30 (October 1951): 60-69.

Hansen, Joseph. "The Attempted Assassination of Leon Trotsky." *Fourth International* 1 (August 1940): 85-89.

————. "Trotsky in Coyoacan." *International Socialist Review* 31 (May 1970): 34-38.

————. "Trotsky's Last Battle Against the Revisionists." *Fourth International* 1 (November 1940): 164-172.

————. "With Trotsky to the End." *Fourth International* 1 (October 1940): 115-123.

Hook, Sidney. "As to Max Eastman's Mentality." *Modern Quarterly* 5 (November 1928-February 1929): 88-91.

————. "On Workers' Democracy." *Modern Monthly* 8 (October 1934): 544.

"The I.B.T.C.W.H. of A." *Fortune* 23 (May 1941): 97-100, 135-142.

James, Ralph and Estelle James. "The Purge of the Trotskyists from the Teamsters." *Western Political Science Quarterly* 19 (March 1966): 5-15.

Kantorovich, Haim. "Notes on the United Front Problem." *American Socialist Monthly* 5 (May 1936): 9-11.

————. "The Left Wing at the Cleveland Convention." *American Socialist Monthly* 5 (June 1936): 11.

Laidler, Harry W. "The Socialist Convention: An Opportunity and a Challenge." *American Socialist Monthly* 6 (February 1937): 52-53.

――. "Some Issues of the Presidential Campaign." *American Socialist Monthly* 5 (October 1936): 5.

Levenstein, Aaron. "The Socialist Convention." *Modern Monthly* 10 (July 1936): 9-10.

Loris, Marc. "On Some Critics of Trotsky." *Fourth International* 3 (August 1942): 229-233.

Malraux, André. "Leon Trotsky." *Modern Monthly* 9 (March 1935): 37-41.

Mayer, Karl. "Lev Davidovitch." *Fourth International* (Memorial Issue) 3 (August 1941): 207-209.

Mini, Norman. "The California Dictatorship." *Nation* 140 (February 20, 1935): 224-226.

Morrow, Felix. "The Minneapolis Sedition Trial." *Fourth International* 3 (January 1942): 4-9.

"M.S." [Max Shachtman?]. "A Head Without a Body." *New International* 4 (June 1938): 175-177.

Muste, A. J. "An American Revolutionary Party." *Modern Monthly* 7 (January 1934): 713-719.

――. "The Problem of Violence." *Modern Monthly* 10 (March 1937): 7-9.

――. "What Mean These Strikes?" *Modern Monthly* 8 (October 1934): 517-521.

Novack, George. "Liberal Morality: The Controversy Between John Dewey and Leon Trotsky." *International Socialist Review* 26 (Fall 1965): 118-124.

Oehler, Hugo. "The Crisis of Capitalism and Revolutionary Marxism." *Modern Socialism* 1 (Winter 1941-1942): 31-35.

Riche, James. "Pragmatism: A National Fascist Mode of Thought." *Literature and Ideology* 9 (1971): 31-35.

Robertson, Jim and Larry Ireland. "The Centrism of the SWP and the Tasks of the Minority." *Marxist Bulletin*, No. 2 (September 1967): 19-28.

Robinson, Jo Ann O. "Pharos of the East Side, 1937-1940: Labor Temple Under the Direction of A. J. Muste." *Journal of Presbyterian History* 42 (Spring 1970): 18-37.

Rodman, Selden. "Third Party Free-for-All." *Modern Monthly* 9 (April 1935): 111-113.

Romer, Samuel and Hal Siegel. "Advance in Chicago." *American Socialist Monthly* 6 (May 1937): 10.

Rorty, James. "Lettuce—With American Dressing." *Nation* 140 (May

15, 1935): 575-576.

Rourke, Walter. "The Murder of Robert Sheldon Harte." *Fourth International* 3 (May 1942): 139-142.

———. "The Trial of the Assassin of Trotsky." *Fourth International* 3 (August 1942): 233-236.

"Sacramento Criminal Syndicalism Cases." *International Juridical Association Bulletin* 4 (November 1935): 4-6.

Shachtman, Max. "Against LaGuardia Socialism." *Socialist Review* 4 (September 1937): 21-22.

———. "Footnote for Historians." *New International* 4 (December 1938): 277-279.

———. "The Fourth International Is Launched." *New International* 4 (November 1938): 325-327.

———. "Towards a Revolutionary Socialist Party." *American Socialist Monthly* 6 (May 1937): 13-18.

———. "Twenty Five Years of American Trotskyism." *New International* 14 (January-February 1954): 11-25.

Schmalhausen, Samuel. "These Tragic Comedians." *Modern Quarterly* 4 (November 1927-February 1928): 195-229.

Schneider, Herbert W. "Recollections of John Dewey." *Claremont Quarterly* 2 (Winter 1964): 23-35.

Solon, S. L. "Largo Caballero." *Modern Monthly* 10 (December 1936): 11-13.

Solow, Herbert. "After Madison Square Garden." *Modern Monthly* 7 (April 1934): 182-184.

Stork, A. "Mr. Calverton and His Friends: Some Notes on Literary Trotskyism in America." *International Literature* 3 (July 1934): 97-124.

Swanson, Dorothy, collator. Special Issue: Holdings on Trotsky and Trotskyism, New York University Libraries, *Bulletin of the Tamiment Library*, No. 47 (April 1971).

Symposium. "Important Problems of the Socialist Party." *American Socialist Monthly* 5 (June 1936): 27-29.

Symposium. "Is Leon Trotsky Guilty?" *Modern Monthly* 10 March 1937): 5-8.

Thomas, Norman. "After the New Deal—What?" *Modern Monthly* 10 (August 1936): 10-12.

Thurber, John N. "People's Front Tried and Found Wanting, Spain, 1936." *American Socialist Monthly* 5 (October 1936): 19-23.

Trotsky, Leon. "Art and Politics." *Partisan Review* 5 (September 1938): 3-10.

———. "Exile in Norway, 1935-1936." *International Socialist Review* 31 (September 1970): 9-11.

———. "A Great Achievement." *New International* 4 (October 1938): 145-147.

———. "His Last Article." *Fourth International* 1 (October 1940): 129-131.

———. "On the Revolutionary Intellectuals: An Open Letter to V. F. Calverton." *Modern Quarterly* 7 (March 1933): 85.

———. "Some Questions on American Problems." *Fourth International* 1 (August 1940): 132-135.

———. "The Task in Spain." *New International* 5 (April 1939): 125-126.

———. "Trade Unions in the Epoch of Imperialist Decay." *Fourth International* 2 (February 1941): 41-43.

Trotsky, Natalia Sedov. "How It Happened." *Fourth International* 2 (May 1941): 100-103.

———. "Mr. Davies and the Moscow Trials." *Fourth International* 3 (January 1942): 9-11.

Tselos, George. "The Farmer-Labor Party in Minnesota, 1918-1944." *International Socialist Review* 32 (May 1971): 94-99.

Tyler, Gus. "How Shall We Conduct Our Election Campaign?" *American Socialist Monthly* 5 (October 1936): 14-16.

———. "Socialist Discipline and Action!" *Socialist Review* 6 (September 1937): 23-25.

Warde, William F. "Capitalist Frame-up: 1941 Model." *Fourth International* 2 (December 1941): 295-297.

———. "The Right of Revolution." *Fourth International* 2 (August 1941): 209-212.

Weber, Sara. "Recollections of Trotsky." *Modern Occasions* (Spring 1972): 181-194.

Villard, Oswald Garrison. "Come Laugh at California." *Nation* 140 (May 15, 1935): 563.

Whitten, Woodrow C. "Criminal Syndicalism and the Law in California, 1919-1927." *Transactions* 54, part 2. Philadelphia: American Philosophical Society, 1969: 1-73.

Zam, Herbert. "Is the Socialist Party Going Revolutionary?" *Modern Monthly* 9 (March 1935): 44-47.

Books

Aaron, Daniel. *Writers on the Left.* New York: Avon Books, 1965.

Adamic, Louis. *Dynamite! The Story of Class Violence in America.* Rev. ed. New York: Viking Press, 1934.

American Committee for the Defense of Leon Trotsky. *World Voices on the Moscow Trials: A Compilation from the Labor and Liberal Press of the World.* New York: Pioneer Press, 1936.

American Workers Party. *Toward An American Revolutionary Labor Movement: Statement of Programmatic Orientation.* New York: Provisional Organizing Committee, 1934.

Arendt, Hannah. *On Revolution.* New York: Viking Press, 1965.

——. *The Origins of Totalitarianism.* 2nd ed. Cleveland: World Publishers, 1958.

Avineri, Schlomo. *The Social and Political Thought of Karl Marx.* Cambridge: University Press, 1968.

Bell, Daniel. *Marxian Socialism in the United States.* Princeton, N.J.: Princeton University Press, 1967.

Bernstein, Irving. *The Lean Years: A History of the American Worker, 1920-1933.* Cambridge, Mass.: Riverside Press, 1960.

——. *The Turbulent Years: A History of the American Worker, 1933-1941.* Boston: Houghton, Mifflin, 1970.

Bingham, Alfred M. and Selden Rodman, eds. *Challenge to the New Deal.* New York: Falcon Press, 1934.

Bittelman, Alexander. *Trotsky the Traitor.* New York: Workers Library Publishers, 1937.

Borkenau, Franz. *World Communism: A History of the Communist International.* Ann Arbor: University of Michigan Press, 1962.

Brant, Irving. *The Bill of Rights: Its Origin and Meaning.* Indianapolis and Kansas City, Bobbs-Merrill, 1965.

Brissenden, Paul F. *The I.W.W.: A Study of American Syndicalism.* New York: Russell and Russell, 1957 (republication of Columbia University Press issue, 1919).

Brooks, John Graham. *American Syndicalism: The I.W.W.* New York: AMS Press, 1969 (reprint of 1913 edition).

Broué, Pierre, ed. Leon Trotsky, *Le mouvement communiste en France, 1919-1939.* Paris: Les Editions de Minuit, 1967.

Browder, Earl. *The Communists and the People's Front.* New York: International Publishers, 1938.

Budenz, Louis F. *Men Without Faces: The Communist Conspiracy in the U.S.A.* New York: Harper Bros., 1948.

——. *The Techniques of Communism.* Chicago: Henry Regnery, 1954.

——. *This Is My Story.* New York and London: McGraw-Hill, 1947.

Burnham, James. *How to Fight War: Isolation, Collective Security, Relentless Class Struggle?* New York: Socialist Workers Party, 1938.

——. *The Managerial Revolution.* New York: John Day, 1941.

Cannon, James P. *The First Ten Years of American Communism: Report of a Participant.* New York: Lyle Stuart, 1962.

——. *The History of American Trotskyism: Report of a Participant.* New York: Pioneer Press, 1944.

———. *Notebook of an Agitator.* New York: Pioneer Press, 1958.

Carr, Edward Hallett. *Studies in Revolution.* New York: Macmillan, 1950.

Chambers, Clark A. *California Farm Organizations: A Historical Study of the Grange, the Farm Bureau, and the Associated Farmers, 1929-1941.* Berkeley: University of California Press, 1952.

Christman, Henry M., ed. *Essential Works of Lenin.* New York: Bantam Books, 1966.

Cole, George D. H. *The Meaning of Marxism.* Ann Arbor: University of Michigan Press, 1968 (first printed 1948).

Coser, Lewis and Irving Howe. *The American Communist Party: A Critical History, 1919-1957.* Boston: Frederick A. Praeger, 1957.

De Caux, Leonard H. *Labor Radical: From the Wobblies to CIO.* Boston: Beacon Press, 1970.

Deutscher, Isaac. *The Prophet Outcast: Trotsky, 1929-1940.* London: Oxford University Press, 1963.

———. *Ironies of History: Essays on Contemporary Communism.* London: Oxford University Press, 1966.

Dewey Commission of Inquiry. *The Case of Leon Trotsky.* New York: Merit Publishers, 1969.

Diggins, John P. *Up from Communism: Conservative Odysseys in American Intellectual History.* New York, Evanston, and London: Harper & Row, 1975.

Djilas, Milovan. *Conversations with Stalin.* New York: Harcourt, Brace & World, 1962.

Dobbs, Farrell. *Teamster Rebellion.* New York: Monad Press, 1972.

Dowell, Eldridge Foster. *A History of Criminal Syndicalism Legislation in the U.S.* Baltimore: Johns Hopkins University Press, 1939.

Draper, Theodore. *American Communism and Soviet Russia: the Formative Period.* New York: Viking Press, 1960.

———. *The Roots of American Communism.* New York: Viking Press, 1957.

Drachkovitch, Milorad M., ed. *The Revolutionary Internationals, 1864-1943.* Stanford, Cal.: Stanford University Press, 1966.

Dubovsky, Melvyn. *We Shall Be All: A History of the Industrial Workers of the World.* Chicago: Quadrangle Press, 1969.

Eastman, Max. *Heroes I Have Known: Twelve Who Lived Great Lives.* New York: Simon & Shuster, 1942.

———. *Love and Revolution: My Journey Through an Epoch.* New York: Random House, 1964.

———. *Marxism: Is It Science?* New York: W. W. Norton, 1940.

———. *Reflections on the Failure of Socialism.* New York: Devin-Adair, 1962.

————. *Stalin's Russia and the Crisis in Socialism.* New York: W. W. Norton, 1940.

Egbert, Donald Drew and Stow Persons, eds. *Socialism and American Life.* 2 vols. Princeton, N.J.: Princeton University Press, 1952.

Emerson, Thomas I. *Toward a General Theory of the First Amendment.* New York: Random House, 1966.

Farrell, James Thomas. *An American Dream Girl and Other Stories.* New York: Vanguard Press, 1950.

————. *Reflections at Fifty and Other Essays.* New York: Vanguard Press, 1954.

Filene, Peter G. *Americans and the Soviet Experiment, 1917-1933.* Cambridge, Mass.: Harvard University Press, 1967.

Fleischman, Harry. *Norman Thomas, A Biography: 1884-1968.* New York: W. W. Norton, 1969.

Foster, William Z. *History of the Communist Party of the U.S.A.* New York: International Publishers, 1952.

————. *Toward Soviet America.* Balboa Island, Cal.: Elgin Publications, 1961 (reprint of 1932 publication).

Freeman, Joseph. *An American Testament: A Narrative of Rebels and Romantics.* London: Victor Gollancz, 1938.

Frisch, Morton J. and Martin Diamond, eds. *The Thirties: A Reconsideration in the Light of the American Political Tradition.* De Kalb, Ill.: Northern Illinois University Press, 1968.

Gates, John. *The Story of an American Communist.* New York and Toronto: Thomas Nelson, 1958.

Gay, Peter. *The Rise of Modern Paganism.* Vol. 1 in *The Enlightenment: An Interpretation.* 2 vols. New York: Alfred A. Knopf, 1966.

Gilbert, James B. *Designing the Industrial State: The Intellectual Pursuit of Collectivism in America, 1880-1940.* Chicago: Quadrangle Books, 1972.

————. *Writers and Partisans: A History of Literary Radicalism in America.* New York and London: John Wiley, 1968.

Gitlow, Benjamin. *I Confess: The Truth About American Communism.* New York: E. P. Dutton, 1939-1940.

————. *The Whole of Their Lives: Communism in America, A Personal History and Intimate Portrayal of Its Leaders.* Boston and Los Angeles: Western Island, 1965 (reprint of Scribner's 1948 publication).

Goldman, Albert. *In Defense of Socialism: The Official Court Record.* New York: Pioneer Press, 1944.

Goodman, Walter. *The Committee: The Extraordinary Career of the House Committee on Un-American Activities.* New York: Farrar, Straus and Giroux, 1968.

Gurr, Ted. *Why Men Rebel.* Princeton, N.J.: Princeton University Press, 1970.

Guttmann, Allen. *The Wound in the Heart: America and the Spanish Civil War.* New York: Free Press of Glencoe, 1962.

Hallgren, Mauritz A. *The Gay Reformer: Profits Before Plenty Under Franklin D. Roosevelt.* New York: Alfred A. Knopf, 1935.

———. *Seeds of Revolution: A Study of the American People during the Depression.* New York: Alfred A. Knopf, 1933.

———. *Why I Resigned from the Trotsky Defense Committee.* New York: International Publishers, 1937.

Hansen, Joseph and William F. Warde, eds. *In Defense of Marxism.* New York: Pathfinder, 1970.

Hentoff, Nat, ed. *The Essays of A. J. Muste.* New York: Simon & Shuster, 1967.

———. *Peace Agitator: The Story of A. J. Muste.* New York: Macmillan, 1963.

Herreshoff, David. *American Disciples of Marx: From the Age of Jackson to the Progressive Era.* Detroit: Wayne State University Press, 1967.

Hicks, Granville. *John Reed: The Making of a Revolutionary.* New York & London: Benjamin Blom, 1968.

Hillquit, Morris. *Loose Leaves from a Busy Life.* New York: Macmillan, 1934.

Hoffa, James R. [as told to Donald I. Rogers]. *The Trials of Jimmy Hoffa.* Chicago: Henry Regnery, 1970.

Hoover, John Edgar. *Masters of Deceit: The Story of Communism in America and How to Fight It.* New York: Henry Holt, 1958.

Howe, Irving. *Steady Work: Essays in the Politics of Democratic Radicalism, 1953-1966.* New York: Harcourt, Brace & World, 1966.

Hulse, James W. *The Forming of the Communist International.* Stanford, Cal.: Stanford University Press, 1964.

Hunt, Robert Nigel Carew. *The Theory and Practice of Communism: An Introduction.* Baltimore: Penguin Books, 1963.

Jacobs, Paul. *The State of the Unions.* New York: Atheneum Press, 1963.

James, Ralph and Estelle James. *Hoffa and the Teamsters.* Princeton, N.J.: Van Nostrand Publishers, 1965.

James, C. L. R. *World Revolution, 1917-1936; The Rise and Fall of the Communist International.* New York: Pioneer Press, 1937.

Johnpoll, Bernard K. *Pacifist's Progress: Norman Thomas and the Decline of American Socialism.* Chicago: Quadrangle Books, 1970.

Johnson, Donald. *The Challenge to American Freedoms: World War I and the Rise of the American Civil Liberties Union.* Lexington: University of Kentucky Press, 1963.

Joll, James. *The Anarchists*. New York: Grosset & Dunlap, 1964.

Josephson, Matthew. *Infidel in the Temple: A Memoir of the Nineteen-Thirties*. New York: Alfred A. Knopf, 1967.

Kampelman, Max. *The Communist Party vs. the C.I.O.* New York: Arno and *New York Times,* 1971.

Kazin, Alfred A. *Starting Out in the Thirties*. Boston and Toronto: Little, Brown, 1962.

Kempton, Murray. *Part of Our Time: Some Ruins and Monuments of the Thirties*. New York: Simon & Shuster, 1955.

Kipnis, Ira R. *The American Socialist Movement, 1897-1912*. New York: Columbia University Press, 1952.

Konvitz, Milton. *Fundamental Liberties of a Free People: Religion, Press, Assembly*. Ithaca, N.Y.: Cornell University Press, 1957.

Kreuter, Kent and Gretchen Kreuter. *An American Dissenter: The Life of Algie Martin Simons, 1870-1950*. Lexington: University of Kentucky Press, 1969.

Laidler, Harry W. *History of Socialism: A Comparative Survey of Socialism, Communism, Trade Unionism, Cooperation, Utopianism, and Other Systems of Reform and Reconstruction*. New York: Thomas Y. Crowell, 1933.

———. *American Socialism: Its Aims and Practical Program*. New York and London: Harper Bros., 1937.

Latham, Earl. *The Communist Controversy in Washington: From the New Deal to McCarthy,* Cambridge, Mass.: Harvard University Press, 1966.

Lens, Sidney. *Radicalism in America: Great Rebels and the Causes for Which They Fought*. New York: Thomas Y. Crowell, 1969.

Lowenthal, Max. *The Federal Bureau of Investigation*. New York: William Sloane, 1950.

Lyons, Eugene. *The Red Decade: The Stalinist Penetration of America*. Indianapolis and New York: Bobbs-Merrill, 1941.

McCarthy, Mary. *On the Contrary: Articles of Belief, 1946-1961*. New York: Farrar, Straus, & Cudahy, 1961.

———. *Sights and Spectacles, 1937-1956*. New York: Farrar, Straus, & Cudahy, 1956.

McCoy, Donald R. *Angry Voices: Left-of-Center Politics in the New Deal Era*. Lawrence: University of Kansas Press, 1958.

McKay, Claude. *A Long Way from Home*. New York: Lee Furman, 1937.

McWilliams, Carey. *Factories in the Field: The Story of Migratory Farm Labor in California*. Boston: Little, Brown, 1939.

Macdonald, Dwight. *Memoirs of a Revolutionist: Essays in Political Criticism.* Cleveland and New York: World Publishing Co., 1957.

Mangione, Jere. *The Dream and the Deal: The Federal Writers Project, 1935-1943.* Boston and Toronto: Little, Brown, 1972.

Markmann, Charles Lam. *The Noblest Cry: A History of the American Civil Liberties Union.* New York: St. Martin's Press, 1965.

Matthews, Joseph B. *Odyssey of a Fellow Traveler.* New York: privately published, 1938.

Mehring, Franz. *Karl Marx: The Story of His Life.* Translated by Edward Fitzgerald. New introduction by Max Shachtman. Ann Arbor: University of Michigan Press, 1969.

Mitchell, Broadus. *Depression Decade.* New York: Rinehart Publishers, 1947.

Morrow, Felix. *Revolution and Counter-Revolution in Spain.* New York: Pioneer Press, 1938.

Muste, Abraham John. *The Automobile Industry and Organized Labor.* Issued by the Christian Social Justice Fund. n.p.

Naville, Pierre. *Trotsky vivant.* Paris: Julliard, 1962.

Nelson, John K. *The Peace Prophets: American Pacifist Thought, 1919-1941.* Chapel Hill: University of North Carolina Press, 1967.

Nollau, Günther. *International Communism and World Revolution: History and Methods.* New York: Frederick A. Praeger, 1961.

Nomad, Max. *Apostles of Revolution.* Boston: Little, Brown, 1939.

———. *Dreamers, Dynamiters, and Demagogues: Reminiscences.* New York: Waldon Press, 1964.

———. *Rebels and Renegades.* Freeport, New York: Books for Libraries Press, 1968.

Olgin, Moissaye J. *Trotskyism: Counter-Revolution in Disguise.* New York: Workers Library Press, 1935.

Oneal, James and George A. Werner. *American Communism: A Critical Analysis of Its Origins, Development, and Programs.* New York: E. P. Dutton, 1947.

Orwell, George. *Homage to Catalonia.* New York: Harcourt, Brace, 1952.

Parker, Albert. *March on Washington: One Year After.* New York: Pioneer Press, 1942.

Philip, André. *Les socialistes.* n.p.: Editions du Seuil, 1967.

Phillips, William and Philip Rahv, eds. *The Partisan Reader: Ten Years of Partisan Review, 1934-1944, An Anthology.* New York: Dial Press, 1946.

Preis, Art. *America's Permanent Depression.* New York: Socialist Workers Party, 1938.

———. *Labor's Giant Step: Twenty Years of the CIO.* New York:

Pathfinder Press, 1972.

Preston, William. *Aliens and Dissenters: Federal Suppression of Radicals, 1903-1933.* Cambridge, Mass.: Harvard University Press, 1963.

Quint, Howard. *The Forging of American Socialism: Origins of the Modern Movement.* Columbia: University of South Carolina Press, 1952.

Rayback, Joseph. *A History of American Labor.* Rev. ed. New York: Macmillan, 1967.

Renshaw, Patrick. *The Wobblies: The Story of Syndicalism in the United States.* Garden City, New York: Doubleday, 1967.

Rideout, Walter. *The Radical Novel in the U.S., 1900-1954: Some Interpretations of Literature and Society.* Cambridge, Mass.: Harvard University Press, 1956.

Rizzi, Bruno. *Il collettivismo burocratico (polemica L. Trotzki, P. Naville, Bruno R.).* Imola: Editrice Galeati, 1967.

Robbins, Jack Alan. *The Birth of American Trotskyism, 1927-1929.* n.p.: published by author, 1973.

Rosenstone, Robert A. *Crusade of the Left: The Lincoln Batallion in the Spanish Civil War.* New York: Pegasus Press, 1969.

Roskolenko, Harry. *When I Was Last on Cherry Street.* New York: Stein & Day, 1965.

Schapiro, Leonard. *The Communist Party of the Soviet Union.* London: Methuen, 1960.

Schlesinger, Arthur M. *The Crisis of the Old Order. The Age of Roosevelt,* vol. 1. Boston: Houghton-Mifflin, 1957.

——. *The Coming of the New Deal. The Age of Roosevelt,* vol. 2. Boston: Houghton-Mifflin, 1959.

——. *The Politics of Upheaval. The Age of Roosevelt,* vol. 3. Boston: Houghton-Mifflin, 1960.

Schneider, David M. *The Workers (Communist) Party and the American Trade Unions.* Baltimore: Johns Hopkins University Press, 1928.

Seidler, Murray B. *Norman Thomas: Respectable Rebel.* New York: Syracuse University Press, 1967.

Serge, Victor. *Memoires d'un révolutionnaire.* Paris: Editions du Seuil, 1951.

Shachtman, Max. *Behind the Moscow Trial.* New York: Pioneer Press, 1936.

——. *The Bureaucratic Revolution: The Rise of the Stalinist State.* New York: Ronald Press, 1962.

——. *The Fight for Socialism: The Principles and Program of the Workers Party.* New York: International Publishing Co., 1946.

Shannon, David A. *The Socialist Party of America: A History.* Chicago: Quadrangle Books, 1967.

Simon, Rita James, ed. *As We Saw the Thirties: Essays on Social and Political Movements of a Decade.* Urbana: University of Illinois Press, 1967.

Socialist Workers Party. *Why We Are in Prison. Farewell Speeches of the Eighteen SWP and 544-CIO Minneapolis Prisoners.* New York: Pioneer Press, 1944.

Solow, Herbert. *Union-Smashing in Sacramento.* New York: National Sacramento Appeal Committee, 1935.

Symes, Lillian and Travers Clement. *Rebel America: The Story of Social Revolt in the U.S.* Boston: Beacon Press, 1972.

Taft, Philip. *Organized Labor in American History.* New York, Evanston, and London: Harper & Row, 1964.

Terkel, Studs. *Hard Times: An Oral History of the Great Depression.* New York: Avon Books, 1970.

Thomas, Norman. *As I See It.* New York: Macmillan, 1932.

———. *Socialism on the Defensive.* New York: Harper Bros., 1938.

Thorez, Maurice. *Fils du peuple: edition revue of mise à jour.* Paris: Editions Sociales, 1960.

Trotsky, Leon. *The Death Agony of Capitalism and the Tasks of the Fourth International: The Transitional Program.* New York: Pathfinder Press, 1970.

———. *Diary in Exile, 1935.* Translated by Elena Zarudnaya. New York: Atheneum, 1963.

———. *Literature and Revolution.* Translated by Rose Strunsky. Ann Arbor: University of Michigan Press, 1966.

———. *My Life.* New York: Grosset and Dunlap, 1960.

———. *The New Course.* Translated by Max Shachtman. Ann Arbor: University of Michigan Press, 1965.

———. *The Permanent Revolution and Results and Prospects.* Translated by John G. Wright, revised by Brian Pearce. New York: Merit Publishers, 1969.

———. *Problems of the Chinese Revolution.* Translated by Max Shachtman. New Foreword by Max Shachtman. Ann Arbor: University of Michigan Press, 1967.

———. *The Revolution Betrayed: What Is the Soviet Union and Where Is It Going?* New York: Pathfinder Press, 1970.

———. *The Spanish Revolution, 1931-1939.* New York: Pathfinder Press, 1973.

———. *Terrorism and Communism.* Translated by Max Shachtman. Ann Arbor: University of Michigan Press, 1963.

———. *Whither France?* Introduction by John G. Wright and Harold R. Isaacs. New York: Pioneer Press, 1936.

———. *Writings of Leon Trotsky, 1934-1935.* Edited by George Breitman and Bev Scott. New York: Pathfinder Press, 1971.

———. *Writings of Leon Trotsky, 1935-1936*. Edited by George Breitman and Bev Scott. New York: Pathfinder Press, 1970.

———. *Writings of Leon Trotsky, 1937-1938*. Edited by George Breitman and Evelyn Reed. New York: Pathfinder Press, 1970.

———. *Writings of Leon Trotsky, 1938-1939*. Edited by George Breitman and Evelyn Reed. New York: Merit Publishers, 1969.

———. *Writings of Leon Trotsky, 1939-1940*. Edited by George Breitman and Evelyn Reed. New York: Merit Publishers, 1969.

Ulam, Adam. *The Bolsheviks: The Intellectual, Personal, and Political History of the Triumph of Communism in Russia*. New York: Collier Books, 1974 (paperback reprint of 1965 Macmillan publication).

U.S. House of Representatives. 92d Congress, 1st session. *Communists in the Trotskyite Mold: A Report on the Socialist Workers Party and the Young Socialist Alliance*. Washington, D.C.: U.S. Government Printing Office, 1971.

Vyshinsky, Andrei Y. *Trotskyism in the Service of Fascism against Socialism and Peace*. New York: Workers Library Publishers, 1936.

Waldman, Louis. *Labor Lawyer*. New York: E. P. Dutton, 1944.

Walker, Charles Rumford. *American City: A Rank-and-File History*. New York and Toronto: Farrar and Rinehart, 1937.

Warren, Frank A. *An Alternative Vision: The Socialist Party in the 1930s*. Bloomington: Indiana University Press, 1974.

———. *The Red Decade Revisited: Liberals and Communists in the 1930s*. Bloomington: Indiana University Press, 1966.

Weinstein, James. *The Decline of Socialism in America, 1912-1925*. New York: Random House, 1969.

Whitten, Woodrow C. *Criminal Syndicalism and the Law in California: 1919-1927*. Philadelphia: American Philosophical Society, 1969.

Wolfe, Bertram D. *Three Who Made a Revolution: A Biographical History*. Boston: Beacon Press, 1948.

———. *One Hundred Years in the Life of a Doctrine*. New York: Dial Press, 1965.

Wolfenstein, E. Victor. *The Revolutionary Personality: Lenin, Trotsky, Gandhi*. Princeton, N.J.: Princeton University Press, 1973.

Wynar, Lubomyr R. *American Political Parties: A Selective Guide to Parties and Movements of the Twentieth Century*. Littleton, Col.: Libraries Unlimited, 1969.

Wyndham, Francis and David King. *Trotsky: A Documentary*. Middlesex, England: Penguin Books, 1972.

Yorburg, Betty. *Utopia and Reality: A Collective Portrait of American Socialists*. New York: Columbia University Press, 1969.

Zinn, Howard. *La Guardia in Congress*. New York: W. W. Norton, 1958.

Index

ABOUT THE AUTHOR

Concentrating on American social and intellectual history, Constance Ashton Myers has taught at California State University at Sacramento, the University of South Carolina, and the College of Charleston. This is her first book length publication.